A Study of Joseph Heller's
Catch-22

Twentieth-Century American Jewish Writers

Daniel Walden
General Editor

Vol. 14

PETER LANG
New York • Washington, D.C./Baltimore • Boston • Bern
Frankfurt am Main • Berlin • Brussels • Vienna • Oxford

Jon Woodson

A Study of Joseph Heller's *Catch-22*

Going Around Twice

PETER LANG
New York • Washington, D.C./Baltimore • Boston • Bern
Frankfurt am Main • Berlin • Brussels • Vienna • Oxford

Library of Congress Cataloging-in-Publication Data

Woodson, Jon.
A study of Joseph Heller's Catch-22: going around twice / Jon Woodson.
p. cm. — (Twentieth-century American Jewish writers; vol. 14)
Includes bibliographical references and index.
1. Heller, Joseph. Catch-22. 2. World War, 1939–1945—Literature and the war.
3. War stories, American—History and criticism. I. Title. II. Series.
PS3558.E476 C339   813'.54—dc21   00-042397
ISBN 0-8204-4599-1
ISSN 0897-7844

Die Deutsche Bibliothek-CIP-Einheitsaufnahme

Woodson, Jon:
A study of Joseph Heller's Catch-22: going around twice / Jon Woodson.
–New York; Washington, D.C./Baltimore; Boston; Bern;
Frankfurt am Main; Berlin; Brussels; Vienna; Oxford: Lang.
(Twentieth-century American Jewish writers; Vol. 14)
ISBN 0-8204-4599-1

PS3558
.E476
C339
2001

The paper in this book meets the guidelines for permanence and durability
of the Committee on Production Guidelines for Book Longevity
of the Council of Library Resources.

Printed in the United States of America

For Lynn, Morgan, Whitney, Marnee, and Gabriel

Contents

Acknowledgments   ix

List of Abbreviations   xi

Introduction   1

1. *Catch-22* and High Modernism   7

2. *Catch-22* and *The Gilgamesh Epic*   39

3. Love and Death in *Catch-22*   65

4. Heller's Religious Vision   103

5. Jewish Mysticism in *Catch-22*   133

Conclusion   153

Bibliography   159

Acknowledgments

All parenthetical page references to *Catch-22* are keyed to the standard Dell pocketbook edition.

I would like to thank Simon & Schuster and Donadio & Olson, Inc. (literary representatives) for permission to quote from *Catch-22*.

This project was completed with assistance from Howard University's University-Sponsored Faculty Research Award Program in the Social Sciences, Humanities, and Education.

I would like to thank Heidi Burns, my editor at Peter Lang Publishing, for her interest in this book and for her many helpful suggestions.

I want to thank Dusty Haller, extraordinary librarian and sibyl, for her generous assistance.

Abbreviations

APIP	*Archetypal Patterns in Poetry*
CB	"Come Back to the Raft Ag'in, Huck Honey!"
JH	*Joseph Heller's Novels*
KU	*A Kabbalistic Universe*
GE	*The Gilgamesh Epic and Old Testament Parallels*
WRU	"Wit and Its Relation to the Unconscious"
ID	"The Interpretation of Dreams"

Introduction

This study takes a new approach to Joseph Heller's novel, *Catch-22*. The idea of leaving behind what has gone before is as fraught with danger and risk in literary study as it is in any other academic field. That being the case, it seems wise to establish why it has become necessary to throw down the fence and to seek the horizon.

In thinking through the steps that have brought me to the completion of this study, I realized that it was because initially I had been entirely unfamiliar with the previous criticism that I was able to come to a different assessment of what Heller was doing. I had not been unfamiliar with literary criticism in general or in the specifics of Heller's novel. It was simply that when I began to see the shape of his text, I was not aware that I was so far from the interpretation of the herd, so to speak. A certain consistent way of looking at Heller had rapidly developed, and that way of doing things served as the foundation for subsequent studies. In the introduction to *Critical Essays of Joseph Heller*, James Nagel is forthright about the character of that endeavor:

> The scholarship on *Catch-22* since these early reviews has been largely confined to the concerns of the initial readers: matters of social satire, black humor, war protest, absurdity, and structural organization, with only the occasional foray into comparative analysis, origins and influence, style, and the aesthetics of the novel. However, in what has become a body of several hundred essays, *Catch-22* criticism has steadily developed in depth and sophistication despite its relatively narrow range. (4)

When I began to acquaint myself with what had been written about *Catch-22,* I discovered two very interesting things. The first was that one problem in the project of coming to understand the novel was Heller's influence. By the time that Nagel wrote his introduction in 1984, Heller had given, by Nagel's count, fifty interviews. Critics have been guided by these interviews, and in the most recent study that I have seen, David M. Craig's *Tilting at Mortality* (1997), it is apparent that they are continuing to listen to Heller and to be guided by him. The imprudence of such a course is suggested by a letter that Heller sent to me in reply to some questions about his attitude toward the reception of his novel: "In the past, for more than thirty years now, I have been reluctant to say anything more about the sources and meanings and techniques of the novel than what little I have said publicly, and so would be reluctant to do so now, except to remind of the old adage that if you see something there, it probably is there" (Sept. 27, 1998). What Heller's letter indicates to me is that against the background of his fifty interviews, the narrow focus taken toward the study of *Catch-22* in the previous several hundred critical articles, and my own reading of the novel is that there is much room to explore in search of sources, meanings, and techniques. The frontier is, in fact, wide open.

The second thing that I encountered is the fact that of the many essays written on *Catch-22*, many of them present glimpses and fragments of the wider landscape that I am trying to render in this study. In other words, I am in no true sense formulating a reading of *Catch-22* that is without considerable, though haphazard, precedence. In fact, what this study advocates has been anticipated by previous writers on Heller, but only in a piecemeal fashion. Should the pieces derived from previous studies be combined, a view of the novel remarkably close to mine emerges, though without the emphases that I would give to some of the fragments, and with certain crucial pieces missing altogether. Nevertheless, it is important that it be understood that my study of *Catch-22* is not without a great deal of support from the critical work that has already been done on the text, if that work is viewed with an eye toward assembling the parts into a whole and consistent exegesis.

My study begins by placing Heller within the context of the relevant contemporary modes of literature and literary study in vogue in the 1940s. Chiefly, it shows the centrality of T.S. Eliot and James Joyce as major authors and of the New Criticism and Myth Criticism as the two major frames for the examination of texts. The chapter then discusses *Catch-22* as a text that is shaped fundamentally by Heller's multifaceted borrowings from *Ulysses*, *The Waste Land*, and *Finnegans Wake*. My first chapter is in line with Raymond M. Olderman's reading that places *Catch-22* in the tradition of T.S. Eliot, seeing Yossarian as both Fisher King and Grail Knight (Nagel 8). Though my first chapter develops its argument more out of a general consideration of Eliot and *The Waste Land*, in my fourth chapter, "Heller's Religious Vision," I discuss Jesse L. Weston's *From Ritual to Romance* as the source of Eliot's material on ancient fertility cults and of the legends of the Fisher King and the Grail Knights. The subject of Heller's relationship to James Joyce seems to have dropped out of scholarly consideration at the commencement of the study of *Catch-22*, for Frederick Karl demonstrated that while Heller had attempted to create an early version of the novel in the Joycean mode, he had later abandoned this direction (Potts 36). In an article published in 1964, Karl located the novel in the absurdist camp, finding that the absurd view of life presented in the novel was not so much a literary invention as a devastating portrayal of modern life (Nagel Introduction 4). From that point on, most discussions of *Catch-22* have assumed its advocacy of an absurdist Weltanschauung. Here we see a prime example of the customary narrowing of critical focus that Nagel identified in his review of the study of *Catch-22*. Seemingly, any further study of that text's relationship to Joyce's novels was cut off in the earliest phase of research, and this crucial aspect of Heller's novel has not been pursued. While my study attempts to present some notion of Heller's broad uses of Joycean techniques, my assessment is preliminary, and a great deal remains to be discovered by further investigations of this topic.

The second chapter of my study establishes a point-by-point analogy of *The Gilgamesh Epic* to *Catch-22*. Here my point is that the relationship of Heller's novel and the ancient Sumerian-Assyrian poem parallels the famous coextension of Joyce's *Ulysses* and Homer's *Odyssey*. I show that Heller's use of narrative parallelism, though hidden in the seemingly chaotic structure of the novel, is the primary location of Heller's use of Joycean techniques. At the same time, though, the added imposition of Joycean technique of free association derived from *Finnegans Wake* requires that another type of further study of *Catch-22* needs to be carried out so as to investigate what I now suppose to be more orderly and direct links between the narratives of Gilgamesh and Yossarian than those I discuss. While I am fairly confident that I have been able to work out the location of every major component of *Gilgamesh* in *Catch-22*, many questions remain, both because of the insufficient space to do so here, and because at this point the technology is not sufficient to allow for the solution of some of the more persistent problems. In carrying out the present study I made good use of a searchable digital version of *Finnegans Wake*, however, no such apparatus yet exists for *Catch-22*. While I had at one time thought of typing the novel into a searchable format myself, other factors intervened, and that task remains undone. Once it is possible to compare these extensive texts more efficiently, I am certain that many interesting features of *Catch-22* will be unveiled, for it is a supremely well-wrought text.

My third chapter reviews the relationship between *Catch-22* and the literary criticism of Leslie Fiedler. In an important article that is highly relevant to the present subject, Fiedler discusses his discovery of an archetype, "the archetypal love of white male and black" ("Come Back to the Raft" 487). According to Fiedler, American men seek out the isolation of the frontier or the ocean and leave behind them their wives and their responsibilities, because they are in search of male-to-male encounters. The thesis of my study is, in the final analysis, that the theme of Heller's novel is Fiedler's archetype and its several repercussions and effects with regard to the psychology and sociology of gender and race. Heller, it seems, is exploring the inability of American men to evolve beyond a relatively primitive form of consciousness. That Heller harbors this concern in *Catch-22* has been registered by Sanford Pinsker, who argues that, unlike other figures in American literature, Yossarian does not mature and thereby remains a perennial innocent (Nagel Introduction 5). My point is not that Pinsker is in agreement with either Fiedler or Heller, for Fiedler shows that the common pattern in American literature determines that male figures do not mature, while what is depicted in *Catch-22* is Yossarian's maturation in the face of the millions of American men caught up in the war who never mature. For Heller it is not Yossarian who indemnifies Pinsker's *puer eternu* but nearly everyone else in the novel—for besides Yossarian, there are in *Catch-22* a few other men who realize the brutish, violent, and atavistic nature of the world that masquerades under the guise of technology, enlightenment, democracy, and the other modern illusions. Heller's use of Fiedler's criticism is remarkably consistent with his interest in Eliot and Joyce, for the texts by Eliot, Fiedler, and Joyce privilege myth, and the conjunction of Joyce and Fiedler makes inevitable a discussion of the archetype-based psychology of Carl Jung. Having stated this, we can now see that when Walter R. Driscoll places Yossarian's desertion within the tradition of other American protagonists who may be said to light out for the territory (Nagel Introduction 9), Driscoll has, along with Pinsker, identified another aspect of the Fiedlerian archetypal theme in *Catch-22*.

In my fourth chapter, "Heller's Religious Vision," I discuss the importance of the theme of rebirth—death and renewal—in the novel. It is by the use of all of the materials mentioned above, Joyce, Eliot, Fiedler, Jung, Weston, and an additional source not previously introduced—Frazer's

The Golden Bough (one of Eliot's most important sources)—that Heller constructs the elaborate allusive structure that is one of the most significant features of the novel's subtext. Fundamental to all of these texts is the theme of various kinds of cycles—agricultural cycles, celestial cycles, and human cycles of reincarnation. Thus, on one level, the text develops the salient theme of the hero's need to escape from the cycles that work to his detriment and his need to find release into timelessness, eternity, and union with higher powers. This reading of the novel is in line with Thomas Allen Nelson's finding that the novel contains a cyclical pattern of action related to the central issue of responsibility (Nagel Introduction 8). Clinton S. Burhans, Jr., also finds unifying patterns of development beneath the seemingly random surface of the text (Nagel Introduction 8). The symbolism that Heller uses to frame much of this religious material is located in the text in many ways, and hence it is not surprising that Fred M. Fetrow concludes that the characters have symbolic functions suggested by their names (Nagel Introduction 11). Fetrow's is an important assessment since the implication of an intricately contrived symbolism belies the relegation of the text as being absurdist in conception: Symbolism is coterminous with the metaphysical not the absurd—a point that I expand toward the end of the first chapter.

In the fifth chapter, I explore the considerable degree to which *Catch-22* is rooted in Kabbalah—Jewish mysticism. New biographical information on Heller and a new study of Kafka's writings have allowed me to reevaluate Heller's appropriation of Kafka and, further, to locate the numerous occurrences of Kabbalistic doctrines that are inserted into the text. Daniel Walden who finds that the values made explicit throughout *Catch-22* grow out of Jewish tradition (Nagel 10) anticipated some measure of this reading of the novel.

Shortly after its publication in 1961 Nelson Algren, Norman Mailer, and Robert Brustein recognized *Catch-22* as a great novel. As the years have gone by, the novel's admirers have won out over its detractors. *Catch-22* is still avidly embraced by each new generation of American readers. The phrase "catch-22" is not only part of the American vocabulary, it turns up in nearly everything that one encounters in the media. Everyone understands that we live in a "catch-22" kind of world. However, despite the universality of the novel, and the ubiquity of the phrase "catch-22," it seems to me that we do not really know what exactly the catch is. We do know that the effects of catch-22 are deleterious, but we go on identifying it all around us without any determination of why it is so pervasive or what might be done to counteract its unfortunate effects. It seems to me that this general ignorance concerning catch-22 is given a further poignancy in my study of *Catch-22*, since I have endeavored to recontextualize the novel from which its name gained entrance into our culture. Therefore, in the final section of the conclusion I attempt to determine the nature of catch-22. Again, this attempt at defining the construct known as catch-22 is not carried out in a vacuum, for I have been anticipated by Leon F. Seltzer's statement that "Catch-22 is not intended to symbolize America but what those in command have reduced it to. And it is not the moral wickedness which Catch-22 stands for that constitutes the greatest threat to Yossarian's existence" (89). For Seltzer the catch is "opportunism, or, on a more basic level, the need or compulsion to assert one's will over others. And the sanction for such tyrannical assertion is catch-22, since in essence it *means* the right to do whatever one can do with impunity" (90). Seltzer locates the problem in the masses that are impotent in the face of the fabrication of the catch by ambitious individuals (90). In a novel that has its intellectual foundation in Kabbalah, *Gilgamesh*, Dostoevsky, Joyce, Eliot, Freud, and Jung, the reductive moralism of such a reading of the text is insufficiently comprehensive to describe a text that does not appear to be definitively classified as absurdist. While I do not deny that *Catch-22* presents an absurd façade to the reader, its absurdity is everywhere undermined by the religious, symbolic, and mystical subtext that pervades every level of the text, for even the accessible and familiar surface level—famously disorganized, unstructured, and chaotic as it is— that harbors the novel's absurdity is under obvious assault by the text's metaphysical elements. The materials that Heller brings to bear on the problem for which catch-22 is emblematic endows his argument with far more depth than Seltzer recognizes. Yet the question that remains is that of the actual nature of the prevailing tyranny—and it is to that topic that the fourth chapter, "Heller's Religious Vision," is addressed.

Chapter 1

Catch-22 and High Modernism

Late in April of 1998 newspapers across the country carried a story headlining Joseph Heller's denial that he had plagiarized *Catch-22* from another novel. The suspected source of Heller's novel, Louis Falstein's *Face of a Hero* (published in England as *The Sky Is a Lonely Place*), was also about an American bomber squadron stationed in Italy during World War II. The allegations were prompted by Heller's having admitted in the pages of his newly published memoir, *Now and Then: From Coney Island to Here* (1998), that he had borrowed actions and settings from other writers. In response to Heller's admission, an amateur bibliophile wrote to *The Sunday Times* of London to point out "the amazing similarity of characters, personality traits, eccentricities, physical descriptions, personnel injuries and incidents" (*Orlando Sentinel* A-8) that the two books supposedly had in common. On the one hand the chronology is suggestive—Falstein's book was published in 1951, while the first chapter of *Catch-22* was written in 1953, shortly after Heller completed his studies at Oxford University. On the other hand, both Heller and Falstein are Air Force veterans from Russian-Jewish families in Brooklyn who served in Italy during the war, so any similarities might be the result of coincidences.

The question of what if any use Heller may or may not have made of Falstein's *Face of a Hero* will be set aside (for discussion in due course) in order that we may focus on resolving the more fundamental question of what Heller's admission of literary borrowing may have meant—to him and to his readers. Once that issue has been resolved and a context for the consideration of Heller's literary borrowing has been more widely established it will be possible to say something useful about any ensuing relationship between the two texts.

We must begin by acknowledging the obvious—that Heller himself brought up the subject of his literary borrowing. That he did so, it seems to me, is indicative of his own view of his relationship to literary history and to what we may understand to be the relationship of his texts to other texts. What, primarily, we must consider in assessing the question of Heller's literary borrowing is embodied in the content of his formal academic study of literature. After his discharge from the Air Force in 1944, Heller was married and studied at the University of Southern California on the G.I. Bill. In 1946 he transferred to New York University. He also attended creative writing seminars and published short stories. In 1948 he received a B.A. In 1949 he earned an M.A. in American Literature at Columbia University, with a thesis on "The Pulitzer Plays: 1917–1935." That same year he studied at Oxford University on a Fulbright scholarship.

As a student of literature at these various schools during this period, Heller necessarily came under the influence of New Criticism and the schools of myth-and-symbol criticism that paralleled it. By 1935 many of the key texts that foregrounded a text-centered discourse had appeared, including works by Eliot, Pound, J.M. Murray, T.E. Hulme, I.A. Richards, F.R. Leavis, William Empson, R.P. Blackmur, and Kenneth Burke (Cain 93–94). The New Critics began to revamp English studies in the late 1930s and through the 1940s, and "by the early 1950s, it was 'the Establishment' itself" (Cain 101). Walter Sutton observes that "In spite of Ransom's poor opinion of *The Waste Land*, there is little doubt that Eliot was the most important early influence upon the theory and practice of the New Critics, even though they did not all accept his ideas. John Guillory shows that the textual canon that emerged in Eliot's' earlier criticism "was presented as a canon in *The Well Wrought Urn*, and has since been institutionalized to a greater or lesser extent in the curricula of university English departments" ("The Ideology of Canon-Formation" 173).

What was installed in the classroom by the disciples of the New Criticism was the pedagogical (and critical) practice of reading a text closely with attention to tone, paradox, imagery, and relative degrees of complex thought and feeling in texts (Cain 101). In its most developed practice this close reading was directed toward opening up the different modernist writings of Yeats, Eliot, and Pound—and an important component of the core curriculum consisted in the "'close reading' of masterpieces" (Cain 119). John Paul Russo states that "The high modernist aesthetics of Hulme, Eliot, and the early Pound furnished its poetic canon and main premises in its theory and poetics: the poem as object, self-reflexivity, craft and technique, economy, complexity, impersonality (antipersonality), antiromanticism" (541). The confluence of New Criticism, high modernism, and myth-archetype criticism perhaps originates in Eliot's highly important essay "*Ulysses,* Order, and Myth" in which he declares that Joyce's "parallel use of the *Odyssey*" has the importance of a scientific discovery" (177). The "mythical method" (178), which for Eliot "mak[es] the modern world possible for art" (178) is "simply a way of controlling, of ordering, of giving a shape and a significance to the immense panorama of futility and anarchy which is contemporary history" (177).

In "*Ulysses,* Order, and Myth" Eliot is speaking of a process that is uniquely carried out by the medium of Joyce's novel: "No one else has built a novel upon such a foundation before" (177)—though he goes on to add that "It is a method already adumbrated by Mr. Yeats" (177). Eliot's interest in Joyce's experimental novel was not carried over into New Critical concerns, nor was the novel the focus of the myth-archetype critics. One important exception to this tendency was Leslie Fiedler: In his study of the American novel, he presented his discovery of an archetypal pattern not of rebirth (which occupied much of the attention of the other myth-archetype critics) but instead "of frustration and perversion resulting from the denial of mature sexuality in American literature, a reflection of the psyche of American society" (Sutton 212). The genres central to the concerns of the New Criticism were the lyric and the long poem (the modernist poetic sequence). Accordingly, the most important modernist poem was Eliot's *The Waste Land.* In *The Well Wrought Urn,* Cleanth Brooks took over the Eliotic literary canon and implicitly installed in it *The Waste Land,* saying that "The structure described—a structure of 'gestures' or attitudes—seems to me to describe the essential structure of both the *Odyssey* and *The Waste Land.* It seems to be the kind of structure which the ten poems considered in this book possess in common" (191).

Besides the New Criticism, the influence of myth-archetype (myth-symbol) criticism was also another powerful influence on the study of literature in the 1940s and 1950s. The growing influence of Carl Jung's development of Freudian psychoanalytic theory, particularly as Jung's thought touched on the relationship of literature and psychology, led to another direction taken by modern literary study—though it was at times looked on as a subset of the New Criticism (Sutton 175–76). Sutton states that "myth and archetype critics are for the most part followers of Jung and share his mystical and religious inclinations, while critics attracted to Freud more often think of themselves as scientifically or historically oriented (176). Jungian thought was conducted into American literary criticism by means of English critic Maud Bodkin's *Archetypal Patterns in Poetry* (1934). Bodkin's study was largely concerned with the "rebirth archetype," which she discussed in connection with *Hamlet* and Coleridge's *Rime of the Ancient Mariner*. She also addressed the archetype as it was manifested in more recent texts. She discussed "the neglected subject of the male ideal (Jung's *animus*) in Virginia Woolf's *Orlando* and the rebirth archetype in Eliot's *The Waste Land*, making use of the parallels from *The Rime of the Ancient Mariner* and the *Inferno*. Her reference to archetypes from Jessie Weston's *From Ritual to Romance* (1920) and her citations of Sir James Frazer's *The Golden Bough* are reminders of the influence of anthropology upon myth study even before Jung's theory was formulated" (Sutton 180). In a sense, the high point of myth-archetype criticism was reached in 1949 with the publication of Joseph Campbell's *The Hero with a Thousand Faces*. Campbell's study was essentially a schematizing of *Finnegans Wake*, for it reproduced as a pattern the central structure of Joyce's novel—that "behind the multiform myths and fragments of myths preserved in art and folklore and ritual, the *one* unifying rebirth myth of the hero involving 'rites of passage,' proceeding through the three stages of 'the separation or departure', 'the trials and victories of initiation,' and 'the return and reintegration with society'" (Sutton 181).

The brief survey of the forces shaping the academic study of literature during the period of time coinciding with Heller's undergraduate and graduate studies given above discloses that both the New Criticism and the myth-archetype schools of criticism held T.S. Eliot in high esteem; it is also made apparent that, in a more general sense, both schools of criticism were rooted in high modernism. The New Criticism was virtually inseparable from Eliot's criticism and his poetry—both of which were used in various ways to define the canon of texts circumscribed by the critical discourse of the New Criticism. In the case of myth-archetype criticism, one of its key texts (Bodkin's *Archetypal Patterns in Poetry*) dealt with *The Waste Land* directly and indirectly (through its component anthropological texts by Weston and Frazer) and another text important to the enterprise (Campbell's *Hero*) was derived from Joyce's fiction. In addition to the above texts, the curriculum of the two critical schools was expanded to include a list of European texts that were considered suitable for critical investigation. Whether these works were a matter of "Monuments of literature [that] form an ideal order among themselves" (N. Frye quoted in Smith 1323) or "the monumental figures of our time" (Trilling 102), major critics of the period, from across the critical spectrum, thought that such a list existed. For example, Marxist cultural critic Lionel Trilling thought the list of major authors included Proust, Joyce, Lawrence, Eliot, Yeats, Mann, Kafka, Rilke, and Gide (102).

When we come to the questions raised by Joseph Heller's development of a novel in progress in the early 1950s, considering what has been said above concerning the tendencies that predominated in literary studies, we should not be surprised to find that Heller's practice paralleled that of such contemporary exemplars as Nabokov and Borges in his pursuit of the high-modernist, post-Joycean approach to the novel. Heller's first attempt to write his novel had incorporated stream of consciousness and a meandering time scheme (Potts 36). The prevailing assumption on the part of Heller's critics is, however, that he abandoned this approach for the "Kafka-Celine-West tradition" (Potts 112), leaving behind only "sudden transitions" (Potts 36) as a vestigial remnant of a style that was abdicated. The thesis of this study is that rather than jettisoning the challenges presented by the Joycean (or post-Joycean) approach, Heller continued with a more or less literal Joycean procedure, incorporating as many of the features of both *Ulysses* and *Finnegans Wake* as the demand for a degree of verisimilitude in his narrative would admit. Heller's embrace of high modernism was designed to result in the creation of a text with a difficult, transcendent poetic language that would lend itself to the close textual analysis that was the method of the New Criticism, a concern playfully announced in the opening pages of the novel, when Yossarian censors mail in such a way that the results "erected more dynamic intralinear tension . . . and left a message far more universal" (8). The New Critics performed their analyses of poems with reference to attitudes, tones, tensions, irony and paradox (Russo 548), and the universal was an important topic, the contrast between the Kantian and Hegelian universal being the subject of an important New Critical distinction (Russo 543).

The specific Joycean attribute that determines the form of *Catch-22* is not those generally associated with Joyce's style (stream of consciousness narration, mythological parallels, involutional time, and linguistic contortion; Adams 196–97) but is nevertheless controlling; it is the self-referentiality of Joyce's texts. Robert Martin Adams states that "Though it imitated minutely the surface of everyday life, as if to prove that it could, *Ulysses* constantly invited the reader to look under or behind that surface" (200). Once resolved to explore this technique, Heller later parted company with Joyce's means of achieving self-referentiality. Joyce announced the superficiality of *Ulysses*'s prose by changing his style: "Its style was often opaque, and by changing so often, called attention to itself" (Adams 200). This was not Heller's method, though he certainly worked to bring to his reader's awareness both the surface of his prose and the universe that it overlay. Heller accomplished this stratagem by substituting literature for popular culture. Instead of a detailed modeling of the world, Heller pursued the imitation of literary texts. This technique is related to Joyce's pursuit of literary textuality in *Finnegans Wake*, however, instead of alluding to the texts by means of puns, while the normal activities of life are carried on (washing, eating, sleeping), Heller incorporates literary texts into the reality of everyday actions, so that his characters perform actions that refer to recognizable events in paramount works of literature. Heller points to the fundamental importance of literature to his novel through the name of his character, Major Major Major. He uses this intrusive, comic, and enigmatic name self-referentially to indicate the presence of "major" literary texts at several levels in his narrative. Despite the importance of such "major" texts to the construction of the novel, we can see that Heller's attitude toward them is irreverent and ironic. We may think of these effects as the playful and self-referential eruption of such New Critical (really Allen Tate's) shibboleths as tension (extension and intension), irony, and paradox into his text.

Far and away the most important "major" text that Heller brings to the reader's attention in *Catch-22* is Eliot's notorious, controversial, and ubiquitous long poem, *The Waste Land*. At this point it is possible to return to the subject of Heller's alleged plagiary, for Eliot represents the origin of the high-modernist practice of composition by means of the appropriation from a "source [that] is not invoked but suppressed, for its identity is not functional. This kind of appropriation, traditionally called *borrowing*, is a kind of higher plagiary" (Sultan 6). We have but to notice that the newspaper story that reported Heller's alleged plagiary on behalf of *Catch-22* quotes his memoir as stating that he "'borrowed' actions and settings from other writers" (*Orlando Sentinel*, Tue., April 28, 1998 A-8) to realize that his use of the word borrowed points to his advocacy of the doctrine of appropriation that Eliot set forth in his essay "Philip Massinger": "Immature poets imitate; mature poets steal; bad poets deface what they take, and good poets make it into something better, or at least something different" (*Selected Essays* 182). In this circumlocuitous manner he himself informs the reader that we must look at his text in a certain way if we are to garner any meaning from it. Heller requires to be seen as a writer who has adopted Eliot's method, which for him is utilitarian and is not subject to controversy. The reader who raised the alarm, the newspapermen who published the story, and, presumably, the readers who bought the paper to follow the sensational story are confined to a neo-romantic, sentimental understanding of literary creation that privileges originality, authenticity, directness, inspiration, imagination, and individuality. Far from being a plagiarist, Heller forged a neo-modernist path, following in the footsteps of Eliot, who plundered Joyce's *Ulysses* in order to write his signal modernist long poem.

In all probability, the Associated Press circulated the story of Heller's alleged plagiary because of the entertainment value of a literary scandal. In the only comment attributed to him in the news story, Heller reacted to the sensationalism, saying, "I'm amused that there'd be such a fuss or that much interest in it. . . . It's irritating because of the implied insinuations" (*Orlando Sentinel* A-8). Moreover, the story did nothing to resolve the question of Heller's alleged plagiary, beyond providing a list of similarities between the two books—diarrhea epidemics, a Texan, a fatal relationship between a flier and a young girl. What, primarily, this episode demonstrates is the conceptual distance between the reading public and modernist and post-modernist writers and critics. This difference in perception is illuminated by Stanley Sultan in his discussion of the possibility that Joyce's *Ulysses* was in some respects borrowed from Dostoevsky. Sultan stated that "borrowing . . . diminishes the indebted work as derivative, a judgment that could scarcely be more irrelevant than it is to *Ulysses*" (75). The same point applied to *Catch-22*: as I show in this study, this novel is a richly complex and original work, that contains borrowings from many other works of literature but is derivative of nothing previous to it.

Because of Heller's adherence to the higher plagiary, T.S. Eliot holds a unique position in *Catch-22*, functioning on a number of levels in the text, and being represented in a number of very different ways. Though Eliot's poem, *The Waste Land*, is not given a direct mention in the novel, the presence of the poem is felt everywhere, and it is a major component of the language, episodes, and themes. It is perhaps one of Heller's many literary jokes that *Catch-22* uses *The Waste Land* the way that Eliot's long poem uses Joyce's *Ulysses*: As we have already seen, this joke follows from Heller's interest in Eliot's doctrine of literary appropriation.

The poet T.S. Eliot is introduced in "Doc Daneeka," the fourth chapter of *Catch-22*, in such a way that the degree to which the text is referenced to the universe of Eliot's waste land is not readily apparent. The comic entrance of the poet into the text belies the importance of what transpires, and it requires careful analysis in order to establish that the T.S. Eliot motif carried through the ensuing patter is more than Marx Brothers-like nonsense. A seemingly random series of comic interlocutions revolving around the asking of disturbing questions take place, with the subject shifting from the question of mortality to the making of money. The interchange is in danger of pursuing the questions about death "through all of the words in the world" (36). However that line of pursuit concludes when Clevinger mysteriously intervenes. Yossarian, we are told, cannot make money and cannot win at gambling even if he cheats: "These were two disappointments to which he had resigned himself: he would never be a skeet shooter, and he would never make money" (36–37). The theme of making money bridges the shift from Yossarian's questions to the question posed by Colonel Cargill's "homiletic memoranda" (37), in which he proposes that "Any fool can make money these days and most of them do. But what about people with talent and brains? Name, for example, one poet who makes money" (37). All of Heller's effects are aimed at achieving an aura of absurdity. The distinction between Yossarian's questions and Colonel Cargill's is that Yossarian wants answers to his questions, while Cargill does not. In fact, Colonel Cargill seems not to have realized that there is a chance that his rhetorical question about the earning capacity of poetry might provoke an answer. This distinction between Yossarian and Colonel Cargill is obliterated by the unreality of the method of narration; duration has been obliterated, so that ex-P.F.C. Wintergreen's answer to Colonel Cargill's memorandum seems to come instantly, as though he had godlike powers of omniscience and can answer any question. This circumstance is, of course, a marked contrast to Yossarian's situation, wherein no answers are forthcoming and which barely allows for the framing of questions. A seemingly immediate reply is provided by ex-P.F.C. Wintergreen, who telephoned his answer and "slammed down the telephone without identifying himself" (37). As the recipients of this unsolicited answer attempt to render meaningful the name T.S. Eliot, the name is repeated another ten times over the course of the following page. General Peckem proposes that perhaps the name is "a new code" (38), and the motif of the decoding of the name T.S. Eliot is dropped after it is verified that "there was no record at Twenty-seventh Air Force Headquarters of a T.S. Eliot (38).

It is difficult to arrive at and any assessment of what colonel Cargill may have meant by the assertion that fools make money while poets—the representatives of talent and brains—do not. If it is true that fools make money, while people of talent and brains do not make money, what is Cargill saying about poets? The statement is not clear as to whether or not the poets are allowed to make money or only allowed to make money through publishing poetry. In fact, if the latter is the subject of Cargill's inquiry, there is the further question of whether it is the fault of the poet or of the reading public that prevents the poet from making money. Thus, Colonel Cargill's inquiry is tautological, and it more resembles one of Lewis Carroll's humorous exercises than a military memorandum "prepared for circulation over General Peckem's signature" (37). We may also wonder why it is that poetry comes so readily to Cargill's mind, and, finally, whether there is any truth to what the officer so breezily advocates concerning money. Conversely, we must also wonder why it is that Wintergreen bothers to respond with Eliot's name, or that the Marx Brothers style of his riposte may or may not be founded on fact. While in the final analysis, the T.S. Eliot motif may be said to exist primarily to install the poet within the text of the novel as explicitly as possible, it may be profitable to consider one or two further points.

It is noteworthy that Eliot enters the text in relation to Cargill's homily on wealth, not through a discussion of literature. We must wonder, then, whether Eliot had money. Paul Foster describes the style of Eliot's life as one of keeping to a "'low profile'" (1):

> He led a regular existence, commuting back and forth to work, first as a banker and later as an employee at the publishing firm of Faber and Faber in London. His domestic, personal, and public life, such as it was, are noteworthy for their high degree of responsibility. His public utterances were few and unspectacular. . . . [P]ublic statements on his own work in reply to justified enquiry are very frequently oblique and, one speculates, deliberately formulated to put the inquirer off the track. . . . (Foster 1–2)

Eliot, then, worked at pursuits outside of poetry to make his living. Moreover, his affairs were kept private and were shielded from the public by misdirection. In the sense that he comes retroactively into Colonel Cargill's memorandum as a person with talent and brains without money, Eliot's case is moot. We do know, however, that ex-P.F.C. Wintergreen offers Eliot as an example of a poet who made money, though we do not see this reflected in the style of life in which Eliot lived. In truth, Eliot had been employed by a bank and a publishing firm. Of course, it is also possible that Wintergreen has no interest in answering the question accurately and that he is only telephoning the words "T.S. Eliot" to irritate Cargill and Peckem. Whatever his motive the result of his actions is nothing but confusion. Strangely, no one besides Wintergreen knows what the name T.S. Eliot means; even Cargill, who might be supposed to know something about poetry, seems not to know who Eliot is. The T.S. Eliot that Wintergreen propels into the narrative has so little context that Wintergreen reports to Cargill that "there was no record at Twenty-seventh Air Force Headquarters of a T.S. Eliot" (38).

The T.S. Eliot that Heller inserts into the text through Wintergreen's practical joke is implicitly the T.S. Eliot of literary history. What remains of interest after all of this elaborate nonsense has been sorted through is that Heller's handling of Eliot's name is reminiscent of the indirect, sideways scuttling method by which Eliot habitually negotiated with the world, and we can see that Heller's Eliot, presented as he is through Wintergreen's ruse, comes across in the amorphous Eliotic mode that more than any other sign indicates the presence of the essential Eliot. Stanley Sultan documents the considerable degree to which. Eliot engaged in jokes, irony, and literary play in *The Waste Land*, concluding that the poem's "Notes" are not serious documentation but another element of the poem, similar to an equivalent element of Joyce's *Ulysses* (163–67). Thus, although the major poet's name is introduced as the trivial, quasi-answer to an absurd question and then reduced to a refrain in a know-nothing dialogue that seems to further underscore the text's absurdity, in actuality *Catch-22* is an intricate subtextual recapitulation of the entirety of *The Waste Land*. At the same time, we are unable to disconnect *Catch-22* from a further association with Joyce's *Ulysses* and with *Finnegans Wake*, because *The Waste Land* recapitulates *Ulysses*, and because Heller makes it clear in several ways that *Catch-22* is polysemically concerned with the Eliot-Joyce intertextualities which represent his foundational "higher plagiaries" from *major* texts and not the secondary appropriation of texts of a lesser order.

In essence, *Catch-22* shares the same dominant theme as both *The Waste Land* and *Ulysses*: "As in Eliot's poem, so in Joyce's novel: after the "First Part" and "Entr'acte" something begins to happen. The constant movement of the protagonist ceases to be repetition of a futile diurnal round, the 'Walking round in a ring' that the other citizens in both works are presented as continuing to do, and becomes a quest for the way out" (Sultan 161). Joyce expresses this theme with Stephen through the enlightened submission of his will and with Bloom through a meaningful life as husband and father (Sultan 161). Heller's text borrows the object lesson entailed in the "Death by Water" section of Eliot's poem, however, in his treatment of this and other motifs from Eliot's poem, they are actualities rather than metaphors. *Catch-22* also breaks new ground by having Orr first invite Yossarian to join his crew (an act which would provide a way out of the war) and later allowing Orr to row to Sweden, which serves as a model for Yossarian's subsequent behavior, prompting him to abandon the war. Sultan sees that the quest for an escape from the futility of life is metaphorically fulfilled in *The Waste Land* by the Buddha's teachings (161). However, my point here is that in *Catch-22* Yossarian's escape is not lodged in the means laid out by *The Waste Land* but in the narrative of Gilgamesh, where Orr enacts both Utnapishtim's escape from mortality, and Gilgamesh's being rowed by Urshanabi to a land outside of time.

Concerning the relationship of Eliot's poem to Joyce's novel, Stanley Sultan states that

> the voluptuous novel and austere poem published in 1922 operate in similar ways; furthermore they do so to achieve a number of similar ends; and they even express similar views of the world in which they were made, similar views of art, and similar views of the relation of art not only to that world but even to the artist himself. It is through the articulation of this rich cluster of similarities, similarities of artistic practice, thematic concern, and conception of art and the artist—a matter of confluence more often that influence, and unimpeded by the difference in composition and outlook of the two works—that their joint central status can be understood and can illuminate the nature of Modernism. (157)

The literary works borrowed by both *The Waste Land* and *Ulysses* include the myth of Odysseus, the Germanic myth of the *Götterdämmerung*, the Hebraic and Christian myths of salvation, the *Commedia* of Dante, Wagner's ring cycle, Shakespeare, the *Arabian Nights*, Goethe's *Faust*, Vergil, Ovid, St. Augustine, Chaucer, Kyd, Spenser, Webster, Marvell, Goldsmith, Baudelaire, Gerard de Nerval, Verlaine, and several English prose works (Sultan 175). Our assessment of what this means to the understanding of *Catch-22* is much advanced by taking into account that Stanley Sultan views the shape behind what Eliot and Joyce have accreted to be that of history; Sultan says that "The groups of myths, masterworks, and the rest conjoin to represent a civilization in its stages—Hebraic, Hellenic, medieval, renaissance, modern" (157). As the chapters of this study demonstrate, *Catch-22* is equally a text that demarcates the successive phase of historical progression, though Heller's concern is more to delineate the stages of human development as the development of the collective unconscious than to register the outward forms of culture and civilization presented as textual artifacts—Eliot's celebrated "fragments I have shored against my ruins" (*The Waste Land* ln. 431).

Because Heller has concentrated more on providing his text with a rich substrate of archetypes than artifactual mastertexts, the inventory of artifacts in *Catch-22* is much sparser than in *Ulysses* and *The Waste Land*. In Eliot's poem, the reader is confronted by civilization in ruins, fragments, and a heap of broken images that have been consolidated into

the supposedly explanatory notes, and though the notes follow the poetry, they are contiguous with the lines of poetry and endow the whole
with what Jeremy Black calls "the impression of a scholarly 'text', a poem
written to be read after the death of poetry" (*Reading Sumerian Poetry*
40). Similarly, in *Ulysses* the reader is confronted by Dublin, a living city.
However "Eliot's wasteland London is Joyce's center-of-paralysis Dublin"
(Sultan 158). By contrasting *Catch-22* with this pair of high-modernist
texts, we see the remove from culture and history from which Heller's
novel operates. The novel, like *Finnegans Wake*, is not located in the
historical world but in a psychic inner-world—a world in which the conscious mind is depicted as neither awake, as in *The Waste Land* and
Ulysses, nor asleep, as in *Finnegans Wake*. In *Catch-22* humanity is
shown in his true state of waking sleep, gifted with an incomplete consciousness.

Striking out in a new psychological direction, Heller conjoins psychic
archaeology and the evolution of consciousness. The theme of his text,
then, is in Erich Neumann's words that "Ego consciousness has, as the
last-born, to fight for its position and secure it against the assaults of the
Great Mother within and the World Mother without" (*Origins* 299). *Catch-
22* is set on a desert island in the Mediterranean—an island that we are
never shown. Contrapuntally, when Yossarian finally reaches Rome in
chapter thirty-nine, "The Eternal City," the city is an *Inferno*, a via
negativa—the city from which Gilgamesh flies in horror. Heller's Rome,
as Yossarian experiences it, is merely another manifestation of the wasteland that the hero must visit during the Götterdämmerung. The postmodern world is at war, a war that progresses technologically with heli-
copters, computers, and psychoanalysts. At the same time, the world is in
the grasp of the World Mother, and man, as mechanized modern warrior,
lives in the psychic clutch of Lilith, the cold, lunar demoness, the Terrible
Mother whose maw is death, whose womb is birth. Heller's departure
from modernism is definitive: Building on the creations of his literary
forerunners, Heller has constructed a vision that is as unlike anything
Joyce and Eliot originated as their texts were to what came before them.

Stanley Sultan explicates the similarities between Eliot's poem and
Joyce's novel by demonstrating that both of them present three specific
kinds of mythic, literary, and historical figures: males/females who are
victims or victimizers; saviors, martyrs, false and true prophets; and
questers. Not only is this pattern consistent with what we find in *Catch-
22* but also in many cases the figures are identical with those in the texts
by Eliot and Joyce.

The motif of male and female victims is present on every level of *Catch-22*. On the surface level are the marriages of Doc Daneeka and his victimizing wife and Mrs. Scheisskopf and her victimizing husband. The text refers to Hippolytus (176), who was victimized by his stepmother, Phaedra, who also victimized her husband, Theseus. The allusion to *A Streetcar Named Desire* (304) brings in the nefarious Stanley Kowalski, who victimizes both his wife and his sister-in-law. The goddess Ishtar, who generates much of the conflict in *The Gilgamesh Epic*, was a celebrated victimizer of a long list of lovers, so that Heller's incorporation of that text into his novel as the narrative parallel of Yossarian's story inescapably invests *Catch-22* with victimization as one of its central themes. In tablet VI, Gilgamesh enumerates these betrayals as being the cause of his rejection of the alluring goddess's erotic advances. Because Ishtar resents being repulsed by Gilgamesh, she seeks revenge, and thereby brings about two cosmic battles, the death of Enkidu, and thus motivates the hero's quest for immortality.

While this observation does not exhaust the treatment that could be given to the martyr motif in *Catch-22,* it will suffice in that regard to indicate that it is doubly ironic that the most apparent presentation of a martyr is General Peckem's "martyred smile" (124).

The most pervasive savior figure in *Catch-22* is the Egyptian god Osiris, who is embodied as the soldier in white, a figure described as a "mummy" (173). The Egyptians thought of all mummies as emblems of the rebirth made possible by Osiris, and it was through the revivifying power of Osiris that the dead could receive their immortality. Other saviors present in the novel are Tammuz, one of Ishtar's lovers, Prometheus, alluded to throughout the text by means of the stolen Zippo lighter (125), Karl Marx (82), and by implication, Christ.

Catch-22 contains a number of prophets, and prophets are demonstrably more important to the text than martyrs. Foremost is the prophet Elijah, who is represented by the ascent of Clevinger into the clouds (170, 206). In contrast to Clevinger, whose status as Elijah is only implied, the chaplain thinks of Captain Flume as "the prophet Flume," though the suggestion made is that he is a false prophet.

It is clearly the questers who predominate in *Catch-22*. The whole of Gilgamesh's epic is recounted in the novel. Another ancient literary work that presents the quest theme in *Catch-22* is the *Odyssey*, although that epic is but fragmentarily present. Allusions to the *Odyssey* include Major _____ de Coverley being wounded in the eye like the Cyclops, Polyphemus (138, 252), the consumption of Odysseus's men by the Cyclops (presented as the orgy of egg eating precipitated by Milo and de Coverley (140), and the concluding episode of Odysseus's dealings with the Cyclops in which Odysseus (in this case Milo Minderbinder) tells the Cyclops (de Coverley) his name (139). By expanding these associations, we may also see that the episode in which de Coverley rented extensive apartments for the troops (135) is a parody of the Cyclops's cave. Thus it is possible to assign significant portions of the events that take place in *Catch-22* to an origin in the *Odyssey* as well as to assign characters the double role of Odysseus. Other important parallel texts that introduce the quester motif into *Catch-22* belong to the category of classic American novels and include *Huckleberry Finn, Moby Dick*, and *The Leatherstocking Tales*. The text alludes to several episodes of *Huckleberry Finn*, and Huck and Jim's raft figures prominently in the narrative. *Moby-Dick* is named in an early chapter (15), so that the compelling quester Captain Ahab is made inescapable. Cooper's stories are alluded to only vaguely, though their presence is signaled unmistakably by characteristic devices; Cooper's contribution is discussed below in greater detail.

Having discussed the manner in which Heller's use of victimizing couples; saviors, martyrs, and prophets; and questers parallels what are to be found in Eliot and Joyce, it must be pointed out that Heller's employment of these important themes and motifs, while significant, do not constitute the most important intertextual relationship between *Catch-22, The Waste Land*, and *Ulysses*. A more basic relationship exists in the method by which meaning is constructed in all three of these texts. Along these lines, Sultan states that

> Allusion so enhances effect and meaning in parts of *Ulysses* and *The Waste Land* as well; but it has a more fundamental task. Neither work was given a coherent complete literal discourse or action. Rather, the very proceeding in both often is by way of the allusive referents of the words, as much as by way of their lexical referents; in both works, sense and integrity depend upon various objects of allusion. The eventual means by which Eliot won his struggle to achieve an articulate and coherent poem vividly illustrates this fact; nor can one conceive of an articulate and coherent narrative the stories of Bloom and Stephen shorn of the allusions in *Ulysses*. (156)

It is exactly the reading of *Catch-22* as a text lacking what Sultan refers to as a "coherent complete literal discourse or action" (156) that has determined the course of the critical investigation and evaluation of Heller's novel, *Catch-22*. The project dominating the critical understanding of *Catch-22* to date has been the recovery of the order in which the events take place in the fabula (the series of logically and chronologically related events that are caused or experienced by the characters) in contrast to the way in which these events are presented in the text as *narrative*. To this purpose David M. Craig's *Tilting at Mortality: Narrative Strategies in Joseph Heller's* Fiction (1997) comes with a large chart of "Joseph Heller's Schematic Outline for *Catch-22*" folded up and stored in a pocket inside the rear cover of the book. Similarly, Stephen W. Potts included a "substantially accurate chart" (27) at the end of his study. Craig makes sense out of the novel by locating in it a discourse that is "The narrative act itself—part of the story as well as the means of its transmission" (47), and he sees a way past "the novel's scrambled chronology" (51) by locating in Yossarian's story "the distinct pattern of an initiation story" (51). The interest that Heller's critics took in locating an overall pattern in the novel served mainly to embroil them in a controversy that provided few insights into the nature of Heller's art. Perhaps the most useful thing that has been said about *Catch-22* by any of its previous critics was Craig's assertion that "contrary to the complaints of early critics and new readers, *Catch-22* is not simply chaotic, but meticulously written to *appear* chaotic, as Heller has insisted in a number of interviews. It is in fact a painstakingly constructed book" (27).

So painstaking is the construction of Heller's novel that it follows in the mode of *Finnegans Wake*, in that nearly everything found in the novel is an allusion to an outside text. (Additionally, the demarcation of the lexical freedom that becomes routine in *Finnegans Wake* is not a pronounced feature of *Catch-22*, wherein, generally speaking, only the names of the characters advertise some degree of ulterior signification; because of the simulated ordinariness of the language, where in fact there is none, the language of *Catch-22* is, in a sense, more subversive than the tumultuous effects that characterize Joyce's text.) Craig observes that "Recording the series of delays in flying the mission, the scenes in the chapter consistently lead away from Bologna and defuse the narrative audience's expectations that the mission is dangerous. In this method of narration, the scenes themselves become delays" (72). On another level, these distracting scenes are narrative fragments contributed from the parallel plot of *The Gilgamesh Epic* and the other parallel narratives, and, as they intersect they do more important work than the atmospherics and narrative indirection to which Craig assigns them. Craig, however, does connect Heller's lack of chronology to the fundamental "primitive and antirealistic" (72) character of the narrative, though he does not connect Heller's interest in acausality with the overarching influence of *The Gilgamesh Epic*, a text descended from "a dead, alien, fragmentary, undateable and authorless literature" (Black 43). The epic to which *Catch-22* owes so much of its form was a fertile source of antirealism, and when Heller inserted it into the events of the contemporary story it invested the text with its complex meta-antirealisms that result from the erosive effects of time on the clay tablets, the distance from the ancient author of present-day scholars and editors, the compilation of at least two disparate texts of the Gilgamesh cycle into the text known as *Gilgamesh*, and the antirealism of the unavailable Sumerian ur-*Gilgamesh* text, with its embodiment of a primitive state of human consciousness that is shockingly evident throughout the text of the epic.

Thus when we come to what will necessarily be a brief listing of Heller's substitutions, we realize that we do so out of an altogether new contextualization of Heller not as an absurdist-materialist stripe of literary coroner empowered only to effect a "comic dismemberment" (Craig 77) of death but as one who followed Eliot and Joyce into the allusive method of narrative construction. This method was basic to Heller's literary procedures because he subscribed to Eliot's "mythical method," and, as I shall show in the chapters that follow, to Joyce's allusive method as well. Heller, however, is not confined to the mythic and the primitive, for these are mere elements of a larger scheme: On the level of intellectual outlook, Heller's practice was shaped by his adherence to Jung's concept of individuation, and on the spiritual level he reaches toward the Jewish mystical system of the Kabbalah. The complex interplay of these methods and themes, in the final analysis, constitute the narrative of *Catch-22*.

To return to the discussion of Heller's use of Eliot and Joyce in *Catch-22*, it is useful to recognize that there is no simple way of reducing this subject to a formula; Heller's complex incorporation of his models is enacted in a manner that can only be described as playful. For example, in the notes to *The Waste Land*, Eliot cites many texts that he proffers as his sources. However, he does not list *Ulysses* as one of them. Nor does he cite many other sources "of important lines, details and phrases" (Sultan 166). While I do not want to emphasize the methodological connection between *Catch-22* and texts by Eliot and Joyce to Heller's authorial detriment, it is striking that while Eliot is given a curiously pronounced and nonsensical presence in *Catch-22*, there would seem to be an equally palpable absence of easily identifiable references to Joyce or to his texts. It is highly suggestive that by so manifestly pushing Eliot upon the reader, while concealing the far more influential Joyce, that Heller is imitating Eliot's occult treatment of Joyce in *The Waste Land*. Not only does Heller conceal Joyce in the background of his text, but like Eliot, he allows the highly observant reader to see that he is extending this treatment to Joyce, so that Heller follows Eliot in engaging in "jokes, irony, and literary play" at the highest level and touching on the very construction of his text. What has been said about Heller's use of Eliot so far has concerned the evident use of Eliot's name in the novel, and before moving on, it should be pointed out that Heller has also inserted Eliot into the text in other ways—through dispersing the poet's initials throughout the text (see chapter four) and through parodies, echoes, and allusions to *The Waste Land*. For example, the opening of chapter twenty-four, "Milo" is a pastiche of openings that parodies the famous lines that open *The Waste Land*: "April had been the best month of all for Milo. Lilacs bloomed in April and fruit ripened on the vine. Heartbeats quickened and old appetites were renewed. In April a livelier iris gleamed upon the burnished dove. April was spring, and in the spring Milo Minderbinder's fancy turned to thoughts of tangerines" (257). Eliot's lines are "April is the cruellest month, breeding / Lilacs out of the dead land, mixing / Memory and desire, stirring / dull roots with spring rain" (lines 1–4).

One legitimate way of looking at *Catch-22* would be to see the entire novel as a recapitulation of *The Waste Land*, for the novel may be thought of as Eliot's long poem treated to a terrific mythic and literary expansion and having been historically updated. The problem with this way of thinking about the novel is that it detracts from what may be a more comprehensive view of the text as an expansion of Eliot's poem by way of *Ulysses* and *Finnegans Wake*. These things are not being said in order to detract from the literary reputation of Heller's novel but to more accurately contextualize a text that has been discussed previously with little connection to Joyce and none to Eliot; for example, neither Craig nor Potts have an entry for Eliot in their indices; Joyce is discussed in Potts only as an influence from which Heller diverged after writing the first draft of the novel, while Craig's index altogether lacks an entry for Joyce.

A close examination of *Catch-22* demonstrates that even prior to the introduction of Eliot's name in the fourth chapter, we find that we are plunged into the Eliotic universe. In the first chapter, we are informed that "across the aisle from Yossarian was Dunbar, and next to Dunbar was the artillery captain with whom Yossarian had stopped playing chess. The captain was a good chess player, and the games were always interesting. Yossarian had stopped playing chess with him because the games were so interesting they were foolish" (9). One of Heller's devices is to explicitly negate whatever in an episode is of salient interest; here, it is chess, which is done away with not because it is boring but because it is too interesting—a condition which is revealing through its senselessness. The absurdity of the conditions that surround the playing of chess direct us to the importance of chess and throw us back upon Eliot, where we find that the second section of *The Waste Land* is "A Game of Chess," taken from Thomas Middleton's play *Women Beware Women*—a section freighted with allusions to lust and lovelessness (Cleopatra's barge in Shakespeare's *Antony and Cleopatra*, Milton's Garden of Eden in *Paradise Lost*, the rape of Philomel) and an overt blandishment of neurasthenia. Reversal, as we might expect, is an Eliotic technique—and he turns the wolf in John Webster's *The White Devil* into a dog and reverses the normal hostility of the wolf making the point of importance the animal's friendliness to man (Brooks 66). But Heller's crowning bit of Eliotic joking is to construct the Eliotic universe out of Joycean materials—namely, the "ultimate parody-pastiche of the hospital chapter" (Sultan 298) found in chapter fourteen of *Ulysses*.

In arranging his own parody-pastiche, Heller also brings in the Bible, *Huckleberry Finn*, *Finnegans Wake*, *Journey to the End of the Night*, and Freud's essays (WRU, ID). Joyce's hospital chapter provides parodies of Shakespeare, Mallory, Bunyan, Journalese, and modern evangelists (Smith 45). Heller in turn parodies Joyce's chapter, and he transforms Mrs. Purefoy's visit to the maternity hospital for the birth of her ninth baby into Yossarian's faked constipation. Above all, Yossarian's comic scatology is serious play with *waste* and thereby reverberates back to *The Waste Land* in several ways, the most obvious being the implied pun on *waste* and the least obvious being that the meaning of the game of chess in Middleton's play is a *double entendre* for rape, the game of chess in question being a device to keep a widow occupied while her daughter is sexually violated (Brooks "Beliefs" 70). Yet there is high seriousness beneath Heller's play. Once the allusion to Joyce's hospital chapter has been seen for what it is (through the parallel stylistic use of parody-pastiche and the similarity of the setting), we can see that Heller presents the theme of rebirth through Yossarian's "constipation." Here the theme of Heller's hospital episode is identical with the theme of Eliot's poem, that life is futile without a component of spirituality that promotes and nurtures rebirth. Eliot's conception—as explained by Brooks—is that "The fact that men have lost the knowledge of good and evil, keeps them from being alive, and is the justification for viewing the modern waste land as a realm in which the inhabitants do not even exist" ("Beliefs" 60). Heller Has taken up the same theme in *Catch-22*, only he has replaced the moral system of Eliot's Buddhism with the systems of Jung's depth psychology and Luria's visionary Kabbalah.

Thus Heller treats *The Waste Land* as "a poem which takes pleasure in the production of waste" (Armstrong 69). Heller sets up Yossarian to deliver the punch line with which he euphemistically puts away Eliot: "'Still no movement?' the full colonel demanded" (7). It is in the conduction of Yossarian's lack of movement and the allusion to Mrs. Purefoy's ninth baby that Heller's burlesque of Eliot's "abject" (Armstrong 69) discourse is to be discovered. All that is required to complete the associative connections is the further identification of Yossarian's behavior in the hospital as Heller's use (or abuse) of Freud to locate Yossarian on the scale of psychic evolution. Freud states that

> One of the surest premonitions of later eccentricity or nervousness is when an infant obstinately refuses to empty his bowel when placed on the chamber by his nurse, and controls this function at his own pleasure. It naturally does not concern him that he will soil his bed; all he cares for is not to lose the subsidiary pleasure in defecating. Educators have again shown the right inkling when they designate children who withhold these functions as naughty ("Infantile Sexuality" *Basic Writings* 389)

The infantilism that Yossarian exhibits belongs to Eliot as well. Eliot's poem is famously lacking "any redeeming vision of social order, or of an internal aesthetic of efficiency" (Armstrong 70). Thus it is his vision of a fragmented world consisting only of incoherent waste without any alternative that Heller satirizes in the hospital chapter that opens *Catch-22*.

As I have stated, the poet T.S. Eliot's presence is met within a disparate number of ways. Besides the fact that *Catch-22* provides the novel an important component of its method and argument, we find that other poems by Eliot appear in the text, such as the pastiche of "The Lovesong of J. Alfred Prufrock" on pages 146–47. The role of Prufrock has been assumed by Captain Black, whose "skinny long legs" allude to the poem's "They will say: 'But how his arms and legs are thin!'"(line 44). The novel presents revisions and even reversals of the major images of the poem— "the cloying yellow stillness" (147) for Eliot's "the yellow fog that rubs its back upon the window-panes, / The yellow smoke that rubs its muzzle on the window-panes" (lines 15-16); "inquired with indifferent curiosity" (147) for Eliot's "To lead you to an overwhelming question" (line 10); and we even find that Heller has supplied a "drug" (146), "the squadron stood insensate" (146), and a "long table of smoothed wood" (147) that makes it possible to reconstruct Eliot's famous line about a "patient etherised upon a table" (line 3).

While the pursuit of Eliot through the sundry levels of the novel reveals the complexity of its intricate intertextual and semiotic structures, it is ultimately a dead end. The significance of Eliot to *Catch-22* does not lie in the degree to which he has been inserted into the text but rather the degree to which Eliot's method has been incorporated into the aspects of the novel by which its meaning is formalized. Heller's particularized use of Eliot in contrast to his particularized use of Joyce establishes the centrality of the difference the two authors with respect to Heller's use of them. While Joyce's text recapitulates Homer's *Odyssey*, the manner of its so doing is radically different from the way that Eliot treats his materials. Bloom and Stephen run through the course of the ancient epic in one day in Dublin. M. Keith Booker states that "one could argue that Joyce's parodic use of Homer as a structural model calls the authority of the epic into question, exposing the cracks and fissures in a genre that would seek to pass itself off as a seamless whole" (25). He goes on to observe that

> Joyce doubly evades the trap of the past in his use of the mythic method. Not only does he refuse to accept unquestionably the authority of past tradition, but also he opposes that authority in a way that remains intensely centered in the present. Moreover, Joyce is not kicking a dead horse by parodying the activities of ancient Greeks and Hebrews like Homer and Jesus. Rather, he is using these parodies to focus his subversive energies on the continuation of ancient ideologies in a present where they are no longer useful or relevant—except as a means of perpetuating the tyranny of the past. (29)

For Booker, "Eliot embodies precisely the traditional respect for authority that Joyce seeks to subvert in his appropriation of Homer" (29)—a point that we will return to presently.

In the final analysis, the perceived disparity between Eliot and Joyce is what Booker calls "Eliot—with his privileging of the eternal—and Joyce—with his privileging of the historical" (29). Thus, Joyce's treatment of his ancient materials is changeably excremental, trivializing, and dissenting. To whatever Bloom may be said to inhabit in the persona of Odysseus, he is no warrior, he has no crew to lose, he fights no battles, and his possibility for risk is very little—as are his possibilities for gains. When Joyce's enraged citizen throws a biscuit tin at Bloom in the "Cyclops" chapter in imitation of the boulder that the Cyclops throws at Odysseus, the episode has suffered an obvious and telling demotion.

In its replication of *The Gilgamesh Epic, Catch-22* has maintained the verities of mystery, passion, struggle, battle, death, horror, defeat, fear, accident, decay, futility, and loss that occupy the narrative of the ancient poem. What it means that Eliot privileges the eternal is that in *The Waste Land* we also encounter the substantiated exigencies of existence heightened by their poetic context. Eliot may offer a fragmented view of the world, but this wasted land is tangibly one in which history has taken place—and the fragments are the remains of events that have taken place in the passage of time. Eliot's eternal plane does not intersect the poem to the detriment of its power to portray life. History is presented as a catalog of "Falling towers / Jerusalem Athens Alexandria / Vienna London / Unreal" (lines 374–77). The poem brings us face-to-face with the First World War and the first Punic War. The unreality of the cities, the hollowness of the loves, and the devastations of the wars are not experienced on the historical and horizontal plane of the poem but only on the eternal, vertical objective plane. Heller recapitulates Eliot's concern with what I will call *the eternal unreal* by introducing into his text an analogous catalog in the mouth of the "evil and debauched ugly old man" (247)—who is reminiscent of Eliot's Tiresias ("Old man with wrinkled female breasts"; McMichaels 1172, line 228). Heller's old man gives Yossarian his version of the unreality of history through a catalog of fallen civilizations: "'Rome was destroyed, Greece was destroyed, Persia was destroyed. Why not yours? How much longer do you really think your own country will last? Forever? Keep in mind that the earth itself is destined to be destroyed by the sun in twenty-five million years or so'" (249). In both Eliot's and Heller's texts there is a struggle that revolves around the attempt on the part of those few who are aware of the contingencies of being to direct the gaze of the protagonist from the panorama of passing, momentary events to the view of life *sub species aeternitatis*.

The Waste Land is essentially a morality tale—little more than a series of warnings: "One must be so careful these days" (line 59), "He who was living is now dead" (line 328), and the bitingly explicit "The awful daring of a moment's surrender / Which an age of prudence can never retract / By this, and this only, we have existed (lines 404–07). Madame Sosostris's warning to "Fear death by water" (line 55) is the poem's organizing trope. She warns her client whose Tarot card is the drowned Phoenician sailor that he is in danger of repeating the events of his former life, which always bring about the same outcome. Like his former incarnation, Phlebas the Phoenician, who drowns in the "Death by Water" section of the poem he is heading for the same fate. The Tarot card reader's warning is synonymous with the Hindu and Buddhist teaching of the law of Karma which proscribes that the quality of one's deeds determines that a person will either become one with the divine Being in his impersonal aspect and no longer suffer human birth or he subject to subsequent human births. The circular imagery (e.g., "And puts a record on the gramophone"; line 256) that inhabits *The Waste Land* is derived from the Buddhist metaphor that describes the human situation as being on the *wheel* of birth, death, and rebirth. Eliot's poem introduces this scheme into the poem through reference to the Buddha's "Fire Sermon," which gives the third section of the poem its name, and through the Sanskrit inclusions in the fifth section, "What the Thunder Said," in which the Lord Brahman speaks through the thunder.

In *Catch-22* the law of Karma is presented comically, pseudo-absurdly, and without Eliot's Hindu and Buddhist trappings, so that it takes the form of a principle of eternal recurrence. Nevertheless, the scheme of eternal recurrence, which served as the concept from which Eliot generated his poem, also served Heller as the origin of his text. In *Catch-22* the motif of eternal recurrence appears under several guises, but its most obvious form is the idea that things are going around twice. In its most trivialized and reduced form, the motif appears when Yossarian takes "his flight of six planes over the target a second time" (141). Yossarian's act of "going around twice" (143) produces incomprehension in the command staff to such a degree that while they are discussing what should be done to punish Yossarian for such an insane stunt, Colonel Korn laughingly observes that "It seems to me that we're going around twice" (143). Korn's speech is a deflated delivery of Madame Sosostris's advice to her client and, equally, the burden of what the whole of *The Waste Land* expresses—that "Gentile or jew / O you who turn the wheel" (lines 319-20)—everyone is going around twice.

In contrast to the travestied handling that eternal recurrence is given in much of *Catch-22*, the motif receives a metaphysical treatment in chapter twenty, "Corporal Whitcomb," where the chaplain's mysticism allows him to contemplate and analyze "a weird, occult sensation of having experienced the identical situation before in some prior time of existence" (209). Having allowed the chaplain to stumble onto this profound insight and to give it a clear expression, the episode then deflates and reverses the chaplain's mysticism and renders his experience as another eruption of nonsense. Despite the chaplain's religious role in society, he understands his numinous experience as paramnesia and worries about its relationship to "such corollary optical phenomena as *jamais vu*, never seen, and *presque vu*, almost seen" (209). The episode shows the chaplain trying to work out the difference between what is real and what is illusion, and in his consideration, we see that he is brought up most sharply by seeing "the naked man in the tree at Snowden's funeral" (210). As we will see, what the chaplain sees and cannot grasp is eternal recurrence, and though the chaplain knows that it was not *presque vu*, *déjà vu*, or *jamais vu*, he does not realize that the phenomenon belongs to an order of reality for which he lacks a category.

Heller's appropriation the law of Karma or eternal recurrence from *The Waste Land* figures importantly in chapter thirty, "Dunbar." The passage in question, the description of Yossarian's encounter with a drowned man, seems anything but Eliotic at first view: "a tufted round log that was drifting toward him on the tide turned unexpectedly into the bloated face of a drowned man; it was the first dead person he had ever seen. He thirsted for life and reached out ravenously to grasp and hold Nurse Duckett's flesh" (347). The conjoined apparition of the drowned man, Yossarian's sudden thirst for life, and his desperate embrace of a woman suggests *The Waste Land,* with its drowned Phoenician in the "Death by Water" section, the lack of water (thus "thirst") in the "What the Thunder Said" section, and the clinging to life through sexuality that is expressed in lines such as "My nerves are bad to-night. Yes, bad. Stay with me" (line 111) and "I raised my knees / supine on the floor of a narrow canoe" (lines 294–95).

One problem in evaluating Heller's appropriation of Eliot is that most critics do not understand the degree of seriousness with which he addressed the subject of reincarnation in *The Waste Land.* Eliot's poem is usually thought of as indicating the futility and depravity of modern life. However, this was not the entirety of Eliot's position. Heller's novel, *Catch-22*, in its intertextual appropriation of Eliot's poem is a reading of the poem, and it is clear that Heller has read *The Waste Land* as a poem that is grounded in Hindu, Buddhist, and occult systems that hold the concept of reincarnation in high regard. Thus, while Heller demonstrates throughout *Catch-22* that his novel recapitulates *The Waste Land,* we are likely to miss much of that activity unless we take into consideration the paramount importance of "going around twice" in *The Waste Land,* for it is contributory to the centrality of that theme in *Catch-22.*

Tom Gibbons states that "When Eliot was a young man, a great many artists and intellectuals were 'drunk' with occultism, just as their successors were with Marxism in the Thirties" (136–37). Prior to the composition of his famous poem, Eliot, like so many of his contemporaries, had been pursuing an interest in occultism. In the spring of 1921, P.D. Ouspensky, a mystic and mathematician much in demand by the Anglo-American literary avant-garde, who had sat out the world war in Turkey, was brought to live and teach in London. A.R. Orage arranged to have groups attend Ouspensky's lectures, and as soon as Ouspensky arrived, weekly meetings were held in Lady Rothmere's study in St. Johns's Wood.

T.S. Eliot was a close friend of Orage's, and he attended some of the meetings (Welch 23). Eliot drafted *The Waste Land* during a rest cure at Margate and Lausanne during the autumn of 1921, subsequent to his attendance at Ouspensky's lectures.

Eliot's serious pursuits of occultism, Buddhist spirituality, and the philosophy of Friedrich Nietzsche (an interest that he shared with Orage) have begun to be investigated, and it has become increasingly evident that the elaborate notes that Eliot attached to *The Waste Land* were supplied in order to confuse his readers about the esoteric nature of the poem. In his reconsideration of the background of *The Waste Land*, Tom Gibbons registers Eliot's evasions, stating that "Eliot appears to have known considerably more about occult literature than he admitted in his notes to *The Waste Land*. He adds that "The Tarot cards appear to play a much more important part in the meaning and organization of *The Waste Land* than is generally allowed" (136). Gibbons, thus, revises the view that Eliot had no great interest in the occult: Some critics have simply accepted on faith Eliot's contradictory statement. In note 46 that he was "not familiar with the exact constitution of the Tarot pack of cards, from which I have obviously departed to suit my own convenience." In order to lend support to his critical revision of *The Waste Land*, Gibbons reassessed Eliot's borrowings from the Tarot, and he shows that Eliot's poem contains several more references and allusions to the Tarot than the ones named in the text and notes: the Sun (lines 22 and 225), Death (lines 55 and 63), the World (line 102), the Fool (line 162), the Moon (line 199), the Lovers (line 250), the Wheel (line 320), the Hermit (line 356), the Tower Struck by Lightning (lines 373, 394, and 429). Kings occur in lines 66, 192, and 192, and a Queen occurs in line 258 (Gibbons 136–37).

It is worth speculating that another of Heller's Eliotic games might be that he included in *Catch-22* the Tarot pack of cards, so that Appleby is a Fool (110), Milo is a King (244), the bombed mountain village (334) is the Tower Struck by Lightning, Flume is a Hermit (133), the soldier in white is Death (171), and Yossarian and Luciana are the Lovers (158), however, given the generality of such comparisons, it is difficult to say whether or not Heller had the Tarot specifically in mind.

For some reason, Eliot felt the need to obscure the influence that his occult pursuits had on his writing, and he, therefore, occluded—and even trivialized—the esoteric contents of *The Waste Land*. As a result of his efforts at concealment, the text that he produced achieved the "evasive" and "ambiguous" quality of the notes that Gibbons noticed, and what an earlier critic, M.L. Rosenthal, described as Eliot's capacity for being "mischievous." Like Gibbons, Rosenthal remarked upon the contradictions that Eliot had made in his notes: Rosenthal notes that Eliot cannot both say that he is "not familiar with the exact constitution of the Tarot pack of cards" and then acknowledge that he has altered it, while stating that the Man with Three Staves is "an authentic member of the Tarot pack" if he wants to be taken seriously. Rosenthal finds Eliot's note 367 "Intriguingly misleading":

> The point is that the poem uses Tiresias, not the other way around. For the moment only, it assumes what Eliot calls a "quasi-dramatic" mode or an "assumed voice." The immediate effect is of subjective, lyrical lament erupting three times in the course of the relatively brisk and objective narrative. This section, with its refrain-like interruptions, is fairly sustained, but of course elsewhere the poem's tonal shifts are extremely rapid. Indeed, it is just such shifts that made *The Waste Land* so explosively original. (162)

A reading of *The Waste Land* in the light of the Ouspensky system suggests that Rosenthal spoke better than he knew: Eliot used Tiresias as a symbol of reincarnation, capitalizing on the Greek seer's unique mythological role of having lived both as a man and as a woman. According to Ouspensky, souls routinely reincarnate as both sexes. *The Waste Land*, then, can be read as a poetic manual that gives directions for escaping from the wheel of death and rebirth, symbolized in the poem by a proliferation of circles and wheels.

It is well established that Eliot was familiar with Sanskrit literature, and this fact has veiled his familiarity with esoteric doctrines. Critics often point out Buddhist doctrines that have been identified in the poem, but the poem's emphasis on reincarnation and the theme of escape from the wheel of birth and death seemed to have escaped notice, as have other, more esoteric references. With regard to Heller, we should note the marked agreement among Ouspensky's occultism, Hinduism, Buddhism, and Kabbalah—all of which teach that repeated lives either gradually bring the soul closer to a state of perfection or eternally recur in a tiring round of incomplete lives in human and nonhuman forms. Thus, the Kabbalistic doctrines that inform *Catch-22* would seem to have injected into the text a component of the doctrine of eternal recurrence from a source different from those used by Eliot but in agreement with them.

Part of Ouspensky's teaching concerned reincarnation. In a novel that he published in Russia in 1915, Ouspensky told the story of Ivan Osokin, a man who realized that the life he was living was the same life that he had repeated countless times; having made this discovery, Osokin tries to change his ways, but finds that he lacks the will. Mieke Bal makes the comment in *Narratology* that Eliot's poem may be termed a narrative poem, but that this does not often happen because its poetic character is more salient and overrides the narrative reading of the poem (9); were the poem given this unusual attention, the result is that one would conclude that Eliot's poem and Ouspensky's novel have the identical plot.

As we have seen, *Ulysses* deflates and trivializes the contents of the *Odyssey* to such an extent that a boulder becomes a biscuit tin. In such a scheme, if we understand Bloom to be Odysseus, we must agree that the events of Bloom's life are not directly equivalent to those of Odysseus's. While reincarnation was probably not in Joyce's mind when he wrote *Ulysses*, the idea that Odysseus is "going around twice" certainly was, and this realization helps us to visualize the differences between a literary form of repetition, eternal recurrence, and reincarnation. In reincarnation the soul is carried over so that the same spiritual essence experiences a new life—and we can see that Bloom (or anybody else) might be a reincarnation of Odysseus. With eternal recurrence, however, the events repeat, so that the drowning of Phlebas the Phoenician is not some disconnected event, it foreshadows what will happen to Madame Sosostris's client who is told to "Fear death by water," for he is Phlebas come again and will again drown. The eternal recurrence in Nietzsche's philosophy, which may have come to Eliot's notice through Orage's interest in that philosopher, is by contrast an abstract form of the concept and bears little resemblance to the "narratives" of Eliot and Heller. Moreover, Nietzsche embraced eternal recurrence as unwavering and irrevocable, and he urged that one must love one's fate: For him there was no escape from the endless repetition of the same life. In both Eliot and Heller, the impetus for knowing that which Madame Sosostris is forbidden to see (line 54) and the absolute truth that the chaplain approaches "in brilliant flashes of clarity that almost came to him" (210) is that they portend a means of escape from the eternal round—Eliot's "crowds of people, walking round in a ring" (line 56). Thus, the attitude to eternal recurrence in Eliot and Heller is, at a certain point, a rejection of one's fate and a determination to choose a fate that, ultimately, overcomes fate altogether. Of course, *Catch-22* is a unique text in that it takes a comic rather than a tragic approach to its protagonist. Osokin and Phlebas the Phoenician fail to save themselves, while we see that at the conclusion of his narrative Yossarian-Gilgamesh resolves to strike out in a new direction. In Heller's text it is the reader who witnesses Yossarian's escape from the wheel of Karma, though it is likely that most readers do not make this connection—only realizing that Yossarian has resolved to live. Through the device of Joycean multi-characterality (see immediately below) we are allowed to see Yossarian, in the guise of the chaplain, come close to working out the delineaments of eternal recurrence. However, we never see that this principle is consciously grasped by any of the "characters." Similarly, Eliot addresses his poem to the reader, reserving the ten lines of the "Death by Water" section of the poem for this purpose: "Gentile of jew / O you who turn the wheel and look to windward, / Consider Phlebas, who was once handsome and tall as you." (lines 319–21).

Having said something about Heller's use of Eliot's long poem in *Catch-22*, the rest of the chapter will discuss his incorporation of Joycean devices into the novel. In *Catch-22* Heller made extensive use of both *Ulysses* and *Finnegans Wake*, and it would require a sustained exegesis in order to provide adequate coverage to this very interesting topic. All that can be done in the essay at hand is to make a few generalized comments and to point toward the significance of Heller's use of Joyce in his novel. Though it may turn out to be criminally reductive to say so, in the absence of other critical exploration of the relationship of Heller's novel to Joyce's, I will venture to say that *Catch-22* may be understood to include one major structural contribution from *Ulysses* and one from *Finnegans Wake*. While other incorporations abound, compared to the two major devices that Heller borrowed from Joyce, the rest are minor appurtenances. *Ulysses*, of course, supplies the idea of the parallel text, here *The Gilgamesh Epic*. Without this device, the novel does not rise above the plane of materialism, determinism, and absurdity and is thereby prevented from symbolizing the collective unconscious and the metaphysical described by the Kabbalah in its depiction of the seven ethereal worlds of the Sephirot (the ladder or tree of life). The contribution to *Catch-22* of *Finnegans Wake* is what Margot Norris calls the "shifting, uncertain nature of characters" in that novel. Addressing Joyce's handling of characterization in *Finnegans Wake*, Tindall states that "In short, the people of the *Wake*, all thousand and one of them, are members or projections of the family, aspects of H.C.E. and A.L.P., who, in a sense, are the only people of the *Wake* and in the world" (quoted in Norris 30). As we have seen from the discussion above, the old man is at one point identifiable as Odysseus and at another as Tiresias, while Colonel _____de Coverley has been shown to be Polyphemus and Prometheus; this feature of the shifting nature of characters runs throughout the text, and the characters constantly change their roles. This aspect of the novel is discussed in detail in the chapter that follows.

Having adopted Joyce's shifting characterization that expands from the two archetypal characters who populate *Finnegans Wake*, Heller then parodies Joyce's use of the device, so that not only is *Catch-22* similarly populated by an archetypal couple, Heller's use of the device also serves to announce the Joycean influence. To insure that the characters may be read as shifting and uncertain and to further connect his use of the device to Joyce, Heller has given some of the characters in *Catch-22* names that are obviously derived from *Finnegans Wake*. The best example of a name that connects *Catch-22* to *Finnegans Wake* is that of Chief White Halfoat, as his ostentatiously curious name is readily identifiable as a derivation from Joyce's permutations of "Whitehead" and "White Hat" (McHugh 535) into "Old Whitehowth" and "whiteoath" (FW 535). Leaving nothing to chance by way of marking a trail back to *Finnegans Wake*, the same page of Joyce's novel that relates to Chief White Halfoat also discloses that the dying "colonel in Communications" (15) of the opening chapter of *Catch-22* is borrowed from "That was Communicator, a former colonel. A discarnated spirit, called Sebastion" (535–36). The redundant nature of the clues in *Catch-22* that refer to *Finnegans Wake* make it clear Heller wanted the reader to be able to connect *Catch-22* to *Finnegans Wake;* at the same time it is evident that to make such a connection is also to realize that Heller's scheme is a critique of Joyce's novel and that *Catch-22* revises Joyce as much as it revises Eliot. Though Heller takes much from Eliot and Joyce, he synthesizes their narrative and architectural methods into something radically innovative, just as he departs entirely from their fundamental ideas on culture, psychology, and metaphysics.

By way of examining this shifting nature of characterization in *Catch-22*, let us briefly interrogate the means by which Heller incorporated archetypal man and woman into his text. As we have seen, H.C.E. and A.L.P. have been wholly imported into the text of *Catch-22*. However, having said this it is difficult to assess Heller's treatment of H.C.E. and A.L.P. In the first place, women have not been given important roles in *Catch-22*, nor does marriage hold the prominent position in Heller's novel that it does in Joyce's. Nevertheless, a careful study of Heller's text reveals that Heller's old man and old woman are indeed Joyce's prime pair. This may be worked out if the moaning that is so prominent in *Catch-22*, occupying the better part of a chapter (twenty-one, "General Dreedle" 225–30) and reappearing at other points (172, 217) is understood to be an important clue that necessitates its prominent, though enigmatic, inclusion in the text. This moaning is Heller's presentation of A.L.P.'s dying moans: "sad and weary I go back to you, my cold father, my cold mad father, my cold mad feary father, till the near sight of the mere size of him, the moyles and moyles of it, *moanoaning*, makes me seasilt saltsick" (628; emphasis added). The old man and old woman make an early entrance to the text as "patriotism" and "matriotism"(9). The comedy inherent in their introduction is completed by the tragedy of their departure at the novel's conclusion, where the old man is dead (416), and we see that the old woman is A.L.P., for "She was talking aloud to herself when Yossarian entered and began moaning as soon as she saw him" (415).

In the face of the identification of H.C.E. and A.L.P. with the old man and old woman of *Catch-22*, we are left to puzzle out that T.S. Eliot—whose initials are T.S.E.—is represented in the text by *The Saturday Evening Post* (194, 198, 201, 202, 290)—which also has the initials T.S.E., though it further disguises an identification with Eliot by the inescapable letter p. Any examination of the text with attention to initials reveals that ex-P.F.C. Wintergreen (38, 108, 124, 140, 331, 414, 458) is the only character in *Catch-22* whose name—as it regularly appears in the text—contains a three-letter abbreviation. This suggestion can be combined with the departure of Milo from his syndicate in chapter thirty-five. At that point in the narrative, Milo describes the operation of his business to Colonel Cathcart through a series of abbreviations: C.O.D., M.I.F., F.O.B., E.O.M. (381), N.M.T.F. (382). The series continues into a subsequent chapter: Q.E.D. (391). On one level of the text, Heller seems to be pointing the reader toward his text's inclusions from Joyce's texts, where similar initials abound. There is also the suggestion that, since at the conclusion of the novel (458), M & M Enterprises (M & M E), and ex-P.F.C. Wintergreen have merged their business operations, we may see in the conjoined names an ironic reflection of the heteronormative archetype expressed by the relationship between H.C.E. and A.L.P. The merging of Minderbinder and Wintergreen is another eruption of the homoerotic theme that is expressed in *Catch-22* through prevalent pairs of men, such as Pilchard and Wren, Yossarian and Dunbar, and Gus and Wes. (Chapter four of this study discusses the treatment of homoeroticism in *Catch-22*.)

Some notion of Heller's complex relationship to so-called high modernism has been broached in this essay, and what has been established in this regard will have to suffice. More than anything else, this exercise demonstrates that it is not possible in one chapter to amend thirty years of critical misinterpretation and misreading. Joseph Heller has shown himself to be a patient, reserved, and esoteric writer. In contrast to Joyce, Eliot, and Pound, he has not troubled himself to direct and oversee the critical reception of his work. The extent to which the reputations of Joyce and Eliot as major authors were the results of astute and tireless public relations campaigns is a matter of record and has been written about many times. Tindall states that "Not altogether reliant upon title as clue, however, Joyce told friends, who, as if horse's mouthpieces, published the news" (128).

Allowing his novel to go its own way, Heller never pursued activities that would determine the reception or interpretation of his novel. Though he has seemed to offer guidance, critics have also commented on the consistent vagueness of his responses to their inquiries. When critics have come to him, he has given them what they have asked for but has not revealed his sources or corrected their assumptions or conclusions. The reasons for this way of handling things are obvious: Heller is a serious, complex, and powerful writer, and as such he knows the limitations of what passes for critical and scholarly opinions. Heller's conduct seems to demonstrate an attitude that his works are there for the use of serious readers, and if these readers prove themselves inadequate, that is none of his affair. The idea that plagiary comes into the picture is but a demonstration that they have been poor readers who have interested themselves in his writings.

Kathleen Raine tells of a poet who "had the humility to admit that he had not understood Muir and proposed to wait until he did before writing about him. The more usual academic mentality is undeterred by any such doubts, as we see in book after book in which ignorance passes judgment upon knowledge" (118). The above quotation comes from an essay, "On the Symbol" in which Raine discusses the problem of the loss of the meaning of the symbol in modern, anti-metaphysical thought. What she has to say in her essay may be applied to the specifics of the critical reception of Joseph Heller, for he like many authors is an example of a writer whose work has been subjected to inadequate critical frameworks. By way of ending this chapter, I will quote the section of her essay that most directly applies to how, in my view, this problem has skewed the prior readings of Heller's novel:

> Visionaries are not iconoclasts. It is immediately evident, to those who are familiar with the universal language of symbolic discourse, whether a poet (writing of sea or river, wind or garden or cave or bird) is using such terms as words within the universal language, or in a personal and imaginatively unlearned way; those who know the secret language immediately recognize it, or miss its presence; while those, on the contrary, who do not know it may read even Shelley's 'Ode to the West Wind' under the impression that its images are merely descriptive of

natural appearances; to such there is no difference in kind between Shelley and Swinburne . . . . We shall do wrong if we think of symbols as single poetic images, used to obtain some literary effect; rather symbol is a language in each of whose parts a whole is implied, and each symbol in some measure makes known to us that whole, as a whole, and in its wholeness. (119–20)

In the following chapters we will move upward along the ladder, from the despair and acceptance of *Gilgamesh* in the following chapter, through the higher evocations of eros, psyche, individuation, and, ultimately, to the Absolute, for the plan of the *Catch-22*, a question that has been the object of so much critical scrutiny, is the plan of the universe as mapped by the ten Sefirot, and it leads from ordinary life to divinity.

Chapter 2

Catch-22 and The Gilgamesh Epic

In his discussion of the stylistic development of *Catch-22*, Stephen Potts quotes Frederick Karl's assertion that an early version of the novel incorporated the Joycean features of free association and stream of consciousness (36). Potts does not insist that in succeeding drafts of the developing text Heller abandoned the direction of high modernism, though Potts leaves the reader to infer such a conclusion from his subsequent assignment of *Catch-22* to the Kafka, Celine, West tradition (112), and, again, to the Kafka, West, and the black humor tradition (114). Potts's placement of Heller in the black humor school is not unqualified, for he does submit that the conclusion of *Catch-22* is more hopeful than this tradition would presuppose.

The thesis that I propose in this essay is that rather than turning entirely away from the procedures of the Joycean style, Heller looked unalterably toward both *Ulysses* and *Finnegans Wake* for his modernist ur-texts. Consequently, in order to read *Catch-22* adequately, we must turn to Joyce in order to establish an intertextual reading that opens up *Catch-22* to its full range of metonymic and symbolic resonances. In reassigning Heller to a new place in the scheme of literary history, my revised reading of *Catch-22* places the text, so to speak, between the high modernist "present" of *Ulysses* and *Finnegans Wake* and the "primitive past" of *The Odyssey*; of course one of Heller's innovations is that, while he had no choice but to extend Joycean procedures into a time beyond the publication of *Finnegans Wake*, he also expands the span of time encompassed by his text by extending the past back beyond the Greece of the 13th century B.C. depicted in *The Odyssey* to the Sumerian culture of 2700 B.C. Should the text which serves as a chronological pole that may be opposed to the modern present of *Catch-22* continue in its undisclosed state, Heller's text would have remained without a second temporal reference in the past and thereby it would have remained as lost to a complexity of interpretation as *Ulysses* would have continued to possess were its intertextual relationship to *The Odyssey* and other mythic veils to have remained undisclosed.

Along these lines it is useful to review what William York Tindall has said about the parallelism of *The Odyssey* to *Ulysses*:

> Of parallels Homer's *Odyssey* is principal, as Joyce's title, helping the reader out, implies. To have called *A Portrait Daedalus*—as, indeed, the French translator did—would have given suitable prominence to a parallel parallel. Not altogether reliant upon title as clue, however, Joyce told friends, who, as if horse's mouth-pieces, published the news. Therefore, readers of French little magazines (T.S. Eliot for example) had some idea of the Homeric parallel from the start. . . . I liked the book at once for its texture and massiveness, but the title, date, and theme remained beyond me when, at the summer's end, I came home on the S.S. Homeric—and for long after. Today, what Joyce told Valery Larbaud and other friends is available to all in a convenient chart, published by Stuart Gilbert, one of those friends, in his study of *Ulysses*. (127–28)

It is a surprise to learn that in order for the parallels between *Ulysses* and *The Odyssey* to come to light it was necessary for Joyce to have announced them. Coming after Joyce in the way he did, Heller is inescapably post-Joycean. However, one might arrive at different conclusions by attributing too much to Joyce's impact. Robert Martin Adams states that "The *Ulysses*-procedure of maintaining a running parallel with a single specific myth (or alternatively, of maintaining an overlay of myth above fable or vice versa) has continued as a working technique of fiction, but not generally with Joyce's effects and never on Joyce's scale." (40); he also states that "the immense pan-mythical resonances of *Finnegans Wake* have no major influence at all on subsequent writers" (40). In such a climate, it would defy expectations to look for both the use of myth on a Joycean scale and the pan-mythical resonances of *Finnegans Wake* in a text that appears to some critics to belong to the absurdist school. It is, then, revelatory to locate the text of *Catch-22* in its proper relationship to *The Gilgamesh Epic* and subsequently to recognize the considerable technical and even spiritual influences (Adams 4) of Joyce's texts on Heller as he came to shape the final form of *Catch-22*.

In its latest version, "*The Gilgamesh Epic* is an epic poem covering twelve tablets and written in Akkadian, the main Semitic language of Babylonia and Assyria. It describes the exploits of Gilgamesh, a king of the Sumerian city-state Uruk. . ." (Tigay 3). By stating that *Catch-22* has a formative and overarching textual relationship to *The Gilgamesh*

Epic, I do not mean to indicate merely that *Catch-22* is an imitation of the ancient text but that *Catch-22* is a modern remaking of the epic along the lines of Joyce's appropriation of *The Odyssey* in formulating *Ulysses*. Robert Martin Adams states that for Joyce "The Homeric incident acts as a container into which Joyce pours just about anything he wants" (41). At the same time, however, Adams notes that Joyce's text is characterized by an innovative use of "the intimate structure of the imitating work, episode by episode in . . . the exoskeleton way that we find Homer being employed by Joyce" (39). While the parallel between *Ulysses* and *The Odyssey* is analogous to the parallel between *Catch-22* and *The Gilgamesh Epic*, the Akkadian influence on *Catch-22*—as we shall see—is just as complex as is the modernist. The strong influence of the Akkadian text on *Catch-22* stems from the fact that the Akkadian version of *The Gilgamesh Epic* is an "instance of creative borrowing which substantially amounts to an independent creation" (Pritchard 73) based on original Sumerian poems, which presented Heller with its own technical and spiritual influences. Thus, there was more involved in the production of *Catch-22* than Heller's substitution of *The Gilgamesh Epic* for *the Odyssey* as the exoskeleton of his text. Additionally, the Akkadian poem is the result of a long literary evolution and a historical deconstruction, and, in a sense, is not available to the contemporary reader; such as it exists, the epic consists of a compilation of the fragments of several versions of the text, and is the result of the work of archaeologists and Assyriologists rather than the work of an Assyrian Homer. *Gilgamesh* has come down to us as a pastiche of ancient texts that has been assembled by Assyriologists who cannot help but apprise the reader of the stylistic evolution of the epic over the two thousand years of its literary centrality in ancient cultures. Furthermore, to read the epic is necessarily to confront scholarly editions that emphasize the existence of the text in its various versions, recensions, copies, and manuscripts—all contributing to many difficulties of interpretation. *Gilgamesh* also presents the experts with insoluble questions as to matters of language, customs, and culture.

Heller's recreation of *The Gilgamesh Epic* in *Catch-22* introduced a further complexity in that, at the modern pole of influence, he is stylistically situated between *Ulysses* and *Finnegans Wake*. For Joseph Heller to employ *The Gilgamesh Epic* as he has in writing *Catch-22* is roughly analogous to what we would have if Joyce had structured *Ulysses* along the line of multidirectional anti-narrative and the "shifting, uncertain nature of characters" (Norris 30) he used in *Finnegans Wake*. Heller bypasses the relatively rigid temporal linearity of *Ulysses* for the "Panmythical resonances" (Adams 40), "atrophy of narrative, ironing out of paper thin characters, [and] multidirectional anti-narrative reading habits" (Adams 69) of *Finnegans Wake*. While the *Wake* tells a story (Tindall avers that it has "the ghost of a plot" [241]), its allusions are not to one central text, as in the *Ulysses-Odyssey* relationship but to an unspecified everything: "*Finnegans Wake* is about *Finnegans Wake*. That is this: not only about everything, the book is about putting everything down in records and interpreting them" (Tindall 237). For his part, Heller accomplishes a simultaneous fracturing of the space-time continuum in two parallel stories—Yossarian's and Gilgamesh's—in such a way that both stories may be independently reconstructed and events from *The Gilgamesh Epic* can be assigned a parallel location in the *Catch-22* narrative, yet there seems to be no simple scheme of relations between *Catch-22* and the epic that will explain why *Catch-22* manifests the particular narrative structure that Heller gave it—a structure over which critics have puzzled for thirty years.

Though it would be both useful and interesting to explicate the many questions arising out of the association of *Catch-22* with *The Gilgamesh Epic*, it is only feasible, while broaching this topic for the first time, to indicate the general outline of the ways in which Heller has utilized *The Gilgamesh Epic* in constructing his text. My examination of *Catch-22* shows that in his use of ancient materials, Heller was not limited to the retelling of the epic. Heller's utilization of Gilgamesh's narrative in his text includes allusions to aspects of ancient Assyrian culture that are beyond the contents of the epic; these extra-epic materials are largely drawn from Frazer and Weston, the same texts that Eliot consulted in writing *The Waste Land*.

Heller, like Joyce, Pound, and Eliot may be shown to have researched obscure aspects of ancient languages and cultures in order to provide his difficult text with the requisite depth of reference. At the same time—it must be urged—Heller inserted into the surface of his text a system of allusions, which serve as either clues or riddles, to alert the reader to his intertextual methodology. Despite these conditions, it is not surprising that *Catch-22*'s connection to *The Gilgamesh Epic* has for so long eluded Heller's critics, even though they have in many instances glimpsed discrete aspects of the text's underlying plan. Now that we are in a position to see the problem whole, it follows that what remains to be done here is to provide some idea of Heller's innovations along the lines of his incorporation of *The Gilgamesh Epic* into *Catch-22*, so that subsequent critical treatments of his oeuvre will be able to take *Catch-22*'s relation to Joyce's fiction into account.

The Gilgamesh Epic opens with a description of the hero, Gilgamesh: he is the one "who saw everything." Gilgamesh's epithet refers to his unique possession of the secrets of the gods, particularly the nature of the Flood that destroyed mankind, a secret that had previously been the preserve of the gods. This opening statement is given to Yossarian in chapter twenty-four, where it is what the naked Yossarian says to Milo as he watches Snowden's funeral from his perch in a tree: "'Come on out here', Yossarian invited him. 'You'll be much safer, and you can see everything'" (269). In presenting this episode in *Catch-22*, Heller has contracted Gilgamesh's cosmic "everything" so that it refers to the individual death of Snowden, in which Yossarian sees, for the first time, that man is mortal. In *Catch-22* the secret of the Sumerian pantheon is demoted to Joycean wordplay as Heller uses anagrams and a pun to divulge that through Snowden's death Yossarian-Gilgamesh comes to "[k]now [the] end."

Despite the shift of the opening sentence of *The Gilgamesh Epic* to the middle of *Catch-22*, much of the novel correlates to early sections of tablet I. Lines 9–21 of tablet I, column i are a description of the walls of "ramparted Uruk." This is the grand city that Gilgamesh built, and the poem describes the pride that Gilgamesh took in his great city: "Go up and walk on the walls of Uruk, / Inspect the base terrace, examine the brickwork: / Is not its brickwork of burnt brick?" (73). In *Catch-22* this city is represented by the officer's club which Yossarian pointedly has not built but which is, nevertheless, given a similarly grandiose description:

> Actually, there were many officer's clubs that Yossarian had not helped to build, but he was proudest of the one on Pianosa. It was a sturdy and complex monument to his powers of determination. Yossarian never went there to help until it was finished; then he went there often, so pleased was he with the large, fine, rambling shingled building. It was truly a splendid structure, and Yossarian throbbed with a mighty sense of accomplishment each time he gazed at it and reflected that none of the work that had gone into it was his. (19)

What previously appears to be Yossarian's profligate and unmilitary lassitude is a decontextualized imitation of Gilgamesh's theocratic realism. As a god-king, none of Gilgamesh's labor went into the building of Uruk, yet it is as justifiable for him to exhibit pride in its walls as it is for Yossarian's enjoyment of the sturdy construction of the officer's club to *seem* inappropriate. At this point we can see that it is Yossarian's closeness to Gilgamesh that is the source of what appears to be either his cynicism or his megalomania—though, too, one realizes that (ironically) the absurdity and comedy of this episode issues from the inexplicable nature of Yossarian's behavior.

Tablet I, column ii is a description of Gilgamesh: "Two-thirds of him is god, [one-third of him is human]." He is "like a wild ox lofty [. . .]; / The onslaught of his weapons verily has no equal" (Pritchard 73). In Heller's text, a parallel passage in the second chapter shows explicit linkages to tablet I, column ii: "They hated him because he was Assyrian. But they couldn't touch him, he told Clevinger, because he had a sound mind in a pure body and was as strong as an ox. They couldn't touch him because he was Tarzan, Mandrake, Flash Gordon. . . ." (20). This sounds insane to his associates, one of whom asserts, "You're crazy. . . . You've got a Jehovah complex" (21)—an ironic inversion, since Yossarian has a Gilgamesh complex. However, when we are no longer positioned to explain away Yossarian's belief in his supernatural identity as mere craziness, the craziness in *Catch-22* may be identified as an effect produced by the intrusion of the epic discourse of the subtext into the verisimilitude of Yossarian's Second World War.

The people of Uruk cry out in distress because their king is oppressing them: "Is this the shepherd of [ramparted] Uruk? . . . [Gilgamesh] leaves not [the maid to her mother]. . . . Day and night [is unbridled his arrogance]" (Pritchard 74, lines 14–24). The section of chapter one in which Yossarian stomps on a ping-pong ball and bandies the phrase "That Yossarian" (101) back and forth with the other officers imitates the complaints of Uruk's citizenry. Yossarian's affair with Lieutenant Scheisskopf's wife is synonymous with "[Gilgamesh] leaves not . . . [the noble's spouse]" (Pritchard 73–74, ln. 28), adultery being yet another manifestation of Gilgamesh's oppression. However, this episode is placed in chapter eighteen, "The Soldier Who Saw Everything Twice." Yossarian's affair with Mrs. Scheisskopf is multivalent and cannot be pinned down to a single episode within the epic. Not only does the affair parallel Gilgamesh's oppression of his people in tablet I, column ii, it suggests Enkidu's socialization by the harlot-lass. The conversation that Yossarian and Lieutenant Scheisskopf's wife have about the kind of god in whom they do not believe—which, on the surface, is the sheerest nonsense—is a parody of the debate over Gilgamesh that transpires between the harlot-lass and Enkidu in tablet I, column v. There, the woman quells Enkidu's boasting by describing the gods' regard for Gilgamesh: "O Enkidu, renounce thy presumption! / Gilgamesh—of him Shamash is fond; / Anu, Enlil, and Ea have broadened his wisdom" (Pritchard 75, lines 20–23). Mrs. Scheisskopf wears Dori Duz's dog tags, and Dori Duz is "a lively little tart" [71], so that we are forced to read Mrs. Scheisskopf-Dori Duz as a floating signifier, and to read the Yossarian-Dori Duz-Mrs. Scheisskopf relationship as one of the many renderings of the seduction of Enkidu. This is particularly reinforced by the fact that Dori Duz slept with Yossarian only once (72), and has crucial implications with regard to the theme of homosexuality. Having seduced and socialized Enkidu, the harlot-lass disappears from the *Gilgamesh* narrative in tablet I, in marked contrast to Nately's whore, who persists to the very end of Heller's text.

As the second column continues, the god Anu answers the cry of Gilgamesh's people by creating Enkidu, Gilgamesh's "double" (74, ln. 31)—the source of the doubling that is an important feature of the novel, as remarked upon by Potts (see below). The plan of the gods is that the two demigods (Gilgamesh and Enkidu) will "contend, that Uruk may have peace" (Pritchard 74, tablet I, column ii, line 34). The preparation of Enkidu is narrated in *Catch-22* in Chief White Halfoat's threat to kill Captain Flume: "Chief White Halfoat proudly regarded the new Captain Flume as his own creation" (58). Flume undergoes "his amazing metamorphosis" (58) and flees to the woods to wait for the Chief to die of pneumonia. Enkidu is described for the first time at the end of column two: "With the gazelles he feeds on grass, / With the wild beasts he jostles at the watering-place" (lines 38–40). In *Catch-22* Enkidu in the wild appears in chapter twelve, when Captain Flume is forced to live in the woods by the Chief's threat: "I saw him in the woods last week eating wild berries" (133). The "Yo-Yo's Roomies" chapter (thirty-two) coincides with Enkidu's former state, in which he lived with animals, and the animal imagery used in the descriptions of Yossarian's "gang of animated roommates" (355) reinforces the identification: the catalog of animal imagery includes "flocks" (354), "swarming," (355), "whale," (356), "horsing," (356) "frisky," (356), "kids," (356), "equine," (356), "asinine," (357), "Donald Duck's nephews" (357), and "loud convivial cries" (359).

Margot Norris observes that "The shifting, uncertain nature of characters in *Finnegans Wake* has long been recognized and documented" (30). What Norris calls "This pervasive cross-identification of characters. . ." (30) is an important feature of *Catch-22* as well and is very likely to have been derived from *Finnegans Wake*. Such a handling of characters, of course, has a decided effect on how the text may be read. In case there is any doubt that his characters are cross-identified, Heller has provided his text with numerous steering devices, such as Dori Duz's dog tags; Yossarian's declaration, "It's my personality. He thinks it's split" (311); and the A. Fortiori episode, in which identities are changed by changing beds (299). The phrase *a fortiori* underscores the principle that identities shift, not only as Yossarian inhabits the beds of other soldiers, but "all the more so." Thus Flume is the wild Enkidu; Enkidu's civilized persona is embodied principally by Dunbar, the Chaplain, and Nately; the dying Enkidu is Chief White Halfoat, Dunbar [see chapter thirty], the soldier who saw everything twice, and the Soldier in White; and the dead Enkidu is represented by the Dead Man in Yossarian's tent, Kid Sampson's legs, and Snowden. The material in tablet I that concerns Enkidu is deferred in *Catch-22* until chapter five, where it is connected to Chief White Halfoat. There is much more in Heller's description of the Indian than meets the eye, for according to Yossarian he is a liar (45), and the narrator underscores the mystery that surrounds him: "Chief White Halfoat was . . . a half-blooded Creek from Enid who for occult reasons of his own had made up his mind to die of pneumonia" (44). Heller's treatment of this character in the main text of the novel is a parody of the scholarly apparatus of *The Gilgamesh Epic*, note 14, which discusses the four Akkadian terms used to describe Enkidu in tablet ii, line 36: one is "uncertain as to meaning", another has "too many possible meanings" (Pritchard 74). Once again, we see that effects that seem to be comic and absurd embellishments are reflections of Heller's interest in the material present at various levels—scholarly, narrative, stylistic, mythological, etc.—in the text of *The Gilgamesh Epic*.

The plan to seduce Enkidu with a "harlot-lass" that takes up much of the third column of tablet I is represented in the novel by the description of General Dreedle's nurse. Heller has put a reverse spin on the description of the plan by making it Colonel Moodus's anti-seduction at General Dreedle's hands, where the General is identified associatively as the creator-god Anu. This passage parallels the contents of column iii, in which the Stalker of Game is first told by his father of the means by which Gilgamesh will trap Enkidu, and then told the same thing by Gilgamesh: "Go, my hunter, take with thee a harlot-lass. / When he waters the beasts at the watering-place, / She shall pull off her clothing, laying bear her ripeness. / As soon as he sees her, he will draw near her" (Pritchard 75). In column iv, the Stalker carries out the plan. He speaks to the harlot-lass: "There he is, 0 lass! Free thy breasts, / Bare thy bosom that he may possess thy ripeness" (Pritchard 75). In *Catch-22* this episode has been lent a comic twist, since Heller reverses what takes place in the *Gilgamesh* passage by allowing General Dreedle to sadistically deny his nurse to Colonel Moodus. Heller is more directly faithful to the epic in another respect: both the passages from *Catch-22* and from *Gilgamesh* are concerned with the irresistible lushness of the two women's breasts. Clearly,

General Dreedle's nurse is derived from the passage quoted above in which the Stalker urges the woman to show her breasts.

Another kind of reversal takes place in connection with the sexual intercourse between Enkidu and the harlot lass. Nately's whore wants nothing to do with him, falling in love with him only in chapter thirty-three, "Nately's Whore," after a prolonged campaign on Nately's part: "The girl smiled with contentment when he opened her eyes and saw him, and then, stretching her long legs languorously beneath the rustling sheets, beckoned him into bed beside her with that look of simpering idiocy of a woman in heat" (365). The seduction of Enkidu is another of *Catch-22*'s far-flung and complex motifs, and it crops up throughout the text. Yossarian's liaisons with Nurse Duckett and Luciana also imitate the same material, for, like the harlot-lass, Nurse Duckett is a bearer of decorum (346), and Luciana will not sleep with Yossarian before carefully cleaning his room (162). There is also a curious parallelism between Luciana's sense of order and Nately's sudden insistence that his girl wear clothes: the congruence between the two events is signaled by the use of he "crazy" motif ("*Tu sei pazzo*"; 163, 366) in both accounts.

Tablet I ends with Enkidu's boast and the lass's caution: "Gilgamesh will see thee in (his) dreams in Uruk" (Pritchard 75, ln. 24). Gilgamesh's mother, then, interprets his dreams. It is noteworthy that dreams, which serve a vital role in the knitting together of the episodes of the epic, play a significant though much different role in *Catch-22*, wherein Yossarian's dreams are interpreted by the psychiatrist, Dr. Sanderson. Gilgamesh dreams that he attempts to hoist "the liegman of Anu"(Pritchard 76, tablet V, line 28)—a star—but it is too heavy for him. With the help of his people, he places it before his mother. A second dream about an axe is also interpreted. The mother's interpretation of the two dreams is that the star and the axe are a wild man, a man that he will love like a woman. Yossarian tells Major Sanderson that his dream about holding a live fish in his hands is "a sex dream" (305).[1] Subsequently, Yossarian reveals that the dream is really one of Dunbar's (305). He next solicits a dream from the chaplain, which is about a shark eating Yossarian's leg, where he has been wounded. Especially significant is the indefinite nature of Yossarian's wound. We have been told explicitly that Yossarian was wounded in the thigh (298), yet Yossarian himself sites the wound in his groin: "I lost my balls!" (29). The implication is that both of these dreams—profoundly disturbing and offensive to Major Sanderson's neurotic squeamishness—are somehow "sex dreams."

In tablet II, column iv, Enkidu arrives in Uruk just as Gilgamesh is about to exercise his kingly right to sleep with a newly married bride: "He is the first, / The husband comes after" (lines 35–6). The corresponding episode in *Catch-22* is the riddling tale of Dr. Daneeka and the newly-weds in chapter five. The doctor's "demonstration" of intercourse with rubber models, for which he is unreasonably punched in the nose by the groom, is revealed in its true light as the parody of the traditional Sumerian and Assyrian custom of the deflowering of the bride by the king, though the act is unconsummated in both the epic and in *Catch-22*. Enkidu intercepts Gilgamesh, and they fight after Enkidu has been repelled by a nocturnal orgy. The fight between Gilgamesh and Enkidu at the orgy is imitated in chapter thirty-four, where the Thanksgiving Day celebration in Pianosa turns into "a raw, violent, guzzling saturnalia" (369), during which Yossarian punches Nately in the nose. This punch resounds throughout the novel, as several other punches are delivered between other pairs of men. Another "seven-day debauch" (137) in chapter thirteen registers a repetition of the same event.

In column vi the two demigods fight. In *Catch-22* there are a number of punches thrown, but the only detailed description of a prolonged fight is given to the struggle between Yossarian and Nately's whore in chapter thirty-eight. That this episode imitates the Gilgamesh-Enkidu struggle is borne out by similarities in imagery between the two texts. The epic's lines "They *grappled* each other, / Holding fast like bulls" (emphasis added) compares favorably with Heller's ". . .they strove against each other frantically in a grunting, panting stalemate, arm against arm," and further down Heller has them "no longer *grappling*" (404; emphasis added). In the epic, "They shattered the doorpost, / as the wall shook;" In *Catch-22* the woman is slammed into one wall and then "banged hard against the other door" (403).

There is also the matter of the conversion of aggression into eroticism in *Gilgamesh*, since Gilgamesh and Enkidu end up as lovers. A similar conversion takes place in Heller's text: "All at once he realized—though the writhing turbulence had not diminished one whit—that she was no longer grappling with him, recognized with a quiver that she was not fighting him but heaving her pelvis up against him remorselessly in the primal, powerful, rhapsodic instinctual rhythm of erotic ardor and aban-donment" (404). Heller has displaced the "inappropriate" homosexual contact between Gilgamesh and Enkidu to a lesser "inappropriate" vio-lent-erotic contact between Yossarian and Nately's girl. What seems to be the displacement, or even the abandonment of the homosexual theme, is illusory. Attention to the phallic imagery of this episode—as the weapon metamorphoses from a potato peeler, to a bread knife, to a steak knife, to a huge carving knife (402–07)—demonstrates a pronounced instance of the text's consistent concern with violent and sadomasochistic homosexual eroticism. We should also note that the fight in tablet II, column vi is imitated by the beginning of *Catch-22*—Yossarian's love-at-first-sight meeting with the chaplain that takes place in the opening sentence of Heller's text and is developed between pages eleven and fifteen.

According to Potts, Heller sees *Catch-22* as being built around the three main bombing missions, Ferrara, Bologna, and Avignon. This is a revealing statement, when it is referenced to *The Gilgamesh Epic*, since the epic's action is focused on three battles, namely, the contests between Gilgamesh and Enkidu, the two heroes and Humbaba, and the two heroes and the Bull of Heaven. Having joined forces with Enkidu after their single combat, Gilgamesh decides to win a name for himself by battling the monster Humbaba. According to tablet III, column ii of the Assyrian *Gilgamesh*, Gilgamesh fights at the behest of Shamash, the sun god, while in the Old Babylonian version he does not. The text provided by Pritchard's *Ancient Near Eastern Texts* gives both versions of the story, so that, presumably, Heller was familiar with them. Later, Gilgamesh's rejection of Ishtar's love causes her to attack him with the Bull of Heaven. These events occupy Tablets Three, Four, Five, and Six. Humbaba is an entrail monster, whose literal appearance in *Catch-22* takes place as Snowden's intestines slide out of his abdomen during the Avignon mission narrated in chapter forty-one. Yossarian sees that Snowden's gut is full of stewed tomatoes (449), which culminates the elaborate and ostentatious "tomato" motif that has run throughout the text. After Yossarian causes a flight of bombers to turn back in chapter fourteen, he eats a pomegranate. Robert Graves states that "red colored food might be offered to the dead only" (95 n. 11) and that "the pomegranate was supposed to have sprung . . . from the blood of . . . Tammuz" (95 n.11; see also 110 n. 10, 72 n.7). Tammuz was one of the victims of Ishtar's love, who were named by Gilgamesh in his rejection of her erotic advances, and, in keeping with this identification, Heller has metamorphosed the pomegranate into the tomatoes in Snowden's gut. The conjoined tomato stew and Snowden's entrails are emblems that identify the disemboweled Snowden as at once Tammuz and Humbaba, for in Assyrian art Humbaba was pictured as a head made of loops of intestines. Snowden's exposed bowels—the decapitated Humbaba—symbolize everything demonic in *Catch-22*, and, in a piling up of narrative situations, the episode also serves to abbreviate the chain of circumstances that bring about the death of Snowden-Enkidu. Though the intestinal revelation that Snowden's death presents to Yossarian in chapter forty-one is the culmination of Humbaba's activities, it is not his first appearance in Heller's text, for throughout *Catch-22*, Humbaba is presented as the demonic Aarfy—"A chubby, moon-faced navigator with little reptilian eyes" (49), "no use to Yossarian as a navigator or as anything else (50)," and "an eerie ogre" (154). Aarfy has plagued Yossarian throughout the narrative, and he finally ends his activities with the rape and defenestration of a prostitute (427).

Another aspect of Humbaba is manifested in Captain Black, a character whose malevolence is more given to verbal assault than that of Milo (who bombs and strafes the squadron), or Aarfy (who murders a young woman); throughout the narrative, Black is given to triumphantly sadistic outbursts: "'That's right, you bastards, Bologna. . . . Ha! Ha! Ha! Eat your livers, you bastards. This time you're really in for it'" (115).

Gilgamesh's dream of a falling mountain in tablet V, column iii, lines 33–35— "[In] mountain gorges [. . .] / [A mountain] toppled [. . .] / Like small reed flies we [. . .]" (Pritchard 82)—is also Humbaba. Enkidu's reading of the dream declares "the mountain, my friend, which thou sawest, / He is Humbaba" (83, lines 39–40). The Humbaba motif first emerges in chapter five—though by no means clearly—with "the flies Orr saw in Appleby's eyes"(47)—the flies being those referred to in line 35 of *The Gilgamesh Epic* quoted above. The Orr-Enkidu victory over Appleby-Humbaba culminates in the first retelling of this episode in chapter six, when Orr "smashed open Appleby's forehead with his [ping-pong] paddle" (57); other repetitions culminate with the Captain Flume-Major Major confrontation on page 104 and the Hungry Joe-Aarfy combat on pages 161–62. In *Catch-22* the mountain is introduced in the nightmarish mission of chapter twenty-five: "The purpose of the mission is to knock the whole village sliding down the side of the mountain and create a roadblock that the Germans will have to clear" (335).

Humbaba possesses a fearsome weapon, "Who is there to face his weapon" (80, line 13); in *Catch-22* this undefined weapon is Yossarian's imaginary "new three-hundred-and forty-four-millimeter Lepage glue gun" (128) that everyone begins to believe is real. The appearance of this weapon in the "Bologna" chapter allows for the association of the Bologna campaign with the fight against Humbaba. Yossarian's cowardice in moving the bomb line (123) and in soliciting forged orders that would get him out of flying to Bologna corresponds to Enkidu's fear in tablet IV, column vi:

"[Let us not go] down [into the heart of the forest]! / [In open]ing [the gate my hand] became limp." (82, lines 25–26). Gilgamesh's speech—"Who my friend is superior to de [ath]? / Only the gods [live] forever under the sun / . . . . Let thy mouth call to me, 'Advance, fear not!'/ Should I fall, I shall have made me a name. . . ." (79, lines 5–13)—which urges Enkidu on to the battle, is given to ex-P.F.C. Wintergreen in Heller's text: "Then you'll just have to be killed . . . so you might as well go out and die like a man" (126). Before he is killed, Humbaba offers a bribe; he will make Gilgamesh rich: "Let me go, Gilgamesh; thou [wilt be] my [master], / And I shall be thy servant" (Pritchard 83, ln. 22–23). The imitation of this bribe in Catch-22 associates Milo Minderbinder with Humbaba, for in chapter twenty-two Milo offers to cut Yossarian into his crooked schemes: "'I have a sure-fire plan for cheating the federal government out of six thousand dollars. We can make three thousand dollars apiece without any risk to either of us. Are you interested?'" (239). Given the importance of Milo's role in the narrative, the implications of his identification as Humbaba are far-reaching.

In tablet VI the goddess Ishtar offers to make Gilgamesh her lover. Most of the women in Catch-22 are aspects of Ishtar, and, as she refracts into a number of moods, the various personalities exhibited by these women reflect the goddess's emotional postures. Nowhere is this better depicted than in the parallel movements of Nurses Duckett and Cramer as they accompany Yossarian to the beach: "Nurse Cramer had stopped speaking to Nurse Duckett, her best friend, because of her liaison with Yossarian, but still went everywhere with Nurse Duckett since Nurse Duckett was her best friend" (364). The inseparably paired nurses represent Ishtar's change of attitude towards Gilgamesh, with Duckett signifying the goddesses desire and Cramer signifying her hatred, after being rejected by the hero. In column i Ishtar says, "'Come, Gilgamesh, be thou (my) lover!'" (83, line 7), corresponding to Luciana's "'Now I will let you sleep with me'" (158). Yossarian's reply, "'Who asked you,'" parallels Gilgamesh's rejection, "'[What am I to give] thee, that I may take thee in marriage? . . . [Thou art, but a brazier which goes out] in the cold'" (84, lines 24–32). This is followed by a long catalog of Gilgamesh's insults that continues into the next column, the thesis being: "'Which lover didst thou love forever?'" (line 42). Gilgamesh's insults appear throughout the text of Catch-22, though they are nearly unrecognizable. The effect of the insults has been reversed, because they are delivered in the narrator's anti-heroic, disparaging irony, and they demote Yossarian-Gilgamesh rather than Ishtar. A good example occurs in chapter fifteen: "She would have been perfect for Yossarian, a debauched, coarse, vulgar, amoral, appetizing slattern whom he had longed for and idolized for months" (159).

To avenge herself on Gilgamesh and Enkidu, Ishtar pleads with Anu to send the Bull of Heaven to dispatch the heroes, threatening to destroy the world if she does not have her way. The battle is described in tablet VI, and corresponds to the mission in which Yossarian is wounded in the thigh that is narrated in chapter twenty-six. Enkidu's response to Ishtar's curse is relevant to this episode: "When Enkidu heard this speech of Ishtar, / He tore loose the right thigh of the Bull of Heaven / and tossed it in her face" (Pritchard 85, lines 160–63). Because he has killed Humbaba and the Bull of Heaven, the gods decree that Enkidu must die. In tablet VII, column iii, Enkidu curses the stalker and the harlot-lass for changing him from his animal state. In a dream the sun-god Shamash upbraids Enkidu, reminding him of the many honors that he has received, "food fit for divinity . . . wine fit for royalty . . . noble garments, . . . a noble couch" (86, lines 35–41). In chapter forty Colonel Korn (speaking for Colonel Cathcart) delivers a similar speech to Yossarian, "'You know in all fairness, we really haven't treated you too badly, have we? We've fed you and paid you on time. We gave you a medal and even made you a captain'" (431). In table VIII column iii, after a long funeral oration, Gilgamesh goes into mourning: "[I shall invest my body with uncut hair], / and clad in a [lion] skin, [I shall roam over the steppe]!" (88, lines 30–1). The corresponding episode in *Catch-22* takes place with Yossarian's refusal to wear clothes at Snowden's funeral in chapter twenty-four; while Gilgamesh is not naked, we must suppose that for a king to don a lion's skin is equivalent to the nakedness of a modern airman. Utnapishtim's advice to Urshanabi in Tablet XI is to have Gilgamesh "clothe his nakedness / That he may arrive in his city" (96, lines 244–45), so it is apparent that Gilgamesh does become naked in the epic. Yossarian's actions at the funeral consist of appearing naked in formation and climbing into a tree. These two actions conflate two episodes connected to Enkidu's death, however, they do not derive from the same Sumerian text. Heller combines the grieving Gilgamesh of Tablet VIII with the Huluppu-tree poem of Tablet XII (which was appended to the eleven tablets of *The Gilgamesh Epic* but is not consistent with its narrative) in which Enkidu is dead and has gone down to the underworld.

A further complication results in that Heller has conflated the demons that possess Ishtar's Huluppu tree with the chaplain's "vision of the naked man in the tree" (279). This is particularly confusing in that Enkidu is killed in helping Gilgamesh and Ishtar (more properly, Inanna) to drive the demons from the tree, whereupon Gilgamesh fails to retrieve his friend from the underworld. Thus, the tree represents the death of Enkidu only by implication.

Realizing for the first time the inevitability of his own death, Gilgamesh starts on a long journey to gain immortality from his ancestor Utnapishtim. Gilgamesh successfully passes the darkness of the mountain range of Mashu guarded by scorpion men. This episode is equivalent to "The Eternal City," chapter thirty-nine, in which Yossarian wanders through the nightmarish streets of Rome. The old moaning woman (415) and the dead old man (417) are the Scorpion People, who in the poem are a man and a woman.

Tablet X reveals that even Lieutenant Scheisskopf is an aspect of Yossarian-Gilgamesh, for Gilgamesh addresses himself to Shamash asking, "After *marching* (and) roving over the steppe, / Must I lay my *head* in the heart of the *earth* / That I may sleep through all the years?" (Pritchard 89, lines 10–11, emphases added). Lieutenant Scheisskopf's name is German for "shit head," and he is obsessed with marching and parades. Here Heller associates the Akkadian "earth" with shit, which is particularly suggestive given that Aarfy's full name, Captain Aardvark (31), is Afrikaans for "earth-pig," and that the dead man in Yossarian's tent is Mudd (111). When Gilgamesh tells his tale to Siduri, the ale-wife, he states that he watched over his friend for seven days and seven nights, "Until the worm fell out of his nose" (Pritchard 91, line 7), suggesting the indefinite death of the Soldier in White, who is not recognized as being dead until Nurse Cramer takes his temperature and determines that he is dead (10). Siduri's advice, to "let thy spouse delight in thy bosom" (Pritchard 90, column iii, line 14) is recapitulated by the chaplain's "longing for his wife and children" (277).

In column iii Gilgamesh encounters Urshanabi the boatman, represented by Orr in Heller's text, the figure associated with the riddles about apple cheeks and the woman who strikes him on the head with her high heels (459). Both Siduri and Urshanabi elicit Gilgamesh's story from him by asking the same formulaic question: "Why are thy cheeks wasted, is [thy face] sunken" (Pritchard 91, line 2). Hungry Joe is the shrunken-cheeked figure in Heller's text who enacts the role of Gilgamesh in search of immortality and traveling the world enduring trials and torments: "Hungry Joe was a jumpy, emaciated wretch with a fleshless face of dingy skin and bone and twitching veins squirming subcutaneously in the blackened hollows behind his eyes like severed sections of snake" (53). His "shrunken face" (55) is referred to throughout the text.

It is with the help of Urshanabi that Gilgamesh reaches Utnapishtim's unreachable realm, though in Heller's text there is an important departure, for Orr undergoes the night-sea journey to Sweden—the impossible sanctuary (318) that is beyond reach—without Yossarian. Urshanabi tells Gilgamesh that he cannot voyage to Utnapishtim's realm because he has broken the "Stone Things" (Pritchard 92, column iii, line 39) that are necessary to sail with: these ambiguous "stone things" appear in Catch-22 as "broken stone pillars" (279) and less clearly as ". . .gray stone farmhouse. "Smashed to bits" (155), though clearly they are uprooted from any significance lent them by Heller's narrative, and they appear only as decontextualized images. There are many parallels between Urshanabi and Orr; for instance, in order to reach Utnapishtim's "Waters [of Death]" (Pritchard 92, [The Assyrian version] tablet X, column iii, line 50) the voyagers wear out all of the punting poles that they brought with them, so that as the goal is neared "Gilgamesh pulled off [his] cl[othing]. / With his hand he holds it aloft as a sail" (Pritchard 92, tablet X, column iv, lines 10–11). Orr is described as sitting in the life raft during one of his many rehearsals for the escape, with "a small magnetic compass and a big waterproof map, and he spread the map open on his knees" (318). We can equate Orr's spread out map with Gilgamesh's clothes. The "stone things" are believed by scholars to refer to lodestones or compasses, thus filling out the association between the voyages of Orr and Urshanabi.

Utnapishtim is of supreme importance in the epic, and therefore Catch-22 is replete with incidents from his story. Utnapishtim is the Sumerian Noah who has survived the destruction of mankind to live immortally with his wife at the end of the world. This aspect of the epic is imitated in the chaplain's disquisition on time in chapter twenty-five (275–76). In Heller's text he is the Old Man in chapter twenty-three who so occupies Nately with his insupportable wisdom. The Old Man appears in several other sections of the text, however, no more ironically than when he turns up dead in "The Eternal City Chapter." Utnapishtim's story appears in the text but not as told by the old man (although he does state that "the earth itself is destined to be destroyed. . ." [249]). Utnapishtim's preparations for the flood comes in chapter twenty-eight, where Sergeant Knight describes Orr "opening up compartments in the raft" (317)—an imitation of tablet XI, column i where Utnapishtim states, "'Her floor plan I divided into nine parts'" (Pritchard 93, tablet XI, line 63). In order to get around the secrecy ordained for the Flood, Anu addresses Utnapishtim from behind a reed-wall, warning him of the flood and the impending destruction of all life on the earth. Similarly, Nurse Duckett tells Yossarian in chapter thirty-four that Dunbar is in danger: "'They're going to disappear him,' she said" (376). She says that she knows this because "I heard them talking behind a door" (376), and we can recognize Utnapishtim's wall in Nurse Duckett's door.

In order to have immortality conferred upon him, Gilgamesh must remain awake for six days and seven nights. Gilgamesh falls asleep immediately, and Utnapishtim gives his wife orders to bake bread each day that he sleeps. After Gilgamesh's sleep, "His first wafer is dried out. . . The sixth (still) is fresh-colored" (95, lines 215–19). This test corresponds to the ordeal that Yossarian and Orr suffer at the hands of Milo in chapter twenty-two. Heller inverts the entire story, and for the six days of Orr's "rest leave" (245), Milo conducts a buying tour of the entire Middle East, during which Yossarian and Orr get little or no sleep, in the reverse of what happens to Gilgamesh. Other inversions follow: Gilgamesh tries to gain immortality and reaps death; Milo sets out for Cairo for eggs and returns with the entire Egyptian cotton crop, which is inedible (234). Heller converts the seven loaves that Utnapishtim's wife bakes to mark the days of Gilgamesh's sleep into Milo's seven purchases: chick-peas (236), artichokes (243), cinnamon sticks and other spices (243), cocoa and coffee (243), red bananas (244), eggs (245), and cotton. When Gilgamesh awakens, Utnapishtim forces him to carefully examine the loaves. Each is described in detail, and "The fifth has a *moldy* cast" (line 228; emphasis added), corresponding to Milo's mention of "mushrooms that were damaged by *mold*" (238; emphasis added). Having failed to remain awake for a week, Gilgamesh is forced to leave, but is recalled after Utnapishtim's wife takes pity on him and forces her husband to give the hero directions to "Man Becomes Young in Old Age" (Pritchard 96, tablet XI, column vi), a plant which will restore his youth. In *Catch-22* this plant is alluded to by the name "Washington Irving," which Yossarian signs to letters he has censored, a motif that begins in chapter seven and continues throughout much of the text. "Washington Irving" is an allusion to Rip Van Winkle in Irving's "The Legend of Sleepy Hollow," a story in which the protagonist is young, while his contemporaries have aged, a device that in this context serves as an ironic version of Utnapishtim's boon. The plant—"Man Becomes Young in Old Age"—is also the subtext of Dunbar's theory on slowing down time (39); the statement, "Today you're an old man" (39); and the question, "How the hell else are you ever going to slow time down?" (40) all of which are located in chapter four. The plant of restored youth is also the subtext of the conversation between Yossarian and Major Danby in the final chapter;

the conversation concludes, "'I guess I don't want to live like a vegetable, then', said Major Danby with a smile of resignation" (456). Not only does this conversation imitate and invert the snake stealing the plant of restored youth, it points toward the speech at the conclusion of the epic in which Gilgamesh resignedly directs Urshanabi to "Go up, Urshanabi, walk on the ramparts of Uruk" (97, line 305).

A serpent steals the plant from Gilgamesh, and leaves the hero without an escape from death. Utnapishtim's counsel to Urshanabi is to have Gilgamesh "put on a cloak to clothe his nakedness, / That he may arrive in his city" (96, lines 244–45). *Catch-22* is fairly close to the epic in its conclusion, and this is unusual, since Heller often inverts the events that take place in the epic: Yossarian states that "'I'm not taking any deals'" (450), when it is clear that Gilgamesh takes any deal he can get: having lost immortality, he accepts restored youth. Orr—who is simultaneously Urshanabi and Utnapishtim—has gone off to "Paradise" in Sweden without Yossarian, so that we can clearly see Yossarian's loss of sanctuary. However, Yossarian is still in grave danger from Nately's whore, while Gilgamesh has resolved the conflicts in his life. Heller has further complicated his text by inserting Tablet XII—the "inorganic appendage"—into his narrative. Even so, tablet XII does not contribute significantly to the concluding chapters of *Catch-22*.

Stephen Potts states that "The conclusion of the novel has proved controversial ever since its publication" (110); no less so is this true of *The Gilgamesh Epic*. In fact Heller has arranged things so that some of the difficulties that scholars have had in interpreting the epic have been allowed to contribute to the contradictions that some critics have located in Heller's text (see Potts 110-14). The varying readings of Heller's text are, in the main, related to whether the novel is "merely 'absurd' or genuinely 'Absurd'" (Potts 112). Given the relationship of *Catch-22* to high Modernism and T.S. Eliot's "mythic method" outlined in his essay "*Ulysses*, Order, and Myth," on the one hand, and on the other hand Heller's use of the same destabilizing elements chosen by Joyce in *Finnegans Wake* ("replicated events, unstable characters, contiguous associations, semantic vagary" [Norris 141), the question that remains to be answered is whether *Catch-22* is absurd in *any* sense.

This is, however, not the place to resolve these controversies, and this essay on Heller's use of *The Gilgamesh Epic* will conclude with a rough appraisal of Heller's reading of the epic itself. In resolving his narrative, Heller seems to have rejected the interpretation given the epic by most experts—that "struggle as he would, man was helpless, his fate and death decreed by the gods. Nor was there any hope of bliss to come. Death led only to an Underworld of dusty gloom" (Hawkes 12). Instead, Heller's view of the epic is nearly identical to that stated by Silvestre Fiore in *Voices from the Clay*:

> The central theme of the epic of Gilgamesh as it appears in the Akkadian version, is not, as has often been sustained, the anxiety of death. In the greater parts of the poem (tablets I–IV), the danger of losing life is envisaged almost with indifference, as an inevitable necessity of human existence. To gain glory and make oneself a name is judged much more important than death: to be afraid of death connotes cowardice. Gilgamesh's principal preoccupation in this part of the poem is with the accomplishment of heroic deeds in the service of his god Shamash. He rejoices in his strength and in the exercise of his kingship over Uruk.
>
> It is not until tablet VII that his tragical apprehension of death begins. Enkidu's dying has filled him with horror at the idea of a final annihilation. During that long vigil over the corpse of his friend, he has been seized with nausea at the sight of physical decay. But he is above all, shaken by metaphysical anguish; the indomitable hero cannot resign himself to the certainty that his existence will one day come to an end. Gilgamesh's fear of death, as expressed in this second part of the poem, has nothing to do with cowardice. During his desperate search for immortality, he faces the dangers of his journey with the same steadfastness that he showed in his previous exploits and does not hesitate to cross the Waters of Death in spite of the risk he incurs. (185)

At this point Fiore and Heller diverge, Fiore's reading being that "the only change [in Gilgamesh] is the natural evolution from early youth to ripe age. The exuberance and carelessness of the first tablets gives way to weariness and despair at the end" (186). Based on Yossarian's revived heroism in the conclusion of the novel, Heller's reading of the epic approximates that of Kluger's psychological reading, that "He [Gilgamesh] picked up his life on earth again, accepting and including death" (207).

Glimpsed at this early stage in the reassessment of *Catch-22*, one of the most striking features of the text is the way that Heller has accommodated his fiction to the material, stylistic, cultural, and aesthetic actualities of ancient Akkadian literature. Writing *Catch-22* between 1955 and 1961, Heller had access to a number of English translations of the epic. Because it was the most widely available version, and because the text of *Catch-22* demonstrates many affinities to it, it seems likely that Heller used *The Epic of Gilgamesh* (translated by Speiser and Grayson) included in James B. Pritchard's *Ancient Near Eastern Texts Relating to the Old Testament*, originally published in 1950 and corrected and enlarged in a second edition in 1955.

The ancient literature of Assyria has been made available to modern readers by means of archaeological discoveries, linguistic research by specialists, and the subsequent publication of translations of whatever discov-

eries had been made: the texts themselves are the products of their shaping by historical accidents, such that many texts are available only as
incomplete clay tablets. The labors of linguists and translators result in
various editions of ancient texts assembled by cross-referencing surviving
texts and often publishing them with the lacunas indicated by brackets
and ellipses ("[. . .]"), logical emendations indicated by inserting words
in brackets ("[they . . .]"), and bearing words that indicate the various
types of incompletenesses inclusive to the text: "(mutilated or missing),"
"(small break)," "(several lines missing)," "(mutilated)," and "(a long gap
follows)." One line in tablet five reads "Of. . . [. . .]. . ." (Pritchard
52). Realistically speaking, it is fair to say that the entire text of *The
Gilgamesh Epic* is provisional.

   In his literary appropriation of *The Gilgamesh Epic*, Heller was faced
with an ancient text that is badly fragmented even in its original version
and, subsequently, was treated to an editorial process, which produced a
collage of the fragments. Moreover, the "original" text of Gilgamesh is an
Akkadian poem, which, while utilizing certain motifs that are featured in
Sumerian poems, does so largely in the course of developing a central
theme that has no Sumerian prototypes (Pritchard 73). Heller's solution
of the problem of textual insubstantiality was to parody the process of
textual destruction and reconstruction in *Catch-22* by representing the
artifactuality of the ancient text as the letters that Yossarian haphazardly
and irresponsibly censored while he malingered in the hospital. We may
particularly note that the letters censored by Yossarian suggest the various states of incompleteness occupied by the various tablets of the epic.
A good example of this is the letter that appears in chapter nine: "Major
Major bent forward slightly and saw a copy of the piece of V mail from
which Yossarian had blacked out everything but the name Mary and on
which he had written, "I yearn for you tragically. A.T. Tappman, Chaplain, U.S. Army" (97). This letter is suggestive of Pritchard's presentation
of the epic in which he omits Tablets Four and Five due to the fragmentary nature of the text: the headnote to the Assyrian version of tablet II in
Pritchard reads "In the Assyrian Version, Tablet II has come down in only
a few disjointed and mutilated fragments" (76). That Heller approximates
the fragmented condition of Assyrian tablets through Yossarian's censoring activities renders *Catch-22* considerably less whimsical than it otherwise appears. Yet another element enters into Yossarian's censoring of V
mail—that of Gilgamesh's habitual oppression of his people. The unspecified oppression represented by Yossarian's extreme method of censor-
ship demonstrates that Heller's text is sylleptic throughout, and there is
always the possibility that at any point one is reading the text superficially.

At the same time, it must be recognized that much of the text of *Catch-22* exists simply to orient the reader and to direct the reader's attention toward the multivalent representations that are indicated.

Similarly, Heller's treatment of time is also a problematic feature of the text's structure that may be partially derived from *The Gilgamesh Epic*. Though, in the final analysis, the tendency of Heller's text to utilize a nonlinear time scheme may be attributed to the influence of *Finnegans Wake*. An additional complicating factor is the provocative fact that *The Gilgamesh Epic* itself introduces an independent nonlinear temporal component that subverts the frame of reference that is in operation throughout the first eleven tablets of the epic. The canonical text commonly referred to by the label *The Gilgamesh Epic* is a late Akkadian text by the poet Sin-leqi unninni consisting of twelve clay tablets, except for the last tablet, which is a portion of a direct translation from a Sumerian poem called "Gilgamesh and the Huluppu-tree." Scholars have recognized this twelfth tablet as "an inorganic appendage to the epic proper" (Pritchard, 1955 97). Because Enkidu is alive in the "Huluppu-tree" poem, the effect of reading the final tablet as an organic component of the epic fractures the conventional handling of time and shifts the poem into quite another range of possible interpretations. We might have expected Heller to have omitted this inorganic appendage, since it does not belong to the epic proper. However, it is evident that Heller has included this twelfth tablet and allowed it to radically alter the form of his text. If Joyce wrote *Finnegans Wake* to demonstrate that time and language are a series of coincidences and that unexpected simultaneities are the rule (Ellman 551), then we might expect that Heller would see the inorganicity of *The Gilgamesh Epic* as an indication that the ancient poem was a precursor of *Finnegans Wake* itself and maintain this feature of the epic in his novel. We can easily recognize Heller's placement of the "Huluppu-tree" episode within *Catch-22*. In the Sumerian poem the action revolves around a tree which Inanna (Ishtar) wants to use for lumber but finds inhabited by demons: a serpent, a Zu-bird, and the demoness Lilith (Heidel 94). This is the source of the episode in chapter twenty-five in which a naked Yossarian watches Snowden's funeral while perched in a tree. To emphasize the supernatural character of the events, which transpire in the tree, Heller has the metaphysically obsessed chaplain witness Yossarian and Milo as they enact a sort of pantomime:

> He would remember them forever, for they were all part and parcel of the most extraordinary event that had ever befallen him, an event perhaps marvelous, perhaps pathological—the vision of the naked man in the tree. How could he explain it? It was not already seen or never seen, and certainly not almost seen;

neither *déjà vu, jamais vu,* nor *presque vu* was elastic enough to cover it. Was it a ghost, then? The dead man's soul? An angel from heaven or a minion from hell? Or was the whole fantastic episode merely the figment of a diseased imagination, his own, of a deteriorating mind, a rotting brain? The possibility that there really had been a naked man in the tree—two men, actually, since the first had been joined shortly by a second man clad in a brown mustache and sinister dark garments from head to toe who bent forward ritualistically along the limb of the tree to offer the first man something to drink from a brown goblet—never crossed the chaplain's mind. (279–80)

A third outstanding feature of *The Gilgamesh Epic* also plays a major role in the form of *Catch-22*, namely, the style of Sumerian and Akkadian poetry. John Maier states that "The technique of exact repetition, using the exact sequence and terminology of the first passage . . . is a characteristic of Sumerian poetry. It is also typical of the late version of *Gilgamesh*. The return to a Sumerian poetic style not found in the Old Babylonian Akkadian *The Epic of Gilgamesh* may, then, be a deliberate attempt to make the Akkadian have the look of a Sumerian composition" (70 n. 18–28). Repetition is one of the chief attributes of the style of *Catch-22*, and there are several types of repetitions, such as the "temporal narratives" (Norris 25) similar to those of *Finnegans Wake*, (i.e., the Soldier in White); *deja vu*; the past events which are told in more detail during each repetition; the repetitious conversations, such as the recurring Yossarian-Orr routine about apple cheeks; and circular conversations in which there is a self-reflexive recognition that the conversation is repetitive (e.g. on 80–1 and on 142–43). In places, Heller's use of repetition is an exact, parallel to that used in Sumerian poetry, a particularly faithful example being the description of General Dreedle's nurse (221–22) and Colonel Moodus's recapitulation of it with only a few minor changes. General Dreedle states that "Back at Wing she's got a uniform that's so tight her nipples stand out like bing cherries. . . . You ought to see what goes on inside that blouse of hers every time she shifts her weight" (222–23). Colonel Moodus says, "Back at Wing she's got a uniform made out of purple silk that's so tight her nipples stand out like bing cherries. . . . You should hear that silk rustle every time she shifts her weight" (222). Thus, *The Gilgamesh Epic* is a narrative constructed out of passages that set up compelling patterns of repetitious narrative, and the same may be said for *Catch-22*.

Having briefly examined how Heller accommodated his text to certain stylistic features of *The Gilgamesh Epic*—textual fragmentation, non-linear time, and the fundamental role of repetition in the style of Sumerian poetry—I will now conclude with a brief indication of the major themes encompassed by the epic and by *Catch-22*. This is not a straightforward matter: in her illuminating study of the hero, Gilgamesh, the Jungian analyst R. S. Kluger states that "We will see that the mother problem is one of the major subjects in the first part of this epic, and that of immortality in the second part" (68). This statement is made in her discussion of the role of homosexuality in moving Gilgamesh beyond the "mother problem," and thus we may say that the narrative of the epic divides into two parts, one dealing with homosexuality, and the second with immortality. Given that Heller's concern with the theme of death-immortality theme is everywhere manifest in *Catch-22*, Kluger's statement leads inexorably to the question as to what has become of the homosexual theme emeshed in *Catch-22*. This question is inescapable given that *Catch-22* opens with "It was love at first sight. The first time Yossarian saw the chaplain he fell madly in love with him" (7). Potts reads this as the deflation of a cliché (35), in other words as comedic rhetoric. At the same time, Potts also notices that

> Many of the characters also appear in doubles or pairs; in the early chapters Appleby and Havermeyer are linked by their similar attitudes, as are Clevinger, and Nately, and Yossarian and Dunbar. In the first section Colonel Cathcart is all but inseparable from Colonel Korn; General Peckem is linked to General Dreedle; Doc Daneeka is contrasted with Doctor Stubbs. Some characters only appear in pairs: operations officers Piltchard and Wren, medical orderlies Gus and Wes. (42)

Admittedly, there are three prominent pairs of women, Nurses Duckett and Cramer, Mrs. Scheisskopf and Dori Duz, and the Countess and her daughter-in-law. However, quite another condition obtains for the women in the text. The men in the text are decidedly paired off, and the implication provided in the opening of the narrative is that at the root of these relationships is "love" of some sort. Discussions tangent to this theme take place rather ambiguously, such as the one between Yossarian and Orr, in which Orr asserts that "Women just don't seem to like you. I think they think you're a bad influence" (324). The women that Yossarian claims to desire are described in disgusting terms: used, decaying, pulpy. Given the importance of Freudian psychology to the generation of significant portions of *Catch-22*, the theme of censoring may be read as having everything to do with the repression of homosexuality in the military culture described by the text. Thus, such statements as "No one but Aarfy ever made reference to the naked men sun-bathing in full view farther down the beach or jumping and diving from the enormous whitewashed raft that bobbed on empty oil drums. . ." (344) seem endowed with a major significance, particularly since Aarfy is a monster whose speech-acts fulfill a transgressive function (Morrison 4–5). In any case, it is Heller himself who makes the theme of repression explicit, for Yo-Yo's roomies, who seem to operate at the instinctual level, "had not brains enough to be introverted and repressed" (357). Having reached the awareness of an operative repression in the text, it only remains for the reader to inquire as to what it is that is being repressed, and the homosexual theme will announce itself. As we will see, the homosexual theme remains latent in Heller's imagery on nearly every page of *Catch-22*.

Note

1 While this allusion may be entirely worked out in connection with *The Gilgamesh Epic*, it also serves as a linkage to Jessie Weston's discussion of the Fisher King's wounded thigh and loss of virility in *From Ritual to Romance*. Weston's statement that "the Fish is a Life symbol" (125) is imitated by Yossarian's "'My fish dream is a sex dream'" (305). Throughout Weston's writings, the word life is used as a euphemism for the word sex

Chapter 3

Love and Death in *Catch-22*

In the essay "Come Back to the Raft Ag'in, Huck Honey!"(1948) Leslie Fiedler presents his discovery of an archetype—"the archetypal love of white male and black" (487)—that inhabits American culture and is expressed in some of the classic works of American fiction. Fiedler's insight has been widely recognized as a contribution to the fundamental understanding of American culture. For instance, in *Blacks and the Jewish Mind* (1998), Seth Forman calls Fiedler "the first critic to identify interracial, homosexual love as a central motif in American literature" (120). Fiedler's unique insight formulated the latent connection between homosexuality and race relations; and it is Heller's use of Fiedler's paring of homosexuality and race relations (and a further pairing of homosexuality with the attempt "to right the imbalance which patriarchy imposes by means of alienation" (Jackson 126) that informs one of the most important subtexts in *Catch-22*. Fiedler includes in this canon of "boys' books" (485) *Moby-Dick, Huckleberry Finn*, the *Leatherstocking Tales* (especially *The Last of the Mohicans*), and *Two Years Before the Mast*.

Fiedler's thesis is so diffused throughout the essay that it is difficult to summarize it in a single quotation, but it is generally encapsulated in his statement that

> The buggery of sailors is taken for granted everywhere, yet it is thought of usually as an inversion forced on men by their isolation from women; though the opposite case may well be true: the isolation sought more or less consciously as an occasion for male encounters. At any rate, there is a context in which the legend of the sea as escape and solace, the fixated sexuality of boys, the myth of the dark beloved are one. In Melville and Twain at the center of our tradition, in the lesser writers at the periphery, the archetype is at once formalized and perpetuated. Nigger Jim and Queequeg make concrete for us what was without them as vague pressure on the threshold of our consciousness; the proper existence of the archetype is in the realized character, who waits, as it were, only to be asked his secret. (487)

The concluding paragraph of Fiedler's essay begins with the declaration that "In each generation we play out the impossible mythos" (489). The mechanism that Fiedler describes in his essay is played out so inexorably because it resides in the collective American unconscious and is not, therefore, subject to a conscious alteration or modification that would be the goal of culture were it directed by more conscious forces. In this vein Neumann states at the conclusion of *Origins*: "A future humanity will then realize the center, which the individual personality today experiences as his own self-center, to be one with humanity's very self, whose coming birth will finally vanquish and cast out that old serpent, the primordial uroboric dragon" (418).

It is this mythos of casting out the Terrible Mother—the dragon—with which we are confronted from the commencement of the text that is the subject of *Catch-22*. Thus, Heller's project in *Catch-22* is to write the history of the uroboric consciousness beginning with the first city, Uruk, and to trace its influence down to the generation that fought in World War Two. Heller's text encapsulates what Fiedler calls the playing out of the impossible mythos as a particularly American form of the eruption of uroboric consciousness, and he presents Fiedler's discovery as one of the central themes with which the text grapples. Having said this, it must be pointed out that Heller does not approach the reader directly with his psychoanalytic materials, but instead confines them to an evocation which is at times satirical, sylleptic, associative, symbolic, even archetypic. This psychological level is perhaps the most developed component of the text, and it is everywhere manifest, but it is accessible to readers only insofar as we are sensitive to the various means by which Heller assaults his readers with the theme of homoeroticism—a theme which might be presumed to strike many of his readers as repugnant and subversive. Where psychoanalysis is addressed in the surface text it is through parody, the intention seemingly to ridicule, demote, and disempower the use of depth psychology by a patriarchal authoritarianism.

Heller presents the theme of Fiedler's homoerotic archetype by elaborately alluding to the "boys' books" that Fiedler used to discover the homoerotic archetype in the first place. However, in order to see that he has concerned himself with Fiedler's canon of "boys' books" requires careful attention, for the texts in the homoerotic canon appear on different levels of the text. *Moby-Dick*, which is the subject of one of the most detailed discussions in "Come Back to the Raft A'gin, Huck Honey" is named in *Catch-22*. Melville's novel appears in chapter one, "The Texan," because a computing error has assigned a cetologist to the medical corps, and the hapless zoologist "spent his sessions with the dying colonel trying to discuss *Moby-Dick* with him" (15). The effect of Heller's substitution of literary analysis for medical care (in a matter of life and death) is that it necessarily provokes a humorous response: the black-comic effect of the passage is produced by the incommensurate seriousness of the dying man's precarious situation having a zoologist who is interested in *Moby-Dick* assigned to his case. Heller's satire is not only directed toward its most obvious target, the military bureaucracy, but also toward science, for Heller's allusion redirects Melville's allegorical inquiry into the nature of good and evil toward an investigation of the moral bankruptcy of modern, value-free science. What Heller signals by the comic conjunction of a cetologist, a dying colonel, and a novel, (rather like Maldoror's conjunction of an umbrella and a sewing machine on an operating table) is a calculatedly reversed significance: it is *Moby-Dick* which is a matter of life and death, and it is to give serious consideration to that text that he invokes it in the first chapter.

Again, another of Fiedler's "boys' books," *The Last of the Mohicans*, is named in the text, in chapter twenty-five, "The Chaplain." That Heller has absorbed Fiedler's canon into *Catch-22* is manifest given that Cooper's novels are named in Heller's novel. However, the certainty that this form of exhibitionistic intertextuality is significant is undercut by the fact that Cooper's books emerge in a list of books that includes the *Bible, Bleak House, and Ethan Frome* (*Catch-22* 293). The subject of this passage that presents the list of books is the chaplain's loss of faith; here the contextless and acategorical list of books represents the flattening out of significance that results with the loss of a belief in absolute truth. The list of books in which *The Last of the Mohicans* is included constitutes the chaplain's evidence that the *Bible* is no more important than other books—a transparently absurd and insufficient proof of absurdity and insufficiency. The list presents another case of an inversion of significance, and thus the books in the list represent texts that are, in some unspecified ways, more significant than the *Bible*.

However, it is not the direct naming of texts that belong to the canon of Fiedler's "boys' books" that is definitive, it is the subtextual handling of an unnamed text, *Huckleberry Finn*, that is definitive. The raft on which Huck and Jim escape into a world without women is for Fiedler the primal site of his archetype, and for this reason he gives it prominence in the title of his essay, "Come Back to the Raft A'gin, Huck Honey." The importance accorded "the enormous whitewashed raft" (344) in *Catch-22* points back to the legendary and iconic raft that is the site of Fiedler's interracial homoerotic: Heller's dreamlike raft is a comically hyperbolic version of Twain's—for not only is it suggestively "enormous," but, tellingly, it is "whitewashed." Moreover, in *Catch-22* the raft is stationary—a permanent fixture of the culture—and in this important respect it stands in marked contrast to Twain's raft which is practically alive in its metaphoric ability to grow, suffer destruction, and even to be reborn as it slips along the Mississippi River. The fact that Heller's raft has been "whitewashed" establishes it as an object, like the white whale Moby-Dick, that has a latent meaning: what is hidden behind Heller's raft is the system of racial and sexual semiosis that Fiedler describes in his essay. This association is further sustained by the extensiveness of the *Huckleberry Finn*-*Catch-22* intertext and by Heller's consistent, though indirect, association of "the enormous whitewashed raft" (344) with homoeroticism.

Catch-22 is infused with characters, settings, episodes, and language that allude to and parody Twain's famous novel. The first chapter of *Catch-22* is called "The Texan," and we may think this a strange opening for a novel about World War Two, even though the first chapter justifies the selection of the Texan as its central character because he is responsible for driving "everybody in the ward back to duty" (16). This pretext is, however, intended to emphasize the Texan so that he may be recognized as the tip of the intertextual iceberg (Riffaterre 131). The subtext of the chapter, "The Texan," is *Huckleberry Finn*, and the Texan himself is a substitution for Huck's father. The Texan first appears on page nine: "Then there was the educated Texan from Texas who looked like someone in technicolor and felt, patriotically, that people of means—decent folk—should be given more votes than drifters, whores, criminals, degenerates, atheists and indecent folk—people without means" (9). The import of this description (rendered more opaque as it is by its echo of Bret Harte's short story "The Outcasts of Poker Flats") is not patent until it is combined with the dialogue of page eleven: "'You killed him because he was a nigger', Dunbar said." To which the Texan replies, "'They don't allow niggers in here. They got a special place for niggers.'" The Texan's speeches have a socially inverted relationship to the diatribe delivered by Huck's father in chapter six of *Huckleberry Finn*:

> "Oh, yes, this is a wonderful government, wonderful. Why, looky here. There was a free nigger there from Ohio—a mulatter, most as white as a white man. He had the whitest shirt on you ever see, too, and the shiniest hat; and there ain't a man in that town that's got as fine clothes as what he had; and he had a gold watch and chain, and a silverheaded cane—and the awfulest old gray-headed nabob in the state. And what do you think? They said he was a p'fessor in a

college, and could talk all kinds of languages, and knowed everything. And that ain't the wust. They said he could vote when he was at home." (42–3)

A comparison of Heller's version with Twain's reveals that Dunbar introduces the anomalous subject of the "nigger" into *Catch-22* in order to bring home the Texan's parody of Huck's Pap's speech. The education applied to the Texan represents another inversion, education having been applied to the "nigger" in the original, but to the Texan in *Catch-22*. Besides inverting Twain's effects, Heller's parody is also inflated, for Pap wants only to auction and sell the P'fessor, but the (seemingly absent") "nigger" is killed in Heller's black-comic imitation, and, therefore, Dunbar pointedly calls the Texan a murderer (11). Again, these assignments only become significant when Heller's text is compared to chapter thirteen of *Huckleberry Finn*. In Twain's text the word *texas* is used to name the upper structure of the wrecked steamboat, and, having taken the skiff and stranded the criminals on the wreck, Huck thinks "how dreadful it was even for murderers to be in such a fix" (83), thus clinching the unlikely association of the words texas and murderer. A further indication that *Catch-22* sustains a consistent intertextual parallelism to *Huckleberry Finn*, we may note the importance of the raft, which first appears on page 148 and has a lyrical presence in the text as "the enormous white-washed raft" (344), until it is the site of Kid Sampson's death. The floating corpse in *Catch-22* (347) imitates both Huck's faking of his own death and Jim's discovery of Pap's body. The significance of the conjunction of all of these elements is brought out in Leslie Fiedler's visit to this same in territory in *Love and Death in the American Novel*: "In both [*Tom Sawyer* and *Huckleberry Finn*] the death of the demonic guardian of the hoard is rendered with special horror: Injun Joe . . . and Pap, naked and stabbed in the back, in the floating house of death. . . . But only in *Huckleberry Finn* is the full Oedipal significance of their deaths revealed, the terrible secret that the innocent treasure can be won only by the destruction of the Bad Father!" (281).

A more veiled, but no less crucial manifestation of Huck and Jim lying side by side on their raft is the equivalence of the hospital and the raft. In the end of the eighteenth chapter of *Huckleberry Finn* Huck states "We said there warn't no home like a raft, after all. Other places do seem so cramped up and smothery, but a raft don't. You feel mighty free and easy and comfortable on a raft" (124). This description compares favorably with what we are told about Yossarian: in the hospital Yossarian censors letters, and then is "free after that to spend the rest of each day lying around idly" and he is "comfortable in the hospital" (7). This identification is suggested, on the one hand, because the raft is "whitewashed" (344), indicating that Jim-Dunbar's "blackness" is not readily apparent, not unlike the "blackness" of the mulatto professor who is the subject of Pap's tirade. On the other hand, it is possible to identify Dunbar as an intertextual substitution for Jim, because Dunbar is so closely established as Yossarian's partner: "It was a good ward this time, one of the best he and Dunbar had ever enjoyed" (9). Not only is Dunbar a name that suggests the African-American poet Paul Lawrence Dunbar, but also "dun" means dull grayish brown in color. The notion here is that another reversal (in the form of a substitution) has been carried out, and that the latent content of the symbol of the whitewashed raft indicates that in actuality the whitewashing has been applied to Jim. Moreover, Dunbar's behavior in the hospital ward imitates the habitual indolence of the stereotypical black man: "Dunbar was lying motionless on his back again with his eyes staring up at the ceiling like a doll's" (9). This is a posture that Jim adopts throughout Twain's text. Heller's sentence imitates Huck's description of Jim and he as they pass down the river on the raft: "It was kind of solemn, drifting down the big, still river, laying on our backs looking up at the stars . . ." (77). Applying Fiedler's terms to this passage allows us to see not only the passive, static, and racially determined condition of Dunbar-Jim's posture, but also that a component of Dunbar-Jim's blackness is his semiosis as an interracial homoerotic subject/object—in other words that he is unalterably one half of a homosexual pair.

Reading Dunbar's "blackness" into the text allows us to reinterpret his role as Yossarian's partner and opposite number. Dunbar's contribution to the drama of *Catch-22* is that he is a questioning presence who shows no acceptance of the system ordained by authority—whether political or military. When Yossarian states, "Maybe they should give him [the chaplain] three votes." (15), we are told, "'Who's they?' Dunbar demanded suspiciously." In chapter twelve, "Bologna," a drunken Dunbar utters the proposition "There is no God" (29) two times, the first time in answer to "My God, it's true!" the second in answer to "I wish to God I knew what it was" (130). Dunbar's paranoia is given a more recognizable shape when it addresses the problem of God's existence, for we can see that Dunbar's assertions are derived from Nietzsche's *Zarathustra* and the proposition that "God is dead" (in fact the graffiti "God is dead, Nietzsche / Nietzsche is dead, God" readily comes to mind). This theme is further developed—though by means of a reversal—when Dunbar is "disappeared," in a sequence of events derived from the Gilgamesh intertext, and Dunbar may be identified as the human race destroyed in the deluge caused by the

Sumerian pantheon: thus, it is mankind not God who does not exist. The racial theme that arises with Dunbar's accusation of the Texan is once again reasserted and given a wider significance when we recall that the Sumerians called themselves the "blackheaded people" (Kramer 151). Furthermore, we may interpret Dunbar as representative of the Sumerian creation story presented in *The Epic of Gilgamesh*. If Dunbar—who is "disappeared" in *Catch-22* is simultaneously a black slave on one level of the text and the first created "blackheaded people" who were killed by the gods on another level of the text, we are drawn to think of other historical disappearances—the decimation of the American Indians, the enslavement and transport of Africans, and that most famous of modern "disappearances," the final solution, the Jewish Holocaust.

The exchanges in which Dunbar interjects the nonexistence of God take the form of inappropriate answers followed by misunderstood questions; this format resembles the back and forth of the comedic pair that are traditional in minstrel shows, Mr. Bones and the Interlocutor, and the racial theme is again reasserted. Heller's treatment of minstrelsy is not pure but suggests a melange of the Marx Brothers and Nathaniel West. Here, Yossarian plays the overconfident straight man to Dunbar's wise clown. The Yossarian-Dunbar relationship is brought to a conclusion in chapter thirty-four, "Thanksgiving." Heller parodies the stock snapping twigs and "stealthy rustle of leaves" (371) so characteristic of Cooper's *Deerslayer* that Twain saw fit to lampoon it in his hilarious essay, "Fenimore Cooper's Literary Offenses." In Heller's send-up of Cooper, he constructs an exaggerated and absurd inflation of the skills of Cooper's woodsmen by arranging it so that Yossarian and Dunbar recognize each other by an exchange of gunfire. The implication of this episode is that gunfire has been substituted for language, for Yossarian is able to recognize his pal because their relationship is characterized by Dunbar's instantaneous ripostes to Yossarian's verbal thrusts, an effect imitated by the gunshots:

"A twig snapped nearby. Yossarian dropped to his knees with a cold thrill of elation and aimed. He heard a stealthy rustle of leaves on the other side of the sandbags and fired two quick rounds. Someone fired back at him once, and he recognized the shot.
"Dunbar?" he called.
"Yossarian?" (371)

Twain concludes his ridicule of Cooper's dependence on broken twigs to demonstrate a mastery of woodcraft by delivering the opinion that "In fact the Leatherstocking Series ought to have been called the Broken

Twig Series" ("Offenses" 436). The twig that snaps in the forest that
Yossarian and Dunbar inhabit calls forth an intertextual regression that
reverberates from Cooper's sentimental heroics, to Twain's anti-romantic
censure of Cooper's so-called "literary offenses," to Fiedler's psychoanalytical reading of Cooper's and Twain's repressed naiveté.

The development of Dunbar's character takes on a pathological dimension, when, thinking that the soldier in white has returned, he becomes manic, and he is taken away never to be seen again. Dunbar's final
appearance shows him "staring with one eye into the lightless, unstirring
void of the soldier in white's mouth" (375). As I have said above, at this
point Dunbar represents mankind just at the point where the gods agree
that men must be destroyed, however, another reading also applies. The
episode has an additional relationship to the soldier in white's identity as
a mummy in the novel's *Book of the Dead* subtext. Given this additional
reading, Dunbar's psychological crisis—in which he is thrust into a final
insanity—is motivated by his direct observation that there is no god of
rebirth (Osiris) and no afterlife. In this second reading, Dunbar is shown
to have looked into the sarcophagus of the god Osiris and verified at first
hand that the god has not been transformed and reborn: instead, as recounted in the myth, the god of agriculture, wine, and dancing has been
sealed up in a box by the god Set. Dunbar's "disappearance" is not only
an imitation of the exile into immortality of Utnapishtim at the hands of
the Sumerian gods but an imitation of the defeat of the god of light,
consciousness, individualism, and the male principle and, thereby, foreshadows the victory of the uroboric dragon.

Dunbar's final assertion is that "They just took him away and left those
bandages there." (375). If now we turn from considering the mythic level
of the text to address the psychological subtext, we can approach the
discussion of Dunbar's racial identity as an African-American. By observ-
ing that the bandages are empty, Dunbar has run afoul of the military's
system of patriarchal authoritarianism that is inexorably driven by the
death wish. Dunbar's alienation from military authority is generated by
his need to repress his racial identity (or to "pass" for white), and this
mechanism has in turn allowed him to understand that the military is not
only inherently pathological but also doubly retributive, because it does
not allow its members any awareness of its true condition. The structural
importance of the episode in which Dunbar is "disappeared" is that it
brings to a completion the "crazy" motif that commenced in chapter two,
where it was stated that "The only thing going on was a war, and no one
seemed to notice but Yossarian and Dunbar. And when Yossarian tried to

remind people, they drew away from him and thought he was crazy" (17). (The text also alludes to Achilles and Patroclus at the point in the ninth book of the *Iliad* where Achilles rejects Agamemnon's envoy, saying he plans on sailing home and advising the envoys to do the same.) Tragically, it is Yossarian and not the armed doctors (375) who declares his companion Dunbar insane; Yossarian shouts, "'You're crazy!'" (375) at Dunbar because he is no longer able to sustain his own former craziness, a state which represents his distrust of and rejection of the system of rules—crowned by *Catch-22*—that directs men smoothly and efficiently to their deaths.

The detailed examination of the relevant intertexts presented above was required to establish Dunbar's racial otherness so that it could be shown that *Catch-22* contains a character in the novel who has assumed the role of the African-American man as "dark beloved" (Fiedler 487). In contrast to the hidden nature of Dunbar's identity, Heller gives a direct treatment to yet another manifestation of Fiedler's "dark beloved," the American Indian. As it did not defy the social mores of the period that an American Indian would be stationed in a white unit, Chief White Halfoat is identified as an American Indian. Chapter five, "Chief White Halfoat," introduces the character of the Chief, who narrates the entire story of his life (44–45).

The Chief's story is a parody of *The Last of the Mohicans*, so in effect Cooper's novel has been so deflated by Heller that it is reduced to a two-page comic monologue. Furthermore, not being content with these effects, Heller has also mingled into the Chief another of Cooper's Indians, *The Chainbearer's* Sureflint, whom Fiedler describes as "advan[cing] with the customary declaration of loneliness, 'No tribe—no squaw—no papoose'" (*Love and Death* 213). It is only through a careful assessment of Heller's embrace of the Joycean interchangeablity of characters that it can be ascertained that the chaplain is also Sureflint. The upshot of the Chief's speech is his declaration that "I was the only survivor," a punchline version of Fiedler's summary of the conclusion of Cooper's novel: "Cooper's Indian smolders to a hopeless old age conscious of the imminent disappearance of his race" (488–89). Heller inverts the fate of Cooper's final Indian by having Chief White Halfoat irrationally become fixated on a cliché belonging to the sentimental novel and vow to die of pneumonia, in unromantic contrast to the pathos with which Cooper treats his Indian.

The Chief's demise by pneumonia is carried out in chapter thirty-five. By these means, Heller sees to the thorough deromanticizing of the Indian as "dark beloved," and we can barely recognize his relationship to the nearly irresistible Indians that Fiedler finds in "boys' books"—such as Sureflint, with whom Mordaunt Littlepage "falls in love at first sight" (*Love and Death* 213). Heller has carried this scene into the opening of *Catch-22*, so that we cannot help but to see that Yossarian's instant infatuation with the chaplain is a caricature of Littlepage's "extraordinary reaction" (*Love and Death* 213) to Sureflint.

We may also note in passing that Chief White Halfoat has a number of connections to *Finnegans Wake*. One of the more telling links between the texts is that the Chief's death by *pneumonia* is a pun on the moaning that occurs at the death of ALP on the novel's final page. Additionally, a connection between the Chief and the writings of Sigmund Freud may be established in that his fixation on dying of pneumonia may be read as a droll, understated, and Eliotic parody of Freud's case study of "The Rat Man" ("Notes Upon a Case of Obsessional Neurosis") that described a soldier who was convinced that he would die in a peculiar and specific manner (a horrific Chinese torture).

Despite Heller's fictional treatment of Fiedler's homoerotic archetype of the white male's passionless passion for the dark beloved, he does not give the theme an unequivocal presentation in the narrative. The occurrences of homoerotic speech-acts contained in the text are not illustrative of the specific joining of white man and dark beloved. Standing in lieu of this latent content is the opening sentence of the novel in which we are told "The first time Yossarian saw the chaplain he fell madly in love with him" (7). Though Dunbar is later paired with Yossarian, and he is both a mulatto and a psychodynamic manifestation of the dark beloved, we are initially told of Yossarian's love for the chaplain, whom we must "normalize" and regard as white. However, before we can regard the "Indian" chaplain as a white man, we must "normalize" Yossarian's love for the chaplain into a love that is not love at first sight. (Admittedly, the first part of this process is paradoxical, as we do not easily become aware that Yossarian falls in love with the chaplain because he is an "Indian"). Here we again encounter the demotional technique that is a prevalent component of Heller's style in *Catch-22*, though in this occurrence it is more problematic than when one of Freud's psychoanalytic cases is burlesqued.

When we confront the opening sentence, with its frank address to the homoerotic theme, we are not told that Yossarian fell in love with the chaplain in a manner that allows us to believe that what we have read is true. The text performs its own self-destruction by presenting the "latent content" of the homoerotic archetype openly, thereby forcing the censor to demote the evident homoeroticism to the mechanism of the joke: this is a verbal equivalence to Harpo's erotic overtures in "Duck Soup" that are read as heteronormatively erotic, when he props his leg on a woman, but eccentric and merely irritating, when he props his leg on a man. The superego efficiently screens out the "obvious" homoeroticism inhabiting the scene. The point that Heller underscores by substituting the chaplain (the invisible "dark beloved" of the Cooper intertext) for Dunbar (the dark beloved in the *Huckleberry Finn* intertext) is that it reinforces Fiedler's assertion that the affection that white men feel for one another is always assumed to be innocent: "To doubt for a moment this innocence, which can survive only as assumed, would destroy our stubborn belief in a relationship simple, utterly satisfying, yet immune to lust; physical as the handshake is physical, this side of copulation" (CB 485). (The violence and betrayal that develops in the Yossarian-Dunbar pairing suggests that it is cast in the mold of what Fiedler calls the "Melvillean sinister homoerotic relationships as those of Redburn and Jackson, Billy Budd and Claggart" [*Love and Death* 214], and we shall see that this is true.)

In the narrator's opening declaration of Yossarian's love for the chaplain, the very bluntness and the clarity of what is expressed negates the possibility that what is being asserted is a possibility; thus the text commences by forcing the reader to haul out the mechanisms of repression and immediately go to work censoring the polysemous and polymorphously perverse text. (Can there now be any wonder that by the bottom of the first page Yossarian—the analyst of psychoanalysts—is in the hospital censoring V-Mail?) Strangely, the confrontation with homoeroticism is not modified when Yossarian is allowed to speak further, saying, "Wasn't he sweet? . . . Maybe they should give him three votes" (15).

The novel's opening is so expressly transgressive and Yossarian's utterances so determinedly flout heteronormality that the reader is forced to conclude that Yossarian cannot mean anything by his statements—that his speech is comic but also nonsense. In other words, laughter is produced by the mechanism of repression and the need for the release of tension that it produces; the statement is funny because if it is not dismissed with humor, the only alternative is to consciously understand its homoerotic content. In addition, the text is equally problematic for alerting the reader to the presence of the repressive process that it generates even while it is generating the repressive function. Heller has approached the presentation of this mechanism early on in his text, because it is such an important feature of Fielder's archetype: "It is this self-congratulatory buddy-buddiness, its astonishing naiveté that breeds at once endless opportunities for inversion and the terrible reluctance to admit its existence, to surrender the last believed-in stronghold of love without passion" (CB 485).

The only use of the word "homosexual" in the text of *Catch-22* suffers a similar syntactical nullification or stylistic undermining of what is tacit: "At the state university he [Major Major] took his studies so seriously that he was suspected by the homosexuals of being a Communist and suspected by the Communists of being a homosexual" (88). This sentence possesses an intonation reminiscent of a Marx Brothers or S.J. Perelman joke that comes about by means of a rhythmic pattern derived from a reversal of the parallel grammatical components. For an example, let us take Perelman's "Our meal finished, we sauntered into the rumpus room and Diana turned on the radio. With a savage snarl, the radio turned on her" (Blair 435). Heller's connection to the humorists of the 1930s, specifically Groucho Marx and S.J. Perelman has been noted from the time of the publication of *Catch-22* (Potts 9), and Stephen Potts indicates that when words and names take on a life of their own in the text the effect is at first comic. However, "the results grow less comic . . . as the narrative moves into the later chapters" (41). Potts defends Heller against the charge that his use of humor is "trivial and redundant" (41) by stating that "not only do the more insistent verbal repetitions and contradictions, as well as the repeated allegations of madness, taper off, they shift in function from mere stylistic devices to motifs embedded in the entire foundation of the book's structure" (41). In Potts's analysis, the central thematic motif developed in *Catch-22* is that "those in the positions of power in this world set the rules of discourse and through them the syllogisms of allowable thought and behavior; thus, they also set the standards for human identity and nonidentity. The reification of the human being is therefore connected to the reification of language: the sundering of words from their meanings, of names from individuals, of signifier from signified" (90).

While it is true that Heller is concerned with this theme, his incremental use of jokes is not confined to building up gradually from the stylistic to the thematic but is, instead, a continual assault on the reader's conscious mind by homoerotic speech-acts, which the text requires that the super-ego censor. The humor expressed in the text is serious humor and masks a psychological component that consists of repressed material: while it may be said that this is true of all humor, here the difference is that although Heller's constructs take the form of jokes, they are formulated as transgressive attacks on tabooed areas of culture. The jokes created by the Marx Brothers and Perelman are verbal play that does little more than entertain. The Perelman joke cited above derives its humor out of the personification of a radio; some additional satire directed at a social class may also be read into the passage, but this is hardly on a par with what Heller arranges in his jokes. Potts cites a passage in which Yossarian acts out a cliché—You scratch my back and I'll scratch yours—and scratches Doc Daneeka's back literally. To introduce the passage he states "An intentionally comic use of this confusion of words and meanings in the interplay from chapter 4 opened by Doc Daneeka" (40). After Potts has quoted the passage, he states "This sort of word play is reminiscent of mainstream comedy, particularly as practiced in Heller's time by the Marx Bothers and S.J. Perelman" (41). What is missing from Potts's analysis is that Yossarian has actually scratched Doc Daneeka's back. This is not and never was an innocent activity, though we necessarily balk at this assessment, for to endow the action with homoerotic content is in Fiedler's words "to compromise an essential aspect of American sentimental life: the camaraderie of the locker room and ball park, the good fellowship of the poker game and fishing trip, a kind of passionless passion, at once gross and delicate, homoerotic in the boy's sense, possessing an innocence above suspicion" (CB 484.). We have already observed the artillery captain who lies "amorously on his belly" (9), and when Yossarian scratches Doc Daneeka's back with his hand instead of resorting to the bribe that is being importuned, we once again meet with the male-to-male embrace where we are least prepared to encounter it.

Interestingly, the problem of repression and awareness is at issue in both the description of Major Major's schooling and in Yossarian's dealings with Doc Daneeka. Because the Major's experience is presented as a joke—"At the state university he [Major Major] took his studies so seriously that he was suspected by the homosexuals of being a Communist and suspected by the Communists of being a homosexual" (88)—it is not readily apparent that we are to take the statement seriously. When it is taken seriously, the statement says something fairly straightforward about the condition of two groups of social outcasts, and something less than obvious about how knowledge is arrived at. The narrator delivers his joke to the reader by virtue of being an insider—an omniscient presence—who has knowledge of how homosexuals and Communists conduct their affairs.

The joke is based on the limited insights of the Communists and the homosexuals and the narrator's superior apprehension of these two groups, which is so penetrating that he can juxtapose them verbally: Communists know who the Communists are, and if they cannot explain aberrant behavior by resorting to their own ideologies, then they must categorize the aberrant agent as a member of the only alternative out-group, and the same process holds true for homosexuals. The joke is that Major Major belongs to neither category (nor, presumably, do the narrator and the reader), but the reason that the joke is operatively funny (and effectively serves to relieve tension) is that, by being aimed at the Communists and homosexuals, it allows the homosexual theme to be safely broached.

There is, however, an important difference between the narrator's joke and a psychologically naive joke, in that the narrator represents an intelligence that understands all too well what Freud said about jokes. The jokes that the narrator delivers are jokes weighted with a Freudian consciousness of the unconscious meaning of jokes, and the narrator subtly communicates to the reader that the reader is not merely to laugh at the joke but to apprehend that the joke is a mechanism of conscious displacement. In "Wit and Its Relation to the Unconscious," Freud states that in the dream-work, "[u]nder the pressure of the censor any kind of association becomes good enough for substitution by allusion" (755), because it works through the dreaming unconscious. However, wit-technique bypasses inhibitions somewhat differently, since its limits are those available to conscious thought: thus wit-technique

> insists upon retaining the play with words or nonsense unaltered, but thanks to the ambiguity of words and multiplicity of thought-relations, it restricts itself to the choice of cases in which this play or nonsense may appear at the same time admissible (jest) or senseful (wit). Nothing distinguishes wit from all other psychic formations better than this double-sidedness and this double-dealing; by emphasizing the "sense in nonsense," the authors have approached nearest the understanding of wit, at least from this angle. ("WRU 755–56)

When Doc Daneeka asks for "a little grease" (34), and says that he wants his hand washed and his back scratched, Yossarian's response is to scratch Doc Daneeka's back, but only after the narrator interposes the comment, "Yossarian knew what he meant" (34). Just as there are several ways to kill a cat, there are several ways to scratch a back, and some of them are erotic. Thus, Yossarian's response to the doctor's cliché may only be interpreted as typical "crazy Yossarian" clowning, if his literal scratching of the doctor's back is understood without reference to the possibility of its erotic "double sidedness."

Taken as components of erotic play, the words "grease," "hand," and "back," which are innocently embedded in the passage (34), contain associations that violate heteronormality in that they communicate an erotic homosexual subtext that is actively being repressed by Doc Daneeka, but which, the narrator implies, Yossarian grasps and responds to by means of a further ambiguous "double-dealing"—he actually touches the doctor. In the final analysis, the reader knows that the narrator knows what Doc Daneeka means, and that Doc Daneeka does not know. And though the reader also knows that Yossarian is a man who falls in love at first sight with other men, the reader does not know whether Yossarian knows consciously what he is doing.

Heller's handling of the homosexual theme, as a seemingly superficial joke about homosexuality in a throwaway line, may be distinguished usefully from his development of Fiedler's archetype of the love of white male and black. Fielder's discovery of the homoerotic interracial archetype was connected to "the idea of sexual fusion as a solution to the American race problem" (Forman 120). Heller's pairing of homosexuality and Communism in the joke directed toward Major Major hints at the dangerously subversive suggestion that homosexuality, like Communism, has a therapeutic content. Graham Jackson observes that "homoeros is viewed by the patriarchy as inimical to its aims . . . because it moves to right the imbalance which patriarchy imposes by means of alienation" (127). Curiously, alienation is a word belonging to both the psychoanalytic and the Marxist vocabularies, and, thus, we may conceive of both the Freudian-Jungian and the Marxist projects as attacks on alienation. In the case of the Freud-Jung therapy we are, in a sense, forced to read homoerotic expression as a semiosis that is synonymous with depth psychology, and the homosexual theme in *Catch-22* seems to be related to the various homosexual stages of psychic and mythic development outlined by Jung, Neumann, and Graham Jackson. In the analysis developed by Neumann, the male-to-male bond makes possible the attack on the Terrible Mother. For Jungians of a less homophobic vision (such as Graham Jackson), homoeroticism represents an alliance to the principles of the Great Mother and an attack on the patriarchy (Jackson 128). Here, we have touched on a veritable politics of homoeroticism, and while a Jungian theorist such as Graham Jackson can set himself apart from the Freud-Jung view of homosexuality as a mother-based neurosis, it is not clear that either Fiedler or Heller embrace either homoeroticism or homosexuality as a stage in a process that unreservedly proceeds to psychic and cultural wholeness. We have only to note the tragic consequences of the male-to-male pairs in the urtexts that underlie the narrative of *Catch-22*—namely, the deaths of Enkidu, Patroclus, Queequeg, Chingachgook, and the separation of Jim from Huck—to realize the price that is exacted for any opposition to the Terrible Father. In *Catch-22* the revenge element receives an even more exaggerated presentation, for it appears as the inexorable and interminable harrowing suffered by the bomber pilots that are Yossarian's companions.

The homoerotic archetype pervades *Catch-22* and generates some of the most compelling material in the text. In chapter thirty there is a description of Yossarian gripped in a frenzy of fear: "He looked desperately about for a gun, a gray-black .45 automatic that he could cock and ram right up against the base of McWatt's skull" (342). We are not used to providing the individual words in a "conventional" novel with readings informed by psychoanalysis, polysemy, and the "lexical deviance" and "semantic density" (Norris 98) of *Finnegans Wake*, so the statement that the description of the enraged and gun-wielding Yossarian is composed at the psychoanalytic level of language (like the narrator's jokes) will at first mean very little. It is rather like Yossarian's position in relation to the doctor's request to have his back scratched. A question arises as to whether the request is literal, metaphoric, or psychoanalytic. The psychoanalytic choice is, however, not a real choice because the censor that is the conscious mind works too well to allow language to be fully understood psychoanalytically. Nevertheless, the sentence under discussion may be shown to contain the words "cock," "ram right up," "base," and "skull." Given Heller's demonstrable and considerable interest in *Finnegans Wake*, an approach to Heller's sentence that treats it as Joycean "double talk" (Norris 101) is not unwarranted, and it allows us to read "base" as ass and "skull" as hole. This interpolation pales in comparison to the gymnastic wrenching that Joyce has performed on language in *Finnegans Wake*. In the *Wake* Joyce renders ass as "harse" (8), "marse" (366), "arias" (11), and "grass" (366); and we also see "skall" (364) for skull, "hooliums" (6) for hole, and "whole" for all. Reading Heller's sentence with an ear attuned to its concealed and repressed content, we learn that Yossarian wants to *ram his cock right up McWatt's ass hole*. The recognition of this violent, homoerotic urge is no less dismaying to heteronormative sensitivities than was the decoding of the homoerotic presentation of the artillery captain whom the narrator depicts in the first chapter reposing amorously on his stomach. In fact the entire text of *Catch-22* is a dizzying welter of homoerotic imagery presented through the various approaches to the double-sidedness of language that a post-Joycean author may take.

As a final example of this multiplicity of approaches to polysemy in *Catch-22*, there is the particularly disturbing sentence in chapter twenty-six, "Aarfy," in which we read, "He was wounded in the thigh, and when he recovered consciousness he found McWatt on both knees taking care of him" (298). This is a superb example of what I have characterized as the narrator's insistent inclusion of the reader in the psychoanalytic reading of the text. The word "consciousness" that the sentence contains is now revealed as straining under the weight of its double-sidedness, and, as we have seen, the narrator dangles before the reader the question of Yossarian's penetration into an awareness of the repressed meanings of the activities in which he and the other characters are engaged, for at times Yossarian outFreuds the Freudians in the game of the "talking cure." In this instance, the word *consciousness*—the term at the center of the Freudian universe—is used to interrogate both reader and character: the meaning of the sentence is undisclosed to the conscious mind, and it is up to both reader and character to come to grips with that missing interpretation, to perceive that something significant has been repressed, and to discover its nature. On the literal level, the activity is the routine dressing of a wound: the undisclosed activity is clearly a homosexual encounter—though it retains its quality of indistinctness and may be regarded as being only "figurative," even after the encounter has been recognized as a homoerotic act.

The passage has an atmosphere of psychic ambivalence to it. McWatt is the target of Yossarian's homoerotic-homicidal frenzy on page 342. Moreover, the "malign and cabalistic and irremovable" (160) Aarfy is supervising the interplay between Yossarian and McWatt: "He [Yossarian] was relieved, even though he still saw Aarfy's bloated cherub's face hanging down over McWatt's shoulder with placid interest" (298). This would be unremarkable except that Aarfy is a marker for the decoding of homoerotic activity: "No one but Aarfy ever made reference to the naked men sun-bathing in full view farther down the beach or jumping and diving from the enormous whitewashed raft that bobbed on empty oil drums out beyond the silt sand bar" (344). As in the encounter between Yossarian and the chaplain on the first page of the text or between Yossarian and Doc Daneeka, and McWatt's "taking care of Yossarian," the narrator's indirect presentation prevents us from apprehending directly the comments that Aarfy makes about the naked men. Similarly, the narrator informs us that Aarfy is looking on as Yossarian becomes aware of "McWatt on both knees taking care of him" (298), however, there is no indication of what Aarfy is thinking, or even of what he sees, for "taking care of him" is a verbal construction designed not to describe what is taking place but to suspend the reader in "the ambiguity of words and multiplicity of thought-relations" (Freud WRU 755). In this way, the narrator repeatedly signals his role as a censor (a censor who is a component of the style of the text).

The narrator-censor is interposed between the unconscious and conscious of the text—the surface text and its Freudian cotext—and, thereby, the narrator constructs the double meaning of the intertext, for to allow Aarfy's comments into the surface text would be to destroy the verisimilitude of the surface text. The repression of Aarfy's comments, however, guides the reader to the homoerotic subtext in a manner described by Riffaterre:

> It should be clear by now that the intertext of the narrative acts as the unconscious of fiction and that readers recover or discover that intertext because the narrative itself contains clues leading back to it. This is in no way different from the process that leads the analyst from anomalies, inconsequences, and nonsequiturs in the analysand's monologue to a key to the latter's symbols and symptoms. It must also be clear that the narrative is produced by repressing and displacing the intertext, and that the visible sign of this repression or displacement at the surface of the fictional text is the loss of narrativity. (91)

Though the text seems to repress Aarfy's use as a marker for homoeroticism, this function is not absolute, for we are further alerted. to the homoerotic thrust of the description of Yossarian's wounding by the description of Aarfy's "bloated cherub's face hanging down over McWatt's shoulder with placid interest" (298). The passage alludes to the use of *putti* in Renaissance and Baroque paintings. *Putti* derived from the figures in classical art that represented Eros, the Greek god of love, thus to describe Aarfy as a cherub is to strengthen his identification as a homoerotic marker. More specifically, we may see Aarfy as the "golden Cupidon" in line 80 of *The Waste Land* that is witness to the episode of trickery, seduction, and rape to which Eliot alludes at the opening of "A Game of Chess," the second section of his poem: this association further supports Aarfy as an indicator of erotic repression, concealment, and doublesidedness.

Finally, the scene involving Yossarian, McWatt, and Aarfy is reminiscent of the ambiguous sexual encounter that is at the core of *Finnegans Wake*. Grace Eckley comments that "The exact nature of the sin of HCE is still clouded in supposition, and perhaps this is the way Joyce wanted it. No matter what precisely did happen in Phoenix Park between HCE, the two girls, and three soldiers, the effects of the guilt engendered there are of primary importance" (88). Compared to the indefinite Joycean sin, Heller's treatment of Fiedler's homoerotic archetype is as explicit as a Renaissance painting. It is also noteworthy that Aarfy's attributes seem to extend back to *Finnegans Wake*, for he is a "cherub" in chapter twenty-six, "Aarfy," and in chapter 15, "Piltchard and Wren" he is "an eerie ogre in a dream, incapable of being bruised or evaded (154): both of these descriptions are combined in *Finnegans Wake*, where "Kevin's just a doat with his cherub cheek, chalking oghres on walls . . ." (27).

Up to this point, the burden of the discussion has been to show the extent to which *Catch-22* is concerned with homoeroticism—a theme derived from Heller's absorption of Fiedler and Jung (and we may include Erich Neumann, Maud Bodkin, and a "Jungian" Joyce). Having examined some of the linguistic, stylistic, and figurative means by which Heller has insinuated the homoerotic theme into *Catch-22*, we will now turn to an examination of what is essentially an extension of this concern into more technical areas—namely, to depth psychology, and specifically, to Freud's case histories. Heller constructs a subtle allusion to these famous case histories by presenting the marriages of four characters as "case histories," and it is helpful to recall that marriage is a crucial subject with regard to Fiedler's archetype of the flight of men from women in that the men are principally fleeing the institution of marriage to women.

Chapter four, the "Doc Daneeka" chapter, presents a sardonic view of the doctor that takes into account his present life in the military, but it is typical of the structure of *Catch-22* that not much about the doctor is disclosed in the chapter which bears his name, and the doctor's "case history" is located in the chapter that follows. The one material comment that is made in chapter four seems on the surface to be about the doctor but is more directed toward revealing an important aspect of Yossarian's character: in the course of relating the doctor's aversion to flying in airplanes, a seemingly inconsequential observation is made: "Doc Daneeka hated to fly. He felt imprisoned in an airplane. In an airplane there was absolutely no place in the world to go except to another part of the airplane. Doc Daneeka had been told that people who enjoyed climbing into an airplane were really giving vent to a subconscious desire to climb back into the womb. He had been told this by Yossarian, who made it possible for Dan Daneeka to collect his flight pay each month without ever climbing back into the womb" (34).

This is not the only passage in the text where we are confronted with Yossarian's application of depth psychology to the analysis of his surroundings. In chapter twenty-seven, "Nurse Duckett," an even more elaborately humorous occasion is constructed out of Yossarian's confrontation of Major Sanderson, the army's psychiatrist; this chapter takes place during the hospital stay following Yossarian's having been wounded in the thigh. So absurd is the exchange between Yossarian and the psychiatrist that the very existence of Yossarian's wound is a matter of their dispute, with the doctor insisting that Yossarian must be mad because he is in the hospital for a stone in his salivary gland not for a wound in his thigh. As this episode develops, it introduces the Freudian technique of the interpretation of dreams, and the specific content of one of the chaplain's dreams. This dream, which involves "a shark eating my left leg in exactly the same place where you have your bandage" (306) suggests two of Freud's case histories, namely, "Little Hans" in which a boy fears castration by horses and "The Rat Man" in which a soldier fears that he will be devoured by rats. (The ambiguity of the dispute between Major Sanderson and Yossarian imitates the various absurd disputes that occur in many of Lewis Carroll's texts, important sources for *Finnegans Wake*. We are also reminded of the ambiguous treatment afforded Yossarian's wounding as well as the ambiguity more generally applied in the text to the treatment of homoerotic wish and homosexual contact. A great deal more might also be said about the wound's symbolic and mythical analogs, particularly with regard to the death and rebirth of Tammuz and the use of the thigh as a euphemism for the phallus by the ancient Egyptians.) The upshot of their disagreements is that Yossarian calls the psychiatrist "crazy" (312), because the psychiatrist has called him crazy. Having extracted this long sought after diagnosis through a nonsensical dialogue, Yossarian asks to be sent home. Major Sanderson agrees to his request (312), but the whole thing comes to nothing, and Yossarian is returned to combat.

The effect of Yossarian's diagnosis of Doc Daneeka's wish to "return to the womb" and Yossarian's confrontation with Major Sanderson in the "dream analysis" episode establishes Yossarian as having a considerable knowledge about depth psychology; in fact, his exchange with Major Sanderson reverses our expectations and demonstrates that Yossarian is endowed with more psychological insight and expertise than the so-called expert. Through his exchanges with Yossarian, Major Sanderson's uncertain grasp of depth psychology is subjected to acidic satire. Heller subjects the Freudian project to an absurd reversal, whereby analysis cannot go forward unless the patient is as much a Freudian as is the analyst. This point is made when Major Sanderson responds joyfully to Yossarian's use of the words *ambivalent attitude*. Detecting the presence of a patient educated in the Freudian discourse, the analyst attempts to convey the frustration of "talking day after day to patients who haven't the slightest knowledge of psychiatry, trying to cure people who have no real interest in me or my work!" (304).

By allowing Major Sanderson to confess his own "terrible feeling of inadequacy" (304), Heller effectively undercuts the authority of the psychiatric profession. Major Sanderson, the figure who represents the practice of psychiatry, is characterized by obvious neurotic symptoms. Moreover, he is revealed to be narcissistic, unsympathetic, and a committed spokesperson for the amoral, absurd, and murderous military-industrial culture that has formed him. Sanderson's posturing is contrasted with Yossarian's headlong veracity, a device that serves to illustrate the inability of the mental health profession to provide accurate and meaningful readings of the nature of reality. Sanderson's response to the threat that his patient poses is to revile Yossarian with a farcical righteous indignation delivered as a rapid-fire catalog of accusations that is reminiscent of the characters that Groucho Marx played in such films as *Animal Crackers* (Captain Jeffrey T. Spaulding) and *Duck Soup* (Rufus T. Firefly): "You're antagonistic to the idea of being robbed, exploited, degraded, humiliated or deceived. Misery depresses you. Ignorance depresses you. Persecution depresses you. Violence depresses you. Slums depress you. Greed depresses you. Crime depresses you. Corruption depresses you. You know, it wouldn't surprise me if you're a manic depressive!" (312).

Major Sanderson evidences the power of unconscious forces in the individual: "The essence of repression lies in the refusal of the human being to recognize the realities of his human nature" (Brown 4). In the struggle between Yossarian and Major Sanderson, the two men represent the necessity of conflict between the unconscious and the conscious minds, for "Every human life unfolds around conflict. . . ." and "[o]ur lives develop and expand by way of conflicts between superior and inferior functions" (Whitmont 135; 147). However, in another characteristic inversion, Heller has allowed Yossarian and Major Sanderson to switch roles, for it is Yossarian who is relatively conscious and the psychiatrist who exhibits a psychopathic inability to grasp the dehumanizing nature of his surroundings. Major Sanderson represents psychoanalysis as a force that oedipalizes the unconscious "rendering it guilty, castrating it" (*Anti-Oedipus* 112), causing the unconscious to desire its own repression, and Yossarian is present as anti-Oedipus, "a nonfascist subject" (*Anti-Oedipus* xxiii).

The relationships between men and women in *Catch-22* are generated out of Heller's appropriation of Leslie Fiedler's reading of American culture in his early essay "Come Back to the Raft A'gin, Huck Honey." Much of what touches on the theme of marriage in *Catch-22* parallels Fiedler's extended treatment of the American homoerotic archetype (and the subsequent flight of men from women) and what he calls the "sentimental love religion" in *Love and Death in the American Novel*. *Catch-22* antedates the publication of *Love and Death*, however, Fiedler's book-length treatment of the archetype is an expansion of what is outlined in the earlier essay, and it is helpful to consult Fiedler's longer study as a means toward explicating the meaning of Heller's appropriation of Fiedler's essay, along with the American novels and psychoanalytic theories that form the basis of the essay.

It is no great feat to recognize in Heller's four case histories of marriages, his black comic parody of Freud's major case histories, "The Rat Man, "The Wolf-man," "Little Hans," "Dora," and "Schreber."[1] Heller has grounded his "case histories" within marriage and within the family: in doing so he compares favorably to the practice of both Freud and Joyce: "James Joyce, with his exploitation of the numerous states of receding consciousness, with his use of words as things, a concept basic to the Freudian interpretation of dreams, with his pervading sense of the interrelation and interpenetration of all things and, not least important, his familiar themes, has perhaps most thoroughly consciously exploited Freud's ideas" (Trilling "Legacy" [quoted in Hoffman 120]).

Despite Heller's parody of Freud, the case histories of certain relationships between men and women that are depicted in *Catch-22* are specifically designed as accurate illustrations of common psychopathic interactions. At this point, it is useful to recall that Fiedler's discussion of the American homoerotic archetype does not present it as an irrevocable fact but an entirely alterable psychosocial condition. Indeed, should American culture neglect to work out a relief for the irrational, inhumane, and self-destructive impulses to which it so easily gives constant and unreflective expression—automation, standardization, conformity, overproduction—it is unlikely that it may much longer endure and sustain the nightmarish system of oppressive social relations to which so many millions of morally, esthetically, and intellectually anesthetized citizens have become acclimated. Along these lines, Lewis Mumford suggests that "the basic conditions for mental stability—accepted criteria of values, accepted norms of conduct, recognizable faces, buildings, landmarks, recurrent vocational duties and rituals—are constantly being undermined; as a result of our whole power-driven civilization is turning into a blank page, torn to shreds from within by psychotic violence" (*Pentagon* 370–71).

Fiedler's thesis is that an unfortunate split in American culture came about and separated men from women; the split expressed itself psychologically as the separation of the animus from the anima. It is this separation of the male component from the female principle and its direction towards itself that accounts for most of the action that takes place in *Catch-22*. Fiedler speaks of the collapse of the sentimental love tradition and the withdrawal of men not only into interracial homoeroticism but also into a pattern of taking revenge on women:

> The nineteenth-century myth of the Immaculate Young Girl has failed to survive in any felt way into our time. Rather, in the dirty jokes shared among men in the smoking car, the barracks, or the dormitory, there is a common male revenge against women for having flagrantly betrayed that myth; and under the revenge, the rather smug assumption of the chastity of the revenging group, in so far as it is a purely male society. From what other source could arise that unexpected air of good clean fun which overhangs such sessions? It is this self-congratulatory buddy-buddiness, its astonishing naiveté that breeds at once endless opportunities for inversion and the terrible reluctance to admit its existence, to surrender the last believed-in stronghold of love without passion. (485)

In *Catch-22* the eruption of war does not shatter a blissful domesticity: rather, it saves the men depicted in the narrative from lives that are unsatisfactory and unfulfilled—loveless, boring, and haunted by the conventionalized fear of social and financial failure that is the dark side of the American bourgeois capitalist, neo-Calvinist culture. Thus, Heller centers on four characters and develops four case histories to illustrate the condition of male-female relationships at the start of the war: Doc Daneeka, the chaplain, Colonel Moodus, and Lieutenant Scheisskopf. Having offered this approach, it must also be said that we cannot take this arrangement as exact or literal, for in the first place, Freud has five case histories to the four that I have located in *Catch-22*. Moreover, marriage is not the explicit problem in any of Freud's cases. The idea is simply that Heller seems to have resorted to the genre of the case history in order to present his material, and to the extent that this is true, he further extends his satire of the apparatus of authoritarian Freudianism that is embodied by Dr. Sanderson.

Doc Daneeka's case history is narrated in "Chief White Half Oat," the chapter that follows the "Doc Daneeka" chapter; there we learn little more about Doc Daneeka than that the doctor collects flight pay even though he does not board the planes that carry him on their manifests. The chapter that initially purports to be a description of the doctor is an account of how modern medicine is corrupted by the requirement of the war machine for healthy bodies: medicine is reduced to a bureaucratic system of organized neglect. We are also shown that the doctor is more committed to the extraction of money from the Army than to any notion of serving his country or of dedicatedly practicing medicine, and it is his greedy pursuit of undeserved danger pay that is the cause of his subsequent downfall. For the doctor, the entire conduct of the war has been reduced to a profit-taking enterprise, and in that respect he may be seen as an adjunct to the themes explored through Milo Minderbinder and his syndicate: we see that reflected in the doctor is the condition of late capitalism in which everything is "thoroughly comodified, normalized, and reified" (Burnham 248).

Doc Daneeka's case history occupies but two paragraphs of the "Chief White Half Oat" chapter and takes the form of a digression within the embedded story of "the newlyweds" (40). Though the Depression is never mentioned, it is apparent that Doc Daneeka's financial problems coincide with the generally poor economy that was in evidence before the war. Significantly, description of his medical practice—except for the narrative about the newlyweds—is given in financial terms: "Bills piled up rapidly, and he was soon faced with the loss of his most precious medical instruments: his adding machine was repossessed, and then his typewriter. The goldfish died. Fortunately, just when things were blackest, the war broke out" (41). The section that I am referring to as Doc Daneeka's "case history" seems to have nothing whatever to do with the (Fiedler defined) relationships between men and women until it is combined with chapter thirty-one, "Mrs. Daneeka." Mrs. Daneeka is a conventional American wife who reacts conventionally and appropriately to the news of her husband's wartime demise. When she learns from his scrawled letter that he is still alive, she dutifully attempts to rectify the situation. However, when money begins to accrue as a result of her husband's death, her attitude begins to change: "Her fantastic wealth just kept piling up, and she had to remind herself daily that all the hundreds of thousands of dollars she was acquiring were not worth a single penny without her husband to share this good fortune with her" (353). Mrs. Daneeka is about to move to save her husband from his living death due to "the depth of emotion in the almost illegible appeal" that he writes to her, when she receives Colonel Cathcart's form letter of condolence: "Dear Mrs., Mr., Miss, or Mr. And Mrs. Daneeka: Words cannot express the deep personal grief I experienced when you husband, son, father or brother was killed, wounded or reported missing in action" (354).

Mrs. Daneeka's response to this automated epistle—which is unsentimental, indifferent, incompetent, and, finally, absurd—is to move with her children to Lansing, Michigan, leaving no forwarding address. What we are left to conclude from the final act in the Daneeka "case history" is that Mrs. Daneeka was forced into a direct apprehension of the insignificant value that is placed on human relationships in the postmodern world. So fictionalized, diminished, and transitory are the bonds between people that her husband's commanding officer cannot disguise his unfamiliarity with her husband or any connection beyond the routines of military life; furthermore, we may usefully recall that these letters were originally composed as part of a cynical plan to get the colonel featured in an issue of *Life* magazine.

We should also note the degree to which Heller uses Doc Daneeka's "case history" to show that language is but one deteriorating component of an illusory system of human bonds. The doctor's letter—an invocation of the epistolary novel—is a "crinkled, grubby tissue of V-mail stationery," (352) that is passionately kissed "a thousand times" (352) in the best sentimental tradition. Further letters from Mrs. Daneeka to her husband are efficiently rubber-stamped "KILLED IN ACTION" (352) and returned to her. It would seem that Mrs. Daneeka's final betrayal of her husband is prompted by the blind inflexibility of the system: Mrs. Daneeka is helpless to alter the military's insistence that her husband is dead. What ensues at this point represents an unmarked cultural shift from the conventions of romance and sentiment to the conventions of the late capitalism. Mrs. Daneeka betrays her husband by moving to another state without leaving behind a forwarding address. We are provided the raw facts of this abandonment, but we are not provided with Mrs. Daneeka's justifications or rationalizations. The aporia marked out by her betrayal of her husband is the most salient characteristic of this episode, for it forces the reader to account for her actions with little to go on beyond the bare facts of her stealthy departure. The sardonic mode in which this episode is narrated establishes a complex and ironic tension between the capitalist convention of commodity fetishism and the convention of sentimental love. In this way we are confronted with insurmountable evidence that it was the pursuit of wealth that was, after all, the essence of Mrs. Daneeka's life with the doctor; we must conclude that what we see is the result of her realization of Doc Daneeka's desire for financial success, that they have been transferred to his wife, who was uniquely endowed with the ability to fulfill them but only through the occasion of the doctor's death.

Through this case history we are shown the failure of the culture of the heart; Mrs. Daneeka's desertion of her husband enacts the truth that feelings, emotions, and passion have no reality in the face of the culture of the bureaucratic military-industrial behemoth.

In *Love and Death in the American Novel* Fiedler provides a very useful psycho-historical overview of the contention between the cultures of eros (Romance) and Thanatos (the war machine). In doing so he introduces the same terms that have been examined above in the discussion of

Heller's use of the archetypes of the collective unconscious. Fiedler states that "The darker motive forces of the psyche refused any longer to accept the names and ranks by which they had been demeaned for almost two thousand years; once worshipped as 'gods', they stirred again in discontent. Especially the Great Mother—cast, down by the most patriarchal of all religions (To the Hebrews she was Lilith, the bride of darkness), ambiguously redeemed as the Blessed Virgin and denied once more by a Hebraizing Protestantism—clamored to be honored once more" *(Love and Death* 35). The Daneekas act out an episode of the sentimental love religion, which is on one level an invocation of the Great Mother. In this case history, however, the Great Mother suffers defeat, as Mrs. Daneeka succumbs to the values and methods of what Fiedler calls the "Machiavellian priesthood" *(Love and Death* 38), and turning her back on love, she takes the money and runs.

Chaplain Albert Taylor Tappman's case history, another brief relation of facts, is presented in chapter twenty-five, "The Chaplain." There is not much in the way of drama in the proceedings of the chaplain's case. The chapter commences with an exposition of the chaplain's Anabaptist faith and the complications that result from wrestling with fundamental questions of faith while serving in the American Army during wartime, where "without dogma, it was almost intolerable" (274). Anabaptist beliefs do not support the bearing of arms, the use of force, or the holding of government offices, though this circumstance is not divulged by the text. At the end of the second paragraph, we are informed, "He was just not equipped to excel. He thought of himself as ugly and wanted daily to be home with his wife" (274).

Three pages concerned with Yossarian and *deja vu* interpose between the above quotation and the narrative's resumption of the "case history" of the chaplain's marriage. Heller is at pains to emphasize the normalcy of the chaplain's marriage, a condition that is everywhere under attack. This is to say that the Daneeka's marriage is not normal, and the doctor is satisfied to have temporarily escaped from his wife. Marriage represents something from which to flee, a condition that has already been presented in connection with Fiedler's discussion of the archetype of the "sacred marriage of males" (CB 487) set in "nature undefiled" (CB 487)— the seas or the wilderness. That it is the chaplain's chief desire is to return home in order to be united with his wife serves to define his role in the text as the indicator of the fundamental pathology of male-female relationships that generally permeates American culture. The chaplain wants to return home, but he is religious, capable of love, and set apart from the other men in the narrative. The chaplain's marriage stands in profound contrast to the other marriages depicted in the text; the mark of his difference is that he is invested in a relationship with a woman that is not a normal relationship because it is so compulsively desired:

> The chaplain's wife was the one thing in the world he *could* be certain of, and it would have been sufficient, if only he had been left to live his life out with just her and the children. The chaplain's wife was a reserved, diminutive, agreeable woman in her early thirties, very dark and very attractive, with a narrow waist, calm intelligent eyes, and small, bright, pointy teeth in a childlike face that was vivacious and petite; he kept forgetting what his children looked like, and each time he returned to their snapshots it was like seeing their faces for the first time. The chaplain loved his wife and children with such tameless intensity that he often wanted to sink to the ground helplessly and weep like a castaway cripple. (278)

Like Odysseus, the chaplain has been unwillingly called away to fight in a distant war. However, as a noncombatant, his role in the theater of combat is in a sense that of a husband: as a giver of comfort, he is never transformed into a warrior like the other men.

This displacement, however, is not specific to the chaplain, for the men engaged in warfare are presented by the text of *Catch-22* not so much as warriors as men inhabiting whorehouses who on occasion drop a devastating load of bombs on the enemy. For his part, we are told that the chaplain's desires are directed toward his wife: "The chaplain's wife was intuitive, gentle, compassionate and responsive. Almost, inevitably, his reveries of reunion with her ended in explicit acts of love-making" (279).

The domestic eroticism of the chaplain's "case history" contrasts with the other "case histories" of marriages in *Catch-22*; it also contrasts with wartime conditions in Italy. Viewed against the background of the war and the indignities served to the chaplain by the atheistic Corporal Whitcomb and by the sadistic and paranoid Colonels, Cathcart and Korn, the chaplain's "case history" implicitly illustrates what Freud says about marriage in *Civilization and Its Discontents*—that "the life of present-day civilized people leaves no room for the simple natural love of two human beings" (52 n.2).

Colonel Moodus does not have his own chapter, and what little there is of his "case history" constitutes a comedic component in chapter twenty-one, "General Dreedle." General Dreedle's nurse has been installed as the central feature of his "case history": the nurse has already been discussed as an important manifestation of the female principle, the young witch aspect of the Great Mother, who presents the negative transformative character. This negative character is evident throughout her appearance in the text:

> General Dreedle was always accompanied by both Colonel Moodus and his nurse, who was as delectable a piece of ass as anyone who saw her had ever laid eyes on. General Dreedle's nurse was chubby, short and blond. She had plump dimpled cheeks, happy blue eyes, and neat curly turned-up hair. She smiled at everyone and never spoke at all unless she was spoken to. He bosom was lush and her complexion clear. She was irresistible, and men edged away from her carefully. She was succulent, sweet, docile and dumb, and she drove everyone crazy but General Dreedle. (221)

Besides the generally unmilitary influence that the nurse has on the men, she also exhibits a particularized effect on Colonel Moodus. The colonel is married to General Dreedle's daughter, and the general occupies himself by torturing Colonel Moodus with the requirement of a conventional marriage that the husband remain sexually faithful to his wife: "'He hasn't gotten laid since we shipped overseas', confided General Dreedle, and his square grizzled head bobbed with sadistic laughter at the fiendish idea. 'That's one of the reasons I never let him out of my sight, just so he can't get to a woman. Can you imagine what that poor son of a bitch is going through?'" (222). What the above passage presents is simultaneously simple and complex. On the realistic surface of the text we see the father justifiably protecting the institution of marriage. The sadistic pleasure that General Dreedle exhibits signals that something additional is transpiring, that on another level he represents the father-god in his most virulent form, as castrator of the son:

> The Terrible Father appears to the hero in two transpersonal figures: as the phallic Earth Father and the frightening Spirit Father. The Earth Father, lord of all chthonic forces, belongs psychologically to the realm of the Great Mother. He manifests himself most commonly as the overwhelming aggressiveness of phallic instinct or as a destructive monster. . . . Patriarchal castration has two forms: captivity and possession. In captivity, the ego remains totally dependent upon the father as the representative of collective norms—that is, it identifies with the lower father and thus loses its connection with the creative powers. It remains bound by traditional morality and conscience, and, as though castrated by convention, loses the higher half of its dual nature. (*Origins* 186–87)

In this episode, there is no address to the subject of marriage; there are no wives present, only women, for the colonel states that "I haven't been to bed with a woman since we shipped overseas . . ." (222). War has so reduced the marriage bond that Colonel Moodus's wife is not mentioned, and his relationship to the general is also established without reference to the wife and daughter who would ordinarily serve as a link between the two men: "'War is hell', he declared frequently, drunk or sober, and he really meant it, although that did not prevent him from taking his son-in-law in to the business with him, even though the two bickered constantly" (221). Colonel Moodus's predicament, thus, represents a degree of pathology in advance of the symptoms presented by the chaplain's "case history": embodied in Colonel Moodus's marriage is the ultimate obliteration of authentic marriage by the preservation of the outer form of marriage through the "overwhelming aggressiveness of phallic instinct" (Neumann *Origins* 186). One important offshoot of the General's aggressive treatment of his son-in-law (and transcendently absent daughter) is that it establishes equivalence between his nameless daughter and the nameless nurse, such that we begin to suspect that (in psychodynamic terms) the daughter is present in the form of the nurse.

We may even glimpse, in General Dreedle's withholding of the nurse-daughter from Colonel Moodus, an allusion to Agamemnon's appropriation of Briseis, Achilles's war prize. The association of this episode of *Catch-22* with the *Iliad* is further supported by Yossarian's withdrawal from conflict (reified by his refusal to wear a uniform [267]) in imitation of Achilles's refusal to fight after Agamemnon took Briseis from him. The implication of these equivalencies is that in General Dreedle's possession of the nurse-daughter and the symbolic usurpation of Colonel Moodus's marriage, we are given an insight into the psychoanalytical meaning of warfare insofar as it marks a stage in the individuation of the personality; in his discussion of this topic Neumann notes that "The 'wicked king' or personal father figure, representing the old ruling system, sends the hero forth to fight the monster—Sphinx, witches, giants, wild beasts, etc.— hoping that it will prove his undoing. This fight is the struggle with the uroboric Great Mother, with the unconscious, to which the hero may easily succumb because it is the seat of the ego's anxiety and holds the threat of impotence" (Neumann *Origins* 176). Marriage has been fractured, canceled, and violated by war, but in separating the wife from the husband, the husband's anger forces him to become a hero and to slay the wicked king, the Terrible Male; in doing so the hero will have advanced to a psychically higher form of marriage. Thus, the psychoanalytical meaning of Colonel Moodus's marriage is that it marks a step in the process of individuation that takes the hero beyond his retreat into the archetypal complex of homosexual eroticism, violence, and eternal adolescence that Fiedler calls "the archetypal love of white male and black"

(CB 487) to the more advanced, pleasurable, and fulfilling stage of marriage that contains eroticism, childrearing, and social responsibility. We are not allowed to see this stage in the literal events involving the triad of General Dreedle, the nurse, and Colonel Moodus. In fact, the absurd surface reality presented by the text seems to demonstrate no connection between the marriages of the chaplain and Colonel Moodus's. However, with reference to the progressive stages of individuation that are outlined in Neumann's *Origins*, it is apparent that the two marriages lie along the same psychic continuum.

The "case history" of Lieutenant Scheisskopf is narrated somewhat differently than the other cases presented in the text. It is presented in chapter eight, "Lieutenant Scheisskopf," and runs from page 71 to page 76, making it the longest of the examinations of marriage in the text. Because Yossarian, the novel's protagonist, is involved in the marriage as the wife's lover and the husband's subordinate, his relationship to the events is closer: this is indicated by a shift in time to when Yossarian and Clevinger "were both at cadet school in Santa Ana, California" (70), before they have completed their training and shipped to the European Theater.

The Scheisskopf marriage is further complicated by the presence of another character, Dori Duz, a woman with whom Yossarian has had a brief fling but is still fixated on, and who Mrs. Scheisskopf pretends to be while she is in bed with Yossarian. Thus the tangible threesome operates as a projective foursome, rather like the "one more member than could actually be counted" that Eliot speaks of in *The Waste Land* in the note to line 360. Early on in the Scheisskopf "case history," we learn that the marriage is a failure: "Lieutenant Scheisskopf was an ROTC graduate who was rather glad that war had broken out, since it gave him an opportunity to wear an officer's uniform every day and say "men" in a clipped military voice to the bunches of kids who fell into his clutches every eight weeks on their way to the butcher block" (70). Mrs. Scheisskopf only resorts to an affair with Yossarian because her husband will not pay any attention to her, although the reason given in the text is that "Lieutenant Scheisskopf's wife was revenging herself upon Lieutenant Scheisskopf for some unforgettable crime of his she couldn't recall" (72). Mrs. Scheisskopf's inability to recall a crime, which is at the same time unforgettable, is reminiscent of Freud's derivation of sadomasochism from an arrest in the development of the Oedipus complex (in *Basic Writings* "The Sexual Aberrations" 572 n.2). This association particularly addresses the case of the Scheisskopfs, for at the heart of the story of Oedipus is a similar forgotten and unforgettable crime.

The Scheisskopf "case history" contains subtle clues that lead us to believe that we must assign Lieutenant Scheisskopf's tendency to ignore his wife to a latent homosexual fixation. For one thing, there is the Lieutenant's obsession with marching and the behavior that it produces in him; in order to win pennants for parading his men, he begins a detailed study of marching, and we are told that "Leonardo's exercises in anatomy proved indispensable" (74), establishing the lieutenant's appreciation of the male anatomy and intimating that there is a deeper issue at hand. For another thing, his wife's healthy sexuality is viewed by the lieutenant with repulsion: "It was the despair of Lieutenant Scheisskopf's life to be chained to a woman who was incapable of looking beyond her own dirty, sexual desires to the titanic struggles for the unattainable in which noble man could become heroically involved" (74). The wife's response to her husband's idealist sublimation is to substitute sadomasochism for heteronormality. Mrs. Scheisskopf, we are told, wants to know why her husband will not whip her; her indignant husband's answer is that he has no time (74). Moreover, we are informed, through a strange conversation that takes place between two characters who are never again encountered, Lieutenants Travers and Engle, that "Lieutenant Bemis whips Mrs. Bemis beautifully every time they have sexual intercourse, and he isn't worth a farthing at parades" (76).

The conversation between Travers and Engle sounds like a parody of one of the case histories in the volume of Kafft-Ebing that Mrs. Scheisskopf reads while amorously waiting in bed for her husband (74), and the suggestion of the discourse of sexology proceeding from two officers who would not be expected to know the intimate details of the marriages of their comrades serves to shift the account of the Scheisskopf marriage from the social sphere, where the pretenses of normalcy are maintained, to a social space where psychopathology is accepted at face value. The effect is completed when in the following paragraphs we learn that it is Lieutenant Scheisskopf's desire to place nickel-alloy swivels in the small of the back of every man in his unit, so that they will be able to keep perfectly in line. Later the solution is modified to a design that would join the knees of his men to their wrists by copper wires and nickel pegs, but the design turns out to be infeasible not because the plan is insane but because "there wasn't time" (75).

Lieutenant Scheisskopf's descent into madness through an obsession with marching represents his unconscious abandonment of his marriage and his fixation with a heavily coded homosexual eroticism. The socially acceptable mechanism of winning parades allows him to engage in his homoerotic activities without eliciting moral censure, though the inclusion of the conversation between Travers and Engle presents the view of those who see through Scheisskopf's disguise: Lieutenant Engle, in particular, has recognized the inner content of what is transpiring, and he gives name to it without flinching: "'I'm talking about flagellation', Lieutenant Engle retorted. 'Who gives a damn about parades'" (76).

By now we have become aware of Heller's consistent use of various types of reversals, or more exactly, a technique of thematic misdirection. Lieutenant Travers insists that he is speaking of flagellation and not parades, but the subtext is not concerned with either of these topics but instead with Krafft-Ebing, perversion, homosexuality, and, ultimately, with the Oedipus complex as an obstacle to psychic development. Should this claim seem exaggerated, let us recall that the third book of *Finnegans Wake*, which has pronouncedly influenced this section of *Catch-22* (see the following chapter), concerns Shawn the postman traveling backwards in the night through the events already narrated; however, it is at the same time about a barrel rolling down the river Liffey (McHugh 403). The entire third book of *Finnegans Wake* is an extended misdirection away from the barrel from which it is generated. The connection between marching and sado-masochism is further reinforced by the fact that it is while Lieutenant Scheisskopf's wife "waited amorously for him in bed thumbing through Krafft-Ebing to her favorite passages" (74) that Lieutenant Scheisskopf developed his ideas on marching.

Richard Freiherr von Krafft-Ebing included homosexuality as one of the types of sexual perversion that he collected in his psychiatric study, *Psychopathia sexualis* (1886). Von Krafft-Ebing distinguished acquired from inborn homosexuality and explained the "perversion" as a case of degeneration. The stages were attraction to one's own sex, effeminacy in men, and masculinization in women, an intermediary phase, and a final metamorphosis in which the man felt like a woman and the woman like a man (Bleys 158–59). The employment of von Krafft-Ebing's book for a pornographic stimulus to sexual excitement by Lieutenant Scheisskopf's wife is highly ironic considering that the degeneration theory that it espoused was mobilized in the form of a catalog of perversions in the hope that it would bring about the regulation of sexual pleasure and eventually propagate a new sexual morality (Bleys 160). The oppressive attitude toward sexual variety espoused in Krafft-Ebing's study is localized in *Catch-22* in the polarities of the Scheisskopf marriage—in the wife's embrace of the pleasure principle and the Lieutenant's definition of her interest as taboo, what he calls "dirty, sexual. desires" (74). The recognition of the crucial disparity between the pleasure principle and the death wish is the subtext to the dialogue between Lieutenant's Travers and Engle: because he embraces the military and rejects his wife and the sexuality that she figures forth, we are allowed to see Lieutenant Scheisskopf as the embodiment of spiritual death.

Scheisskopf's refusal to acknowledge his wife's sexuality is a repeat of Gilgamesh's rejection of Ishtar; and Mrs. Scheisskopf's insistence on being whipped recapitulates Ishtar's aggression, however, with the polarity reversed. We may also note the manner in which Heller's imitation of this episode in a military context skews the relationships between Gilgamesh, Enkidu, and Ishtar. In the original version, Enkidu assists Gilgamesh in repulsing Ishtar's overture, and the homosexual nature of the grounds for rejecting the goddess are patent. When Yossarian resists Luciana's romantic and erotic advances in chapter twenty, he has left Orr behind. However, Yossarian's repetition of this scene is incomplete, for it combines two episodes from the epic. Yossarian initially responds to Luciana's overtures by saying "Who asked you," which seems to imitate Gilgamesh's rejection of Ishtar. Yossarian then gives in to Luciana and makes love to her, however, when he does so, Yossarian is imitating the education of Enkidu by the prostitute—an episode that also serves as the source of Yossarian's affair with Mrs. Scheisskopf. Because the epic's episodes are distorted when they are imitated in *Catch-22*, we have only an indistinct sense of Gilgamesh's rejection of Ishtar and a homoerotic embrace of Enkidu. The novel's complex use of anti-narrative devices—blended episodes from the epic; the fragmentation of Ishtar into Lieutenant Scheisskopf's wife, Dori Duz, and Luciana; the division of Gilgamesh into Yossarian and Lieutenant Scheisskopf; and the division of Enkidu into Yossarian, Lieutenant Scheisskopf, Hungry Joe and Orr—effectively serve to conceal the homoerotic subtext of the events that are being presented.

Though Lieutenant Scheisskopf's rejection of his wife's Krafft-Ebing inspired propositions appears later in the text, the event represents what Lieutenant Scheisskopf understands to be required by the dictates of a more culturally advanced stage of civilization. On the other hand, speaking psychoanalytically, the stage of development that Lieutenant Scheisskopf represents is regressive. This is not surprising, since the war that is embodied in the narrative of *Catch-22* marks the failure of male-to-male friendships beginning with the relationship between Gilgamesh and Enkidu, Achilles and Patroclus, Ishmael and Queequeg, and Huck and Jim that are imitated in the intertext of *Catch-22*. In the surface text, the narrative details the relationships between Yossarian and Dunbar, Yossarian and the Chaplain, and Yossarian and Orr, to name the most important male pairs. We have already commented on the numerous pairs of men that are found throughout the text—pairs such as Piltchard and Wren or Travers and Engle. Thus, in the episode in which Lieutenant Scheisskopf may be said to repeat Gilgamesh's homosexually inflected rejection of Ishtar, Scheisskopf's repressed homosexuality is presented as an abreaction in which the lieutenant obsessively embraces Frederick Winslow Taylor's efficiency engineering desiring the "nailing" (74) of his men to beams, as well as attaching swivels "in the small of every man's back" (75).

The homoerotic import of Lieutenant Scheisskopf's research is under-scored by the comically understated treatment of his toy soldiers as mail-order sexual aids: Scheisskopf performs his marching experiments with "a set of plastic cowboys he had bought from a mail-order house under an assumed name and kept locked away from everyone's eyes during the day" (74). Scheisskopf's concern with the perfection of his marching com-panies and the insufficiency of his time brings to mind the methods-time-motion studies carried out by the inventor of efficiency engineering. Taylor's presence in the text of *Catch-22* is further reinforced by the chaplain's name—Albert Taylor Tappman, a name that may be abbreviated A.T.T. The conflation of the Chaplainesque chaplain with one of America's great business monopolies, A.T.& T., compounds the further suggestion of Charlie Chaplin's satiric attack on big business in *Modern Times*, and the implied pun relating to the tapping of telephones made by the chaplain's initials, A.T.T., an approximation of AT&T, in combination with his sur-name, Tappman, underscores Heller's interest in the threat of monopolis-tic businesses. Thus, Scheisskopf's sublimated flight from woman and marriage into what he calls "the titanic struggle for the unattainable" is revealed by Heller as an investment in paranoia, regimentation, and op-pression by the military-industrial complex. Heller shows us that whereas in the past men fled into the wilderness or out onto the ocean, postmodern man is cut off from the natural world and, therefore, absconds to the battlefield, the parade ground, the reviewing stand, and the war room.

The dialogue between Lieutenants Travers and Engle comes down to a choice between flagellation and parades: taken literally these are forms of castration, and offer no choice at all. The dispute between Travers and Engle, so reminiscent of Tweedle-dum-Tweedle-Dee, runs into a welter of interpretative possibilities. Engle suggests Joyce's "engiles" (FW 416), a combination of angel and engine. Engle also suggests the other half of the (Karl) Marx and (Friedrich) Engels pair. The word "travers" may be found on page 278 of *Finnegans Wake*; "travers" may be a compound of "travel" and "reverse" so as to intimate the manner of Shawn the postman's travels as he proceeds "backwards in the night through the events already narrated" (Joyce quoted in McHugh 404). The concern with travel perhaps points as well to *The Gilgamesh Epic* intertext. The recognition of the insupportability of the duality represented by the whip and the parade (on the literal level) is sustained by Scheisskopf's words, containing as they do an allusion to the Titans and their struggle. Neumann states that

> If [the hero] acts in the arrogance of egomania, which the Greeks called hybris, and does not reverence the numinosum against which he strives, then his deeds will infallibly come to nought. To fly too high and fall, to go too deep and get stuck, these are alike symptoms of an overvaluation of the ego that ends in disaster, death, or madness. An overweening contempt for the transpersonal powers above and below means falling victim to them, whether the hero crashes to earth like Etana . . . or does penance like the Titans. (*Origins* 188)

The Titan's penance appears in the novel as the pun on the "pennants" that Scheisskopf wins; having won the red pennant, Scheisskopf is "beside himself with rapture" (75). This rapture comes about because we are also given a pun on "parades," which allows us to read the word as *pardes*, the Hebrew word for garden and, as such, a symbol of Jewish mystical practice. With the imposition of the dialogue between Lieutenants Travers and Engle, the case history of the Scheisskopf marriage is brought to a conclusion. A compressed parody of Kafka's *The Trial* interrupts and distorts the conclusion of Lieutenant Scheisskopf's "case history," in the form of the "parade" episode, much in the way that Yossarian's rejection of Luciana/Ishtar is interrupted by his sexual intercourse with Luciana as a repeat of Enkidu's sexual intercourse with the prostitute.

Thus, in *Catch-22* not only is marriage destroyed by the flight of (married) men, in combination with the destructive social forces that impinge on marriage relationships, but in each of the case histories developed in the novel, the men who are propelled out of their marriages intersect with homoeroticism. This is handled through various distancing techniques, so that the homoerotic content of the behavior exhibited by the men who are in flight from marriage is not revealed as homoeroticism without a considerable examination of the case histories. Heller does not arrange these case histories in an escalating order as I have done in my discussion of them. However, it is clear that in the four case histories the bone has, so to speak, been buried at increased depths, and I have presented them in the order of their difficulty in reaching their latent contents. Yossarian falls in love with the chaplain. However, the seeming directness of this instance in which heteronormality is openly flouted is deflected by comic deflation. Heller allows the latent homoerotic content of his text to be hidden by a series of mediocre jokes. The worst joke is the opening sentences of the text, "It was love at first sight" (7), a provocative sentence that sets up the punch line that the object of Yossarian's sudden passion is a diffident Anabaptist chaplain. It is an interesting, though indeterminable, question as to whether or not these jokes are intentionally weak, for their primary characteristic is not that they are very funny but that their shocking homoerotic content compensates for their blandness and renders it nearly imperceptible that they are not very funny. Heller's jokes have a similar effect to the laughter produced by Harpo Marx's bit of physical comedy in which he allows his victim to hold his leg: instead of each repetition becoming less funny, it becomes funnier as his persistence threatens to overwhelm the viewer's "censor" and divulge the forceful erotic component of his behavior that compels him to continue indiscriminately thrusting his "leg" into the hands of men and women. This type of joke is a feature of the opening pages, with the joke about the captain "still lying amorously on his belly" (9) running a close second to the opening joke. Close examination of the jokes reveals that they are "funny" as a result of a latent content of threatening homoeroticism that counteracts the comic mildness of the surface text. Freud's comment, that "*every exposure of* . . . an unconscious fact affects us in a comical manner" (*Basic Writings* "The Relations of Wit to Dreams" 754) says much about this feature of Heller's construction of the novel's opening passages.

As we have seen, Yossarian's back-scratching approach to Doc Daneeka is covered over by wit—puns and double-entendres. Accordingly, we may think of Freud's comment that "The substitution of the inner associations (similarity, causal connection, etc.) by the so-called outer associations (simultaneity, contiguity in space, assonance) is particularly conspicuous and characteristic of the dreamwork. . . . All these means of displacement also occur as techniques of wit, but when they do occur they usually restrict themselves to those limits prescribed for their use in conscious thought; in fact, they may be lacking even though wit must regularly solve a task on inhibition" (*Basic Writings* "The Relations of Wit to Dreams" 755).

The intertextuality between *Catch-22* and the *Iliad* is used to cast Colonel Moodus in the role of Achilles (one half of the Achilles-Patroclus pair), so that we do not encounter the homoerotic content until we search far beneath the surface and its depiction of the Oedipal struggle and the ravages of the Terrible Father. Lieutenant Scheisskopf's homosexual panic is expressed through his obsession with anatomy and his obsession with dreaming up bio-engineered methods for drilling and piercing the bodies of the men who serve under him. These interests serve to sublimate his deeply repressed homoerotic longing, through the winning of pennants (penance). In the final case history (Lieutenant Scheisskopf''s), the process of repressing the homoerotic desire becomes pathological and is expressed on a mass scale through methods that are military-industrial and, thereby, the homosexual panic becomes institutional and a general threat to human survival.

Note

1   The cases to which I refer were published, respectively, under the titles: "Notes
upon a case of Obsesional Neurosis" (1909), Std. Ed., x, 153–318; "From the
History of an Infantile Neurosis" (1918 [1914]),m Std. Ed., XVII, 3–122; "Analysis of a Phobia in a Five-Year-Old-Boy" (1909), Std. Ed., X, 3–149; "Fragment of
an Analysis of a Case of Hysteria" (1905 [1901]), Std. Ed., VII, 3–122; "Psychoanalytic Notes on an Autobiographical Account of a Case of Paranoia" (1911),
Std. Ed. XIII, 3–82.

Chapter 4

Heller's Religious Vision

The subject of *Catch-22* is modern warfare, and Heller has subjected warfare to a black comic treatment. However, this assessment of the text's theme and presentation does not adequately describe the contents and form of the text. The black comic world that Heller's protagonist, Yossarian, inhabits occupies a narrative structure that forgoes the conventions of the realistic novel. Heller's text also employs a post-Joycean panoply of stylistic techniques: a running parallel with a specific myth, achrony, substitutable characters, a dense allusiveness, linguistic disruption, and a complex intertextuality. As an attempt to offer a more comprehensive description of the novel, we may say that in addition to being a black-comic treatment of modern warfare, *Catch-22* is a pan-mythical, symbolic presentation of the essential phases in the history of consciousness, and, as such, delineates the dynamic of the conflict between the dualities of captivity and freedom as they are unconsciously played out in human cultures (Neumann *The Great Mother* 65). We can use a comment by Leslie Fiedler to illuminate what is meant by the symbolic construction of *Catch-22*: "In . . . projective or symbolic fiction, character, setting, and incident alike are "true," not in their own right but as they symbolize in outward terms and inward reality" (*Love and Death* 140).

Thus, it is not war that Heller interrogates but the mythological and psychological meaning of war both in individual and collective terms at a particular moment in the evolution of Western culture. Modern crises produce a culture of fear in which projections of anxiety, aggression, and repression becomes a canalized system that self-perpetuates itself through ritual. Touching this theme, Erich Neumann states that "The creativity of consciousness may be jeopardized by religious or political totalitarianism, for any authoritarian fixation of the canon leads to sterility of consciousness" (*Origins* xix). It is not difficult to realize that many of the elements included in *Catch-22* represent such "authoritarian fixations" in that they are pursued for their own limited and destructive purposes in fulfillment of unconscious needs—primarily relief of the feeling of danger from projected shadows. The compulsive raising of missions by Colonel Cathcart is one determining example of such a fixation, one that is important to the entire narrative structure of *Catch-22* in that this particular fixation can be said to propel much of the subsequent action in the story.

Another, though less determining, "totalitarian fixation" is the incipient authoritarianism implied by the Glorious Loyalty Oath Crusade of chapter eleven. Neumann's outlook, though, is optimistic and illuminates the actions taken by Yossarian in his quest for liberation:

> Such fixations, however, can only be provisional. So far as Western man is concerned, the assimilative vitality of his ego consciousness is more or less assured. The progress of science and the increasingly obvious threat to humanity from unconscious forces impel his consciousness, from within and without, to continual self-analysis and expansion. The individual is the bearer of this creative activity of the mind and therefore remains the decisive factor in all future Western developments. (*Origins* xix)

While the most visible form of the freedom/captivity duality is embodied in the wartime military culture, at a more fundamental psychic and mythic level, Yossarian's world shows itself to be a religious world. This is not to say that Heller's desire is to depict a religious world because he requires a religious vision in order to site his own ideological predilections, but that in generating his text he has necessarily commenced with the primordial religious systematizing of *The Gilgamesh Epic*. Over this primary level he has superimposed subsequent phases of development, though, admittedly, it is difficult to distinguish the mythic from the psychic: "The evolution of consciousness by stages is as much a collective human phenomenon as a particular individual phenomenon. Ontogenetic development may therefore be regarded as a modified recapitulation of phylogenetic development" (Neumann *Origins* xx).

A pronounced achrony prevails throughout *Catch-22*, with respect to the three stages of mythological development (unity, separation, and transformation). This arrangement contrasts with Heller's handling of the three stages of personality development (centroversion, differentiation, and self-realization), for symbols from the successive stages appear in the text roughly in the order called for in the scheme presented in the works of Jung, Neumann and other depth psychologists. For example, the mummy, a symbol of the third mythic and psychic stages, first appears in the text in the initial chapter, in connection with the uroboric hospital (where Yossarian "had everything he wanted" [7]), a symbol belonging to the first mythic and psychic stages. However, one is able to assign to the first appearance of the Soldier in White a different meaning from that symbolized by his reappearance in a later chapter. Thus, *Catch-22* employs the dreamlike logic and dreamlike humor of James Joyce's *Finnegans Wake* in the project of bringing into consciousness the repressed contents of the precivilized self represented by Yossarian's "supraman" (20): those repressed contents include homosexuality, sexual perversion, murder, fear of otherness, misogyny, and the death wish.

The style of *Catch-22* is a type of *skaz* in which contents are suspended in an imagery that seems created out of a dreaming process unmediated by a socialized self. Usually these images are "not understood." However, whenever they are interrogated consciously, they divulge a repressed content. An example of such an image is "In the bed on Yossarian's right, still lying amorously on his belly, was the startled captain with malaria in his blood and a mosquito bite on his ass" (9). The humor is as unpremeditated as anything expelled by the punning unconscious; therefore, the captain is "startled." He is startled because he does not admit the erotic content of his encounter with the mosquito; the captain has desired a bite on the ass from a man and received it from an insect. Heller's method at this point consists of the narrator's Freud-informed mockery of the captain in combination with a witty mockery of Freud's method:

> Wit and humor in the dream or in waking life result from the unconscious resistance to the repression of pleasure. The thrust of the dream is wish-fulfillment, Freud tells us, and the unconscious produces puns and comic effects in its attempts to outflank the censor. This causal relationship between repression and wit is best delineated in Freud's theory of errors as presented in "The Psychopathology of Everyday Life" and the *General Introduction*. Many of the errors are hilarious, particularly slips of the pen such as "clown prince" for "crown prince." The error is caused by repression of the writer's true feelings and their unconscious eruption in the misprint. The humor resides in the incongruity or discrepancy between the two descriptions of the same man—an incongruity existing originally between the honest and hypocritical expressions of the writer. (Adams 115)

In *Catch-22* an achronic treatment similar to the handling of the developmental stages of myth and psyche is also given to Frazer's cultural stages: thus later conceptions of reality belonging to the phases of magic and science are found intermixed with materials belonging to the religiously informed stage that produced *The Gilgamesh Epic*. In his foreword to the 1993 edition of *From Ritual to Romance*, Robert A. Segal states that

> Frazer is likely best remembered for his tripartite division of the development of culture into the stages of magic, religion, and science. In both magic and science events in the physical world are caused by the behavior of impersonal, mechanical forces. Magic and science differ over what those forces are and by what laws they operate. In religion, which oddly comes between magic and science rather than either before or after them, events in the physical world are caused by the decision of the gods. Both magic and science offer the prospect of direct and certain control over nature—once one discovers the forces and the laws that regulate nature. Religion, by contrast, provides only indirect and uncertain control: one must persuade the gods to do one's bidding, and no matter how much one supplicates, obeys, flatters, or bribes them, they may still demur. (xxiii)

The fundamental grounding of Yossarian's world is such that the ancient Sumerian pantheon is alive in *Catch-22,* for the divinities that belonged to the unconscious of the distant past described in the epic are manifested as projections into the conscious world:

> The ego can see and experience the archetypal constellations of the unconscious directly or indirectly—directly by perceiving them on the inner projection plane as psychic images, indirectly by experiencing them in their projection into the world. Modern man with his reflective consciousness speaks of a direct psychic experience when a content of the psyche, e.g. an archetype, appears in a dream, a vision, or in the imagination. We call it an indirect experience when an intrinsically psychic content is experienced as belonging to the outside world, e.g. a demon as the living spirit of as stone or a tree. . . .
>
> The archetype is experienced indirectly also through individuals upon whom it is projected. . . . The Gorgon is projected into a woman who, for example, transfixes one with terror in an anxiety neuroses. Similarly there are individuals in whom the projector unconsciously experiences the figures of Sophia or Isis. Such projection phenomena, as modern depth psychology discovered, are of crucial importance not only for the genesis of psychoneuroses and for their therapy but also for normal development. (Neumann The *Great Mother* 22–23)

Thus the animation of archetypes is the metatextual system from which *Catch-22* is generated. Often the archetypes are given their substance by associating them with the contents of literary texts, and these associations constitute the subtext of *Catch-22*. It follows that *Catch-22* is a highly intertextual text containing allusions to numerous works of literature (for example, *Huckleberry Finn*, *The Waste Land*, the *Bible*, *Oedipus Rex*, *Hamlet*, *Julius Caesar*, *Crime and Punishment*) and to several authors (Twain, T.S. Eliot, Euripides, Shakespeare, and Dostoevsky); other literary texts are simply named in the text: *Moby-Dick* (15), *Bleak*

House (293), *Treasure Island* (293), *Ethan Frome* (293), *The Last of the Mohicans* (293). Clearly, *Catch-22* may be read enjoyably and profitably—even inspirationally—without resorting to the explication of those allusions and citations, and many millions of readers have done so. In fact, to explore the meanings of Heller's humor is to decode the humor in the text and thereby to render the experience of reading witless and flat; however, there is, apparently, little danger of the common reader performing this type of analytical reading. We may even say that to all practical purposes most of those allusions are invisible, for they are present as "subconscious" materials that exist only in the literary intertext. Also subliminal is the mythological material out of which the metatext is constructed, for it is no exaggeration to state that *Catch-22* is built up out of an intricate interweaving of myths, legends, and rituals that belong to the collective unconscious and the individual unconscious. As materials belonging to the collective and individual unconsciousnesses, they are beyond conscious detection by Yossarian as he experiences the events that take place in the narrative, and they are equally to a large degree undetectable by the reader who absorbs the text in the act of reading for pleasure.

So impervious to detection is the metatext that Heller indulges in a type of self-reflexive, comic reification of myths and rituals in order to bring them into the reader's consciousness; one example of this practice is the elaborate joke of the Soldier in White. The Soldier in White undergoes a long development as a character throughout the text (though he can hardly be said to exist as a *character* in the conventional sense), even undergoing a revival in chapter thirty-four, "Thanksgiving." His description in chapter seventeen, "The Soldier in White," resorts to the use of a double-meaning *wit* to identify the soldier as a mummy: "The soldier in white was constructed entirely of gauze, plaster and a thermometer, and the thermometer was merely an adornment left balanced in the empty dark hole in the bandages over his mouth early each morning and late each afternoon by Nurse Cramer and Nurse Duckett right up to the afternoon Nurse Cramer read the thermometer and discovered he was dead" (171). The description of the Soldier in White continues over the next few pages in the same morose, understated tone: "The soldier in white was more like a stuffed and sterilized mummy than a real nice guy" (173).

The Soldier in White is not only said to be like a mummy. To anyone familiar with Egyptian rituals it is apparent that he *is* an Egyptian mummy, attended by Isis and Nephthys (the two nurses) and a priest ("the educated Texan" [9]); this passage enacts the Opening of the Mouth ceremony, as it is recorded in *The Book of the Dead* ("The Book of Opening the Mouth" 248–56), in which the dead man inhabits the role of Osiris in the god's mythic cycle of dismemberment, reassembly, and resurrection. In the ritual described in *The Book of the Dead*, "One priest, holding a miniature *adze* that possessed special mystical powers, approached the mummy. To the chanting of religious formulas, he touched the mummy's head: the eyes, to open them so the man could see; the ears, so he could hear; the mouth, so he could speak; the jaws, so he could eat" (Pace 54).

This Egyptian ritual is recapitulated in the series of questions beginning with Dunbar's, "'Does he even know what you're talking about?'" (172), and it continues with a series of queries that touch on the Soldier in White's ability to hear, move, breathe, see, and "wiggle his toes or move the tips of his fingers" (173). Dunbar's questions are a parody of the Egyptian ritual that was intended to allow the dead man to "live in the other world as he had on earth" (Pace 54). So exact is Heller's rendition of this ritual that the "thermometer balanced in the empty dark hole in the bandages over his mouth" (171) imitates the miniature adze, "the iron tool with which the mouths of the gods were opened" (*The Book of the Dead* 250). The two "stoppered jars," (174) that were connected to the inside of the soldier's elbow and to his urethra can be recognized as a somewhat scatological version of the four Canopic jars used by Egyptian embalmers to store the organs of the eviscerated mummy.

What we reveal by bringing into "consciousness" the *Book of the Dead/* Soldier in White intertext is that patterns of discourse that imitate ancient literature are consistently in effect throughout *Catch-22*, such that imitations of *The Book of the Dead* and *The Gilgamesh Epic* comprise the novel's dialogic norm. In other words, text that we might otherwise ascribe to be a component of Heller's construction of a realistic-absurdist mode of discourse in the interest of pursuing a black-comic send-up of World War Two is, in actuality, the product of the intrusion of ancient rituals into modern discourse. Thus, in *Catch-22* what are ordinarily assumed to constitute the emblems of modern life are revealed (by their hidden contents) to be living enactments of atavisms—exactly the point made by Frazer in *The Golden Bough*. In the view of Robert A. Segal, Jessie Weston contends that "literature comes from myth, not that it *is* myth" (Segal xxi) and that "the keenest difference between literature and myth is that literature stands severed from literature" (Segal xxi).

In *Catch-22* an entirely different set of conditions prevails from what we expect to find in a realistic-absurdist novel, for the characters seek a revelation that is beyond literature; for example, the chaplain realizes that

"the Bible was a book, and so were *Bleak House, Treasure Island. . .*"
(293). Where there is a lack of ritual in literature, in the world of *Catch-22*, life itself is both myth and ritual. Progress is unveiled as nothing more
than novel and sensational experiences poured into primordial mythic,
archetypal, ritual, and psychic structures. And we can note as a point of
major significance that Heller's use of an Egyptian ritual brings him even
closer to *Finnegans Wake*, for *The Book of the Dead* is a determining
text in the *Wake*: because it "[implies] death and renewal" it is "an epitome
of *Finnegans Wake*" (Tindall 289). Similarly, Erich Neumann states that
"all these symbols with which men have sought to grasp the beginning in
mythological terms are as alive today as they ever were: they have their
place not only in art and religion, but in the living processes of the individual psyche, in dreams and in fantasies" (Origins 11).

What at first seem to be calculatedly meaningless black-comic situations that express a nihilistic outlook may be shown to symbolize a content that is vitally important for the psychological development of characters in a universe of spiritual dimensions. The characters have little or no
conscious awareness of the significance of their actions, for these situations are filled with a vitality that is largely symbolic and, thereby, expres-
sive of potentials and possibilities. On these outwardly absurd actions
depend the individual transformations toward which characters may pos-
sibly evolve—either toward psychic dissolution or toward vision and inspiration. The most trivial aspects of their world turn out to be the shapes of
its inner, more real formations: nowhere is this more clearly seen than in
the Soldier in White's jars. Seemingly the most offensive element of "The
Soldier in White" chapter, these two jars, are said to contain clear liquid
dripped into the soldier and then reversed and fed in the opposite direction. The process that represents the Soldier in White's maintenance is
described in terms that are so profitless that the artillery captain is motivated to ask, "'Why can't they hook the two jars up to each other and
eliminate the middleman? . . . What the hell do they need him for?'"
(174). It is the extreme assertiveness of the artillery captain's outraged
deflation of the Soldier in White's maintenance that signals the importance of his question. The comic description of the seemingly interchange-
able jars inverts the significance of what is being shown in this episode,
for the episode summarizes the great mystery of creation as described by
the mystical wisdom of Kabbalah. In the Kabbalah/Soldier in White
intertext, the Soldier in White is cosmic man:

> . . . the reason for the process of human incarnation is that mankind should act
> as a bridge between the upper and lower worlds. In this way, the Divine Presence

may be realized consciously, even in the lowest depths of physical reality, as mankind raises, for example, the metal and mineral kingdoms in to the upper levels of the Asyyatic Tree and imbues them with an intelligence they would never have experienced while buried and in an unrefined state in the earth. This is also true of the plant and animal kingdoms, whose stock, despite periodic error, is slowly being improved and protected against disease. Thus, the planet is gradually lifted in its state of awareness as mankind husbands its surface and resources. (Halevi *A Kabbalistic Universe* 195).

Ironically, Yossarian's militarized world, as presented in the primary fabula, operates as a religious system, but it is a religious system with no cosmic resonances. Nevertheless, the apparatus for strategic bombing veils the subtextual cosmic world, and it is from the barbarity, malevolence, and tyranny sustained by that religious world that Yossarian desperately wishes to escape: indeed, it is because Yossarian's world is religiously delineated that he finds himself in need of escape from it. In contrast, the religious world of *The Gilgamesh Epic* is not the only mirror text operating in the subtext (or operating as a subtext), present also is also the magico-religious world of *The Waste Land*, as described by Jessie Weston in *From Ritual to Romance*. This world operates by means of different systems of "laws" and "rituals" than the "laws" of *The Gilgamesh Epic*, offering escape in the form of the healing of the land and the restoration of fertility to the realm by means of the magical healing of The Fisher King. Kluger shows that "*The Gilgamesh Epic* . . . mirrors a significant era in the history of religion, a time when the Great Goddess Ishtar was defeated by the hero under the aegis of Shamash, the archetype of consciousness. This marks the beginning of the transition from polytheism to the monotheism of the Bible" (207–8). Thus the two mythic systems (and their attendant religions) are in conflict throughout the text of *Catch-22*, and the problem that Yossarian faces is that in order to preserve his life he must cross from the primitive and "unconscious" religious world of *The Gilgamesh Epic* to the magico-religious world of the Fisher King, in which there is a possibility of salvation and redemption.

I have said that Heller has no interest in presenting a religious world per se, because the religious nature of his conception is derived from the recapitulation of the developmental stages of psychic consciousness, such as outlined the scheme presented in Erich Neumann's *The Origins and History of Consciousness* and not because Heller is a religious thinker. Heller's primary fabula, set as it is in World War Two, has a close relationship with its three ur-texts, James Joyce's *Ulysses* and *Finnegans Wake* and T.S. Eliot's *The Waste Land*, and it is to Joyce and Eliot that we may turn in order to acquire a better idea of the nature of Heller's ideology. Robert Martin Adams states that "He [Joyce] looks past ideologies, conventions, and intentions, beyond morals, manners, character, and individuality, to the visionary substructure of human life; by which I mean the primitive instinctual patterns and tropisms by which life is and always has been controlled" (34). Joyce's approach to the novel is very close to Heller's starting point, a condition announced early on in his text. Heller's innovation, however, is to pursue the theme of development, to look beyond Joyce's reduction to the instinctive context. To accomplish this Heller traces the primordial beginning through the subsequent stages of evolution, emerging fully into the paradisal light (*or* [Hebrew for light]/Orr [the character in *Catch-22*]) of consciousness, whereas *Finnegans Wake* contains rebirth but no *wakening* beyond the level of instinct and unconscious dreaming.

In the first of his many "crazy" speeches Yossarian states "'I am a bona fide supraman'" (20), to which Clevinger replies "'Superman?'" Clevinger's query is "corrected" by Yossarian: "'Supraman,' Yossarian corrected" (20). This, of course, is more than an extended pun; the intention is to bring to the reader's attention the distinction between superman and supraman. Supraman is an unfamiliar word that may at first appear to mean the same as superman but which, for Heller, has far different implications than superman supplies. Super and supra both mean above, but supra contains the additional meaning of anterior and earlier. We should also note that the word supra occurs on the second page of *Finnegans Wake*— "building supra buildung pon the banks" (4). The word is connected with the building of a wall, so that Yossarian's non-building of the officer's club, which we have discussed as a reversal of Gilgamesh's building of Uruk, may also be read as a (distinct but distant) reversal of Finnegan's work as a hod carrier in Joyce's novel. Heller's use of the word supraman can be, perhaps, more usefully explicated by turning to a passage in Erich Neumann's *The Origins and History of Consciousness* (1954), which may have supplied Heller with some of the Jungian ideas and mythological examples that appear in *Catch-22*:

> Any attempt to outline the archetypal stages from the standpoint of analytical psychology must begin by drawing a fundamental distinction between personal and transpersonal psychic factors. Personal factors are those which belong to one individual personality and are not shared by any other individual, regardless of whether they are conscious or unconscious. Transpersonal factors, on the other hand, are collective, supra- or extra-personal, and are to be regarded not as *external* conditions of society, but as *internal* structural elements. The

transpersonal represents a factor that is largely independent of the personal, for
the personal, both collectively and individually, is a late production of evolution.
(xix–xx)

What Adams terms Joyce's "visionary substructure of human life" (34)
is the same as the "supra-personal" and the "*internal* structural elements"
that concern Neumann: this psychic area of evolutionary anteriority is
what Heller means to indicate, when Yossarian insists that he is a supraman.
It may be added that this is also what Eliot refers to in "Tradition and the
Individual Talent," when he states that "The progress of an artist is a
continual self-sacrifice, a continual extinction of personality" (143).

It is Heller himself who determines that T.S. Eliot must be introduced
into this discussion, for the poet's name makes a mock-comic appearance
in chapter four, "Doc Daneeka" (37–38), significantly, in answer to a
question—a situation that imitates the forbidden "overwhelming question"
(line 3) in "Prufrock." The intrusion of Eliot's name, which General Peckem
seizes upon as "a new code or something" (38) alerts the reader to the
presence of the many allusions to *The Waste Land* and others of Eliot's
poems throughout the text. The Waste Land theme (as well as the incorporation of The *Waste Land*) may be glimpsed in such a passage as:
"Yossarian had once stood on a jetty at dawn and watched a tufted round
log that was drifting toward him on the tide turn unexpectedly in to the
bloated face of a drowned man; it was the first dead person he has ever
seen. He thirsted for life. . . ." (347). The passage combines thirst with
drowning in such a way that it alludes to both the "Death by Water"
section of *The Waste Land* and to the drought that is described in the
fifth section of the poem, "What the Thunder Said": "Here is no water
but only rock / Rock and no water and the sandy road" (ln. 331–332).

Eliot's poem may be read as a narrative in which a hero suffers several
incarnations, all of which are failures in that rather than escaping the
wheel of rebirth and death he drowns only to be born again: the final
movement of the poem advises that the way out of the world is through
"Datta. Dayadhvam. Damyatta" (46)—give, sympathize, control. Eliot's
poem has layered the transcendental and impersonal Buddhist system of
spiritual liberation over a more primitive ethos, that of the Waste Land as
described in Jessie Weston's *From Ritual to Romance*. This is exactly
Heller's method in *Catch-22*, and we see that the events which take place
in Yossarian's story illustrate material extracted from the myths and rituals which mark the evolution of mankind through the various phases of
his passage from instinctive "suprahumanity" to the crucial (if tragically
insufficient) modicum of conscious awareness that is attainable in the

modern period. Thus, by insisting that he is the "supraman," Yossarian indicates that he is locked into a religiously based system of social relations in which there is no transpersonal salvation; the most that can be extracted from the life of the instinctual level of the supraman is the resignation that Gilgamesh comes to at the end of his epic. At the same time, however, it is crucial to realize that even this resignation was a spiritual attainment of noteworthy magnitude: "Gilgamesh, in accord with the heroic role, did step into the future, far ahead of the consciousness of his time" (Kluger 208).

A further problem arises in that the modern world, of which the military culture is an expression, is dangerously lacking in self-knowledge—in fact its prime directive is repression. When Yossarian is not flying his destructive missions at the behest of industrialized and omnicompetent death wish, he is set to censoring V mail. Heller's dissections of the psyches of Lt. Scheisskopf (171), Doc Daneeka (33–35), Major Major (90–96), and Colonel Cathcart (213–20), demonstrate, among other things, the one dimensionality, paucity of imagination, and general unattractiveness of these highly conventional men, for whom *life* is a magazine. The degree of undeveloped consciousness that they represent stands in marked contrast to the chaplain's compassion, introspection, and sensitivity (274–81). The same thing may be said for the ethical heroism of Yossarian, whose "crazy" character departs from the amoral normality of the world depicted by *Catch-22* by virtue of the intensity of his insight and the energy with which he reacts to his perceptions:

> . . .Clevinger enumerated Yossarian's symptoms: An unreasonable belief that everybody around him was crazy, a homicidal impulse to machine-gun strangers, retrospective falsification, an unfounded suspicion that people hated him and were conspiring to kill him.
>
> But Yossarian knew he was right, because, as he explained to Clevinger, to the best of his knowledge he had never been wrong. Everywhere he looked was a nut, and it was all a sensible young gentleman like himself could do to maintain his perspective amid so much madness. And it was urgent that he did, for he knew his life was in peril. (21)

The metaphor of the world at risk is established through the *Catch-22/ Waste Land* intertext. The Waste Land is a Medieval grail legend concerning the drought brought on by the sexual impotence of the land's ruler, The Fisher King. A partial solution to the king's malady will come about when the Fisher King is asked a question. In *Perceval* the task of the Quester becomes that of healing the king (Weston 13–14); in another version of the legend, "the task of the hero consists in asking concerning the Grail, and by so doing, to restore the Fisher King (Weston 14). This suggests the importance of the manifold questions that are asked to seemingly little purpose throughout *Catch-22*, such as Orr's queries to Yossarian about apple cheeks, the questions that erupt at the "education session" in chapter four, or even Colonel Cargill's question that solicits the answer, "T.S. Eliot"—"'Name, for example, one poet who makes money'" (37). The symbol of transcendence in the legends of the grail cycle is rain, the subject of an entire chapter in Weston's study: she states that

> a very considerable number of the *Rig Veda* hymns depend for their initial inspiration on the actual bodily needs and requirements of a mainly agricultural population, i.e., of a people that depend upon the fruits of the earth for their subsistence, and to whom the regular and ordered sequence of the processes of Nature was a vital necessity.
>
> Their hymns and prayers, and as we have strong reason to suppose, their dramatic ritual, were devised for the main purpose of obtaining from the gods of their worship that which was essential to ensure their well-being and the fertility of their land—warmth, sunshine, above all, sufficient water. (25–26)

Catch-22 is above all a symbolic (or metasymbolic) system embedded within the fictional text: the system of symbols constructs a separate metalinguistic discourse of mytho/psycho-evolution (Riffaterre 53)—and the most important symbol in that system is water in the form of rain. Not only is it necessary to realize that Yossarian's World War Two Europe has been construed as a Waste Land, it must also be realized that the problem of Yossarian's Waste Land must be solved by rain. Rain is first announced as a problem in chapter twelve, "Bologna," where Heller reverses the situation that prevails in the medieval tale (and in Eliot's poem), in which a drought has wasted the land. The counter version in *Catch-22* proffers, "Their only *hope* was that it would never stop raining, and they had *no hope* because they all knew it would" (122; emphases added). The rain that falls in the "Bologna" chapter is ineffectual rain, a condition underscored by the plunge into drunkenness undertaken by Yossarian and his colleagues, as they drive through the rainy night in Chief White Halfoat's stolen jeep.

After they have crashed and been found by Clevinger and McWatt (131), their subhuman condition is presented in understated terms as they are shown "'Lying there like a bunch of drunken animals.'" This episode corresponds with the qualities assigned to the Terrible Mother, the negative transformative character of the Great Mother, whose rites are celebrated in the "mysteries of drunkenness" (Neumann *The Great*

Mother 73): to these mysteries Neumann assigns the qualities of madness, stupor, impotence, and ecstasy. By virtue of his drunken ride in the
rain, Yossarian has turned toward regression and loss of consciousness;
thus the rain is dedicated to the death mysteries of the Mother. As a
confirmation of the negative character of this episode, it is at this point
that Chief White Halfoat resolves to die of pneumonia. Clevinger, who
reifies the superego throughout the episode, suggests that they be removed from the mud "before they all die of pneumonia," to which the
Chief rejoins, "'I think I will die of pneumonia'" (131). Thus, the drunken
Chief, who would not turn on his headlights (131) and has, consequently,
crashed in the rain and mud, turns away from hope: in Neumann's terms
he has been overwhelmed by the negative animal (Neumann *The Great
Mother* 75). What is fundamentally at issue in *Catch-22* is the problem
that in the face of what seems the prevalence of the death wish, there
must be hope; the rain brings the men hope (for temporarily the rain
makes missions impossible), but they do not recognize the hope that the
rain brings as being more than a transitory hope. The men ritualistically
invoke the rain by means of the nursery rhyme "Rain, rain, go away /
Come again some other day" (130), but, significantly, the Chief crashes
the jeep before the song can be sung all the way through. They end up
trapped in the negative phase, so that "The more it rained, the worse
they suffered" (12). The rain in chapter twelve is not the rain of hope,
because it only postpones the battle.

"The Eternal City," the thirty-ninth chapter of the forty-two chapters
that comprise the text, sets up the last four chapters that critics have had
such a hard time integrating into the rest of the text (Potts "The Problem
of the Ending" 110–14). One portion of the symbolic level of the text has
been used to pursue the Grail theme, and another has been concerned
with the Waste Land theme: the resolution of the Waste Land motif is
presented by means of the sentence "A frigid, fine rain was falling" (421).
Because he has chosen to rescue Nately's whore's kid sister, Yossarian
has transcended the supraman—the heroic stage symbolized by *The
Gilgamesh Epic*. Yossarian then walks in the hopeful rain, a rain that is
different in quality than the "heroic" and hopeless rain of the "Bologna"
chapter, and for the first time Yossarian sees the world. The world has
not changed, the Eternal City is still a Waste Land, where *every* injustice,
cruelty, and inhumanity is enacted, but Yossarian has been transformed:
he is the transfigured bearer of hope.

The rain of renewed life now falls because Yossarian has asked a ritual
question; in asking the question he has risen to the selflessness of "Datta.

Dayadhvam. Damyatta" (*The Waste Land* ln. 64; give, sympathize, control):

> Yossarian hurried back to Milo and recanted. He said he was sorry and, knowing he was lying, promised to fly as many more missions as Colonel Cathcart wanted if Milo would only use all his influence in Rome to help him locate Nately's whore's kid sister.
>
> "She's just a twelve-year-old virgin, Milo," he explained anxiously, "and I want to find her before it's too late. (418)

The formulaic phrase "Nately's whore's kid sister," which resounds so comically throughout the text, is a powerful magical formula and is the essence of the Grail. One aspect of the interchangeablity of Yossarian's character is that he is Tammuz, who Weston observes "typified the vivifying waters" (38): like Tammuz, Yossarian was wounded in the thigh and—by virtue of the Ishtar-Dori Duz substitution—was the goddess's lover. However, he is also the son of the virgin/whore goddess, for he is connected with pomegranates (147), and Frazer states that Attis was conceived by Cybele (a pair that were parallel with Tammuz and Ishtar) when she placed a pomegranate in her bosom (403).

The identification of Yossarian as Tammuz-Attis and the parallel identification of various women as Ishtar are carried out in the text by means of a number of substitutions and reversals. Frazer states that at Babylon every woman "had once in her life to submit to the embraces of a stranger" (384); Heller's reversal of the single encounter transforms Ishtar's religious ritual into "the maid-in lime-colored panties that she was always rolling off for any man who wanted her" (137). The woman dedicated to Ishtar awaited her lover in a window and was identified with the aspect of the goddess Ishtar called Kalili of the Windows. In *Catch-22* Ishtar's ritual suffers a further reversal, when Aarfy throws a prostitute from a window and kills her (428). Certainly, Ishtar is Nately's whore also; in the guise of "Nately's whore's kid sister" Ishtar is a "twelve year old virgin" whose title says everything, when it is read as an example of General Peckem's "a new code or something" (38): the name "Ishtar" is present as an anagram in the word "sister," and "birth" (natal) is hidden in Nately. The sacred identity of Nately's whore's kid sister is further confirmed by Yossarian's insistence that she is "a twelve year old virgin," for as such she represents one half of the virgin/whore duality that we may also recognize in the otherwise inexplicable pairing of Nurse Cramer with Nurse Duckett. Thus Nately's whore is the principle of virgin birth, and as such she is one component of what Neumann calls the "polyvalence of the archetypal structure of the Feminine" (*The Great Mother* 75): "The four polar points on the third circle of our schema are not static or conceptual quantities. At each pole an archetypal figure is situated, e.g., the Good Mother, the Terrible Mother, the negative anima (or, more simply, the seductive young witch), and the positive anima (or, more simply, the Sophia-virgin)" (75).

Heller has introduced characters into *Catch-22* that are manifestations of these four archetypes, and they may be identified as the chaplain's wife, Nately's whore, Dori Duz, and Nately's whore's kid sister, respectively. Since the text, describes a "dynamic" (Neumann *The Great Mother* 75), we see that in many cases the archetypes do not appear in a pure form, so that, for example, Nurse Duckett and Lieutenant Scheisskopf's wife exemplify a combination of the Good Mother and the seductive young witch-anima: the two women symbolize Yossarian's ego consciousness, as it detaches from its fascination with the witch and aligns itself with the fertility rituals of the Good Mother.

Initially, the text of *Catch-22* presents an exploration of the pre-individual stages of consciousness, the transpersonal factors that mark the first of the three stages through which both individuals and cultures must pass on the route toward individuation (Neumann xx). These stages of evolution in both myth and psyche—unity, separation, and transformation—are integrated into the novel in a rough chronology that contrasts with the achronic handling of the events narrated in the primary fabula. In other words, the chromometrical difficulties of Yossarian's story have been submitted to the organization of an overarching psychological scheme. For instance, Yossarian's querulous and whining inquiry, "Why in the world did He [God] ever create pain?" (184), may be taken *seriously* and assigned to the unitary or Uroboric psychological stage of personality development, which is the first stage. Erich Neumann states that "Pain and discomfort are among the earliest factors that build consciousness. They are 'alarm-signals' sent out by centroversion to indicate that the unconscious equilibrium is disturbed" (297). Neumann adds that "the manner of their development [the pain signals] is as mysterious as that of' all other organs and systems" (297). Yossarian's exploration of the question as to why God did not substitute "a doorbell" or a system of blue-and-red neon tubes right in the middle of each person's forehead" (184) for pain is a comic address to the same topic. It should be noted that it is not until we are 184 pages into Heller's text before we reach a discussion of the first of the three stages of psychological development. Prior to this the Uroboros has been symbolized by the womblike hospital, the setting where Yossarian resides at the opening of the text.

We may consider that food is also important in the early phase of the narrative: on the first page the narrator comments that "his [Yossarian's] meals were brought to him in bed" (7). As Milo Minderbinder takes over the running of the mess hall, food itself becomes the subject of a quest in chapter thirteen, and Milo's assumption of the duties of overseeing the feeding of the men represents the commencement of his development as a character. Milo first appears "taking shelter behind the hardboiled egg raised protectively before his face like a magic charm" (138). By page 140 there is "an insatiable orgy of fresh-egg eating." In his discussion of "The Uroboros" Erich Neumann states that "The first cycle of myth is the creation myth. . . . In the beginning is perfection, wholeness. . . . One symbol of original perfection is the circle. Allied to it are the sphere, the egg, and the *rotundum*—the 'round' of alchemy. . . . The round is the egg, the philosophical World Egg, the nucleus of the beginning, and the germ from which, as humanity teaches everywhere, the world arises" (*Origins* 8). Moreover, we see that food as food is indicative of a psychic plane of the lowest order: "The instinct to eat—hunger—is one of the most elementary of man's psychic, instincts, and the psychology of the belly plays a correspondingly large part, with primitives and children. One's state of mind is the more dependent upon whether one is satisfied or not, or thirsty or not, the less one's consciousness and one's ego are developed. For the embryonic ego the nutritional side is the only important factor, and this sphere is still very strongly accentuated for the infantile ego, which regards the maternal uroboros as the source of food and satisfaction" (26–27). While it is clear that Heller invokes uroboric symbolism, this is not done to enforce this psychic state but to imitate the creation and evolution of the cosmos: while it would seem that the text invokes the uroboric level for hundreds of pages, in actuality the text commences with the dissolution of the uroboric whole from the first page.

One way of framing Yossarian's problem is to see his situation as that of his not being a god: as the uroboric whole, he is not a god, because he is unmanifested. Thus, his problem is one of manifestation, or in Neumann's terms, "The Separation of the World Parents: The Principle of Opposition"—the splitting off of opposites from unity (*Origins* 103). The theme of manifestation is introduced on the second page of *Catch-22*: "When he had exhausted all possibilities in the letters, he began attacking the names and addresses on the envelopes, obliterating whole homes and streets, annihilating entire metropolises with careless flicks of his wrist as though he were God" (8). One reading of this sentence is that it parodies Yossarian's routine duties as a bomber pilot. This episode is placed at the opening of the text, but at this point in the story Yossarian has already flown fifty missions. Yossarian has accomplished in reality what he resorts to in play to relieve the monotony of not exercising his godlike powers of destruction—"obliterating whole homes and streets, annihilating entire metropolises with careless flicks of his wrist as though he were God" (8).

Repression of the ego level is the mechanism at work in this episode, a condition of which we are informed by the text as we are shown Yossarian *censoring* letters. Furthermore, we are shown the consequent displacement of guilt, as it is funneled first into Yossarian's guilty escape into the hospital and thence the displacement into language, through Yossarian's playful and regressive attacks on the structure of his society: "To break the monotony he invented games. Death to all modifiers, he declared one day, and out of every letter that passed through his hands went every adverb and every adjective. The next day he made war on articles. He reached a much higher plane of creativity the following day when he blacked out everything in the letters but *a, an* and *the*" (8). The passage is difficult to read because it carries out a number of subtle reversals. Yossarian's energetic and aggressive treatment of the letters is motivated by the return of the repressed: that which he has censored by resorting to the uroboric hospital has surfaced and again demands his attention. By entering the Uroboric whole, Yossarian has made it possible to make war on the articles of war—the meaning of his "war on articles" in the above quotation.

In another reversal, Yossarian's play at textual destruction "creates" *The Gilgamesh Epic*, the work of literature that comprises one of the subtexts that the main text imitates. By crossing out the text, Yossarian imitates the historical events that have caused *The Epic of Gilgamesh* to exist as fragments, for the text referred to as *The Epic of Gilgamesh* consists of what remains after the destruction of Nineveh by the Medes in 612 B.C. The passage also parodies another important ancient text, the Bible, however in the parody of the Bible's account of the creation of the universe, Yossarian also (ironically) takes on the godly task of metaphoric creation. Insofar as *Catch-22* engages the Bible subtextually, it establishes the Bible as a subset of *The Gilgamesh Epic* and other Sumerian and Babylonian poems containing myths. This is because the Bible presents later versions of Noah and the flood story (Kramer *History* 150-54), the divine paradise of *Genesis* (Kramer 145), the creation of woman from a rib (Kramer 146), and the first resurrection (Kramer 155-169). In effect, the passage narrates Yossarian's parodic "creation" of his own psychological world by "destroying" the letters of his comrades in arms. Heller inverts the six days of creation that are described in the first verses of the Bible: Yossarian's "higher plane of creativity," phrased as a burlesque of the ontological methodology of the New Criticism, is far more formidable than a mockery of a school of literary criticism, for it constructs an operative anti-*logos*— "death," "made war," and "blacked out everything"—that is juxtaposed against Yahweh's, "Let there be light."

Yossarian is a god after all, but what kind of god is he? Is he God or a god? What manner of divinity produces "serious repercussions" from his surroundings, for that is the response to Yossarian's activities: "Censoring the envelopes had serious repercussions, produced a ripple of anxiety on some ethereal military echelon that floated a C.I.D. man back into the ward posing as a patient" (8). One way of reading this passage is to take into account Neumann's depiction of the sociology of the uroboros stage as "the dominance of group consciousness": "In this state the ego was not an autonomous, individualized entity with a knowledge of morality, volition, and activity of its own; it functioned solely as a part of the group, and the group with its superordinate power was the only real subject" (109). This is a description that applies equally to the military, particularly during wartime, when all goals are group goals: thus Yossarian has elicited the notice of the group consciousness, making it aware that a portion of its substance has somehow emerged from the collective and needs to be reabsorbed. The C.I.D. man—dressed in "official hospital attire" (207), the red robe sacred to the cult of Ishtar and Tammuz (Frazer 379)—may be recognized as a priest of the cult of the Terrible Mother; it is because society is fixated at the level of consciousness symbolized by the Terrible Mother in her aspect as goddess of death that the C.I.D. man represents an authority that must be heroically engaged and resisted. Yossarian's heroism is given a divine aspect in the early chapters. However, as a god Yossarian is tightly constrained by the fact that his powers are individual and psychological: in his dealings with the outside world he belongs to an order which he did not create—the reality principle—and he is constantly forced to consider that he is only a man. Indeed, as he becomes more conscious of his surroundings, he is increasingly aware that his world is fundamentally a religious world. Increasingly, his world becomes defined by such things as prayers for tighter bomb patterns and atheists who argue enthusiastically about the nature of the god in whom they do not believe.

Nowhere is the centrality of religious conceptualizing more evident in *Catch-22* than in regard to the catch itself. It follows that it is only by

examining the nature of the catch—catch-22—that we may understand
the religious ramifications of Yossarian's evolutionary condition as a man
faced with the problem of developing an individual self in Milo
Minderbinder's collectivistic world system, in which "Everyone has a share"
(238). Having ascertained the nature of catch-22, many of the riddles and
paradoxes offered by Heller's text may also be assigned their places.

The catch is initially described as a manifestation of the army's bureaucratic organization of behavior; its first intrusion into the primary fabula
occurs early in the opening chapter: "When he had exhausted all possibilities in the letters, he began attacking the names and addresses on the
envelopes, obliterating whole homes and streets, annihilating entire metropolises with careless flicks of his wrist as though he were God. Catch-
22 required that each censored letter bear the censoring officer's name"
(8). In the above sentence the word "Catch-22" follows directly after the
word "God" in the previous sentence. The sentence in which catch-22
appears seems to be a non sequitur. If we accept an "absurd" reading of
these two sentences, we will not trouble ourselves for much more than
the non sequitur relationship between the two sentences, and they seem
little more than indications of Yossarian's justifiable boredom. On the
other hand, a religious reading of the sentences takes their meaning into
another direction. Read as an allusion, the words presented by the two
sentences refer to the Kabbalistic mystic Abraham Abulafia, who was a
master of letter permutation: "Using a pseudonym corresponding in numerical value to his own name, Abulafia circulated his meditation manuals
under titles like *Splitting of Names*. . . . Abulafia freely sprinkled his
texts with codes, acrostics, and number-letter puns to simultaneously
befuddle his persecutors and communicate freely with knowledgeable
Spanish mystics. . ." (Epstein *Kabbalah* 81). The description of Yossarian
"exhaust[ing] all possibilities in the letters" exploits the double meaning of
"letters" to refer to correspondence or to the alphabet. Yossarian's censoring is, thus, an allusion to Abulafia's Kabbalistic mystical practices:
Epstein's description of Abulafia's practice states that "[He] permutated
the twenty-two Hebrew letters to gain prophetic wisdom" (83), and what
Heller refers to as exhausting the possibilities in the letters is equivalent to
Abulafia's permutations of the Hebrew alphabet. Moreover, Jewish mysticism is often referred to as the path of letters (Epstein 73).

Heller repeatedly signals his interest in codes, puns, and acrostics similar to Abulafia's permutational techniques: when Corporal Wintergreen
telephones only to say "T.S. Eliot" (38), General Peckem wants confirmation that "it's a new code or something'" (38); similarly, Flume's words to

the chaplain are "cryptic" (294) and have "esoteric import" (286). An Joyce-inflected reading of Yossarian's name is to understand that except for the addition of a diversionary letter o, Yossarian is an anagram of "Assyrian": the *Finnegans Wake* subtext of *Catch-22* readily admits such a rendering. Additionally, to indicate some further examples of Heller's use of permutations, Nately is an extension of natal. Orr is also a homonym for oar, which suits him, since he is the boatman Urshanabi in *The Gilgamesh Epic* subtext. Heller's treatment of Urshanabi's name rivals the wordplay of *Finnegans Wake*, though it takes a form not characteristic to Joyce's novel. "Urshanabi" is presented in a phonetically coded sentence in chapter twenty-eight: "Orr hasn't got brains enough to be unhappy" (315). In order to extract the name from the sentence, it is necessary to unscramble "shan" from "hasn't" and precede it with "Ur" from its homophone "Orr." Extracting the sounds "abi" from "happy" derives the rendering of the final syllable of Urshanabi. It is also noteworthy that Heller's indulgence in wordplay suggests the Kabbalistic practice of "reading scripture without separating phrases into logical order" (Epstein 89) so as to derive a meaning beyond meaning.

The system behind Heller's permutations is the mystical handling of language explored by the Kabbalah; Heller's interest in this system is indicated specifically, for the word "cabalistic" turns up on page 160 in a description of Aarfy. The association of Aarfy and the Kabbalistic practice of the permutation of letters is completed when Aarfy's name is subjected to "cabalistic" permutation and rendered in the text as "eerie ogre" on page 154. Aarfy's name suggests a number of other associations with Kabbalah. The sixteenth-century Kabbalist and mystic Isaac Luria was known as the "Ari," the Lion. If we apply the mechanisms of Joycean condensation (see Norris 99—118) to Captain Aardvark's nickname, the permutation from "Aarfy" to "eerie" suggests that a further permutation to Ari is permissible. An earlier Kabbalist, Isaac Abulafia wrote manuals on the meditation on the letters:

> Moving from gross material visualizations to finer spiritual ones, the Abulafian mystic reached a state of ecstasy in which he was actually confronting the premanifest "spirit" behind each formed letter. *Dillug*, or skipping, consisted of observing the mind as it free-associated from one idea to another according to a set of flexible code words. Here, instead of forcing away distracting thoughts and images, the Kabbalist followed them by constructing them into sentences, and the letters into light. (Epstein 77)

The most radical view of *Catch-22* is that the entire text is an exercise in the most advanced form of Kabbalistic letter permutation—permutating the Specific Name. This feature of the text is not visible at every point; however, the repetition of certain words suggests that they are code words that progress toward mystical illumination, light. We have already seen that Orr's name equates to the Hebrew word for light, *or*, and it is Orr that brings about Yossarian's salvation, so it is not stretching the point to read Orr as "light." Another set of words may also have a mystical meaning: we have seen that Aarfy is connected to the mystic, The Ari. To perform the most extreme letter permutation "the Abulafian mystic began permutating the letters of the Tetragrammaton (YHVH) with each of the five vowel sounds until he had accomplished every combination of the twelve possibilities given him by the master" (Epstein 96). We see something of this technique reflected in the way that the words Aarfy, eerie, Irving, Orr, [Urshanabi] progress through the vowels in connection with the consonant r.

In contrast to the disorder that Yossarian perpetrates as he censors letters, the intervention of catch-22 seems to represent the restoration of an order. However, it is an order, which Yossarian acknowledges only so that he may flout it through his infantile handling of the letters: "Most letters he didn't read at all. On those he didn't read at all he wrote his own name. On those he did read he wrote, 'Washington Irving.' When that grew monotonous he wrote, 'Irving Washington'" (8). Yossarian's behavior is equally indicative of Kabbalistic permutation and infantile regression. In fact, the next sentence tells us that by use of this method Yossarian is able to extract "serious repercussions" from his surroundings. Thus, by violating catch-22, Yossarian has opened himself up to pursuit from the godlike but indefinite authorities in "some ethereal military echelon" (8).

Even so, there is a serious and progressive side to Yossarian's activities, for his play is no less than cosmic creation; Yossarian's letter permutation is paralleled by Havermeyer's assassination of field mice, which is yet another imitation of the Kabbalistic description of cosmic creation. The line of string running to the light bulb (31–32) that forms part of the equipment used by Havermayer in his play preserves the identical Kabbalistic terminology that describes creation. Kabbalists state that manifestation came about when "God willed that the Line of Light should penetrate beyond the First Crown. . . (Halevi *Kabbalistic Universe* 8). The mystical attainment of "light" is the goal of Kabbalistic study, a condition which is described in terms of Havermeyer's game: "The line was taut as a banjo string, and the merest tug would snap it on and blind the shivering quarry in a blaze of light" (32). We have noted that his mystical light is named throughout the text, whenever Orr's name is mentioned.

This mystical light is also divided into the hierarchy of the Sefirot, the stages along the Line of Light at which various types of angelic beings are to be found, and since Yossarian's military chain of command is analogous to the hierarchy of angelic beings in Kabbalah, it is possible for a C.I.D. man to be floated by "a ripple of anxiety on some ethereal military echelon" as a result of his creative activities (8): "The hierarchy of angelic beings conforms to the order of the Worlds. In Genesis 1, the fowl of the air are the archangels of Beriah or Creation, while the fish of the sea are the angels of Yezirah or Formation. According to tradition each World is divided into its own hierarchy of levels and Pillars" (Halevi *Kabbalah* 75).

In the opening chapters of the text Yossarian is depicted giving creative order to the world, yet his creation is disguised as destruction, play, regression, chaos, and death. Opposed to Yossarian's play is catch-22, which gives name to the fundamental lawlessness and disorder inherent in the religious worldview in a definitive, comic, and ironic manner that wholly obscures the true nature of the catch. Moreover, the catch obscures the chaotic nature of the world that the text presents. Catch-22 seems to indicate the direction in which Yossarian must look for order; catch-22 is continually invoked to explain why things, usually terrible things, must happen. In those contexts it seems to indicate a type of order prevailing over events, a first cause. Catch-22, though, effectively obscures the nature of that first cause because the catch has been made to sound as though it belongs to a rational world.

In mythology a great deal is made of the origin of the gods and their role in banishing chaos. An examination of the gods in comparison with magic and science reveals that the gods—whatever the gods—have substituted their brand of chaos for some other preexisting chaos. In fact, if we reflect upon this point sufficiently, we realize that at various points we have come upon the idea that the reign of these gods is provisional, with their hegemonies always in danger of collapsing. Thus, taken out of context, catch-22 reveals itself as the principle of the lawlessness of the world to which it gives name. The catch is, then, precisely the direction in which one must look for an understanding of the prevailing orderlessness of the world of *Catch-22*.

To return to the exposition of the stages of development, the second stage is the hero myth (phylogenetic) and the separation of the systems (ontogenetic). Neumann divides the hero myth into three phases: the birth of the hero, the slaying of the mother, and the slaying of the father. By imitating *The Gilgamesh Epic*, *Catch-22* has established a major intertextual relationship with the hero myth; in this way the *Catch-22/*

Gilgamesh intertext becomes a narrative rendering of the second phase of mythic and psychic development, the slaying of the mother. In Gilgamesh's epic, the goddess Ishtar represents the mother, and it is her monstrous surrogates, Humbaba and the Bull of Heaven, that the heroes, Gilgamesh and Enkidu, must kill. In the second chapter of this study we have examined how the goddess and her monsters appear in Heller's text. Though *Catch-22* is largely informed by the heroic work of the slaying of the mother, the text includes elements from the other phases. However, they are confined to a symbolic level of the text.

In myth the mother of the hero is often a "virgin mother . . . who gives birth to the hero after being impregnated by a god. . . . She has many forms, ranging from the innocent virgin . . . and the young girl . . . to the sorrowful figure of Sophia" (*Origins* 137). With the help of Neumann's comment, we are able to recognize that it is Nately's whore's kid sister who is Yossarian's mother, and that it is his own birth on the higher psychic planes that Yossarian struggles toward in the concluding chapters of the narrative. This topic alone could be expanded into a lengthy discussion; however, it is necessary at this point to turn to the phase of the slaying of the father.

The slaying of the father plays an important role in *Catch-22* in that it inhabits one of the most significant motifs in the text, namely, that of the appearance of men in pairs that has been taken note of in the first chapter. These pairs are representations of what Neumann assigns an advancing form of man-to-man relationships as masculine self-consciousness "asserts its independence and no longer allows itself to be made the tool of *rituals inimical to it*" *(Origins* 180; emphasis added). Looked at in this way, the slaying of the mother is a practical advance, for her rituals are sometimes the sacrifice of sacred kings. In the text such a ritual is represented by the death of Kid Sampson, whose dismemberment is an accident only on the surface level of the text. Frazer indicates that Kid was one of the names applied to the god Dionysus (453) who was "cut to pieces by the murderous knives of his enemies" (451) just as Kid Sampson is "sliced half away" (347) by McWatt's propeller. We cannot but note the ritualistic import implied by the information that "Kid Sampson had rained all over" (348). Moreover, Heller makes it clear that the "sacred phallus . . . 'remains'" (*Origins* 225), for the "bloated and decaying" (335) legs are "still joined by strings somehow at the bloody truncated hips" (347–48).

The moaning episode (225–30) of chapter twenty-one is another occurrence of ritual worship of the mother-goddess in her Ishtar aspect, and the episode nearly ends with the sacrifice of Major Danby. As if the chthonic import of this episode were not sufficiently established, we can further establish that the mother-goddess in her aspect as the Terrible Mother is at the center of the moaning episode. The moaning that issues from Yossarian as General Dreedle's nurse arouses him is an imitation of the "moananoaning" (*Finnegans Wake* 628) pronounced by the dying A.L.P. (Mrs. Earwicker or Anna Livia Plurabelle) on the final page of Joyce's novel. According to Tindall, A.L.P. is "Eve, the Virgin Mary, Pandora, Noah's wife, Napoleon's Josephine, and the Moon" (249). It is to slay the Mother literally that Aarfy murders the prostitute by throwing her out of a window sacred to Ishtar.

Because the mother fixates culture at a barbaric level, social and psychic liberation into the light of fuller consciousness requires a removal from such bloody rituals of fertility and renewal. The institution of homosexuality is "a cultural necessity to break away on a larger scale from the mother realm, to get the libido out of the mother" (Kluger 68). The important theme of homosexuality and cultural evolution has beeen given a detailed discussion in the third chapter. However, it is useful at this point to take under consideration Neumann's observation that

> Accentuation of the man-to-man relationship eventually leads to the overthrow of the matriarchate by patriarchal rulers. Just as in Sparta, with its late matriarchal conditions, a strongly marked masculine relationship is to be observed among pairs of young warriors, so, at a much earlier date, we find the same thing in the Gilgamesh epic and numerous other hero myths. The countless male friendships in Greek mythology vindicate themselves, like that between Gilgamesh and Engidu [sic], in the hero's fight with the Great Mother dragon. (*Origins* 180–81)

The next phase is the slaying of the father. Neumann states that "The Terrible Male who has to be killed and whose final form is the Terrible Father . . . is always old and evil, and to be overthrown—at any rate for the hero, whose task it is to achieve something out of the ordinary" (*Origins* 185–86). This theme is addressed in *Catch-22* in chapter twenty-seven, "Nurse Duckett," wherein Dobbs attempts to enlist Yossarian's aid in assassinating Colonel Cathcart: "We can kill him the first thing tomorrow morning when he drives back from his farm" (308): this sentence reveals that Cathcart is the phallic Earth Father and "lord of all chthonic forces, belong[ing] psychologically to the realm of the Great Mother" (Neumann 186).

Neumann calls the third phase in the evolution of consciousness "The Transformation Myth," which he divides into "The Captive and The Treasure" and "The Transformation, or Osiris." In the individual, this phase corresponds to the attainment of "[s]tructural wholeness, with the self as center as the psyche" (417). The description of "the captive and the treasure" phase illuminates the final third of *Catch-22* with startling clarity: "The mythological goal of the dragon fight is almost always the virgin, the captive, or, more generally, 'the treasure hard to attain'" (195). Chapter thirty-eight is titled "Kid Sister": in her only appearance in the chapter, the girl tries to kill Yossarian with a bread knife (405). She is reintroduced when the monstrous figure of Captain Black reappears with the intention of further insulting the dead Nately: "You know, just to keep that kid Nately's body spinning in his grave, ha ha!" (412). Black tells Yossarian that the Roman whorehouse is empty and the whores have vanished. Yossarian's response is such deep concern for Nately's whore's kid sister that Black states: "'If I knew this was going to make you so unhappy, I would have come right over and told you, just to make you eat your liver'" (413).

We are not shown Yossarian's attainment of the virgin; it is enough that her salvation has become his goal, for he is thereby saved. (Neumann suggests that this is not entirely satisfactory, for "The nonliberation of the captive expresses itself in the continued dominance of the Great Mother" (*Origins* 206). Yossarian's sympathy for the girl is contrasted with Captain Black's aggressive sadism and Milo's greed as he forgets that the virgin is the goal and rushes off in pursuit of illegal tobacco (420); the values that are ranged in opposition in this episode serve to establish the unique quality of Yossarian's compassion for Nately's whore's kid sister. Moreover, we are now in a position to recognize that the kid sister emerges during the fight with Nately's whore, because that fight imitates the hero's fight with the Great Mother's dragon. As Yossarian battles Nately's whore, the Great Mother in her deadly aspect makes a more direct appearance.

The meaning of "transformation of Osiris," i.e., Osirification, may be readily grasped in that "It is related of Osiris that he led the Egyptians out of the state of savagery and cannibalism and gave them laws, not only teaching them to honor the gods, but to plant corn, to gather fruit, and to cultivate the grape" (*Origins* 211–12). Thus, an Osiris figure, Yossarian comes not to honor the gods but to overthrow the primeval gods; and he comes and not to establish laws but to violate primordial laws. The god of this ancient dispensation is catch-22, and the laws are the rules of combat—the articles of war. Heller's point is that the prevailing systems have degenerated and are expressions not of evolution and the life force but of

devolution and the death wish. World war—total warfare—does not represent a liberating project for culture: it is the final expression of psychic
repression and social fixation, and its ultimate principle is revealed to be
catch-22.

Yossarian grasps the provisional nature of the order provided by catch-
22 in "The Eternal City" chapter, a chapter that is the turning point in the
action that is narrated in the text:

> Yossarian left money in the old woman's lap—it was odd how many wrongs
> leaving money seemed to right—and strode out of the apartment, cursing Catch-
> 22 vehemently as he descended the stairs, even though he knew there was no
> such thing. Catch-22 did not exist, he was positive of that, but it made no differ-
> ence. What did matter was that everyone thought it existed, and that was much
> worse, for there was no object or text to ridicule or refute, to accuse, criticize,
> attack, amend, hate, revile, spit at, rip to shreds, trample upon or burn up. (418)

While *Catch-22* may not seem to reflect a religiously constructed world,
religion is an inescapable theme in the text: the chaplain, a principal
character, is introduced in the first sentence. His most important contribution is to embody the priestly function in modern society, a position
that he finds troubling and his commanding officers find incomprehensible. The chaplain is about to give in to despair because there is nothing
he can do about the increasing number of missions that his friends are
being required to fly. He is restrained from despair by the memory of his
wife and by

> the lifelong trust, he had placed in the wisdom and justice of an immortal, om-
> nipotent, omniscient, humane, universal, anthropomorphic, English-speaking,
> Anglo-Saxon, pro-American God, which had begun to waver. So many things
> were testing his faith. There was the Bible, of course, but the Bible was a book,
> and so were *Bleak House, Treasure Island, Ethan Frome* and *The Last of the
> Mohicans* Did it indeed seem probable, as he had once overheard Dunbar ask,
> that the answers to the riddles of creation would be supplied by people too igno-
> rant to understand the mechanics of rainfall? (293)

An important subplot revolves around prayers for a tighter bomb pattern, and Yossarian prays for the first time in his life in chapter thirty-five.
We may also note that several discussions of religious beliefs occur in the
text.

What is not so obvious is that the concerns that occupy Heller in
Catch-22 are only slightly deflected from the questions raised in *The
Gilgamesh Epic,* for the same gods are in attendance in both texts. Ini-
tially, we are distracted from realizing the metaphysical similarity of the

two texts, because in *Catch-22* the discussions of religious themes are couched in a comic discourse that sounds absurdist and that evinces a nihilistic assessment of reality. For example, when the nonexistent Lepage glue gun that Yossarian invents as a "humorless, glum joke" (128) comes back to him in the words of Captain Black, Yossarian shrieks "'My God, it's true!'" In turn, the drunken atheist, Dunbar, answers, "There is no God'" (129). The demotion of God is nowhere more in evidence in *Catch-22* than in the "intellectual conversation" (183) between Yossarian and Lieutenant Scheisskopf's wife, "who had henpecked Yossarian sententiously for being cynical and callous about Thanksgiving, even though she didn't believe in God just as much as he didn't" (183).

When we look closely at the topics discussed in the "intellectual conversation," we recognize that there is nothing comic, absurd, or nihilistic about what is transpiring. Lieutenant Scheisskopf's wife asserts that the god in whom she does not believe is "'a good God, a just God, a merciful God. He's not the mean and stupid God you make him out to be'" (185). The comic zenith in this conversation is reached just prior to the conclusion quoted above, when Lieutenant Scheisskopf's wife urges Yossarian to desist from listing examples of God's "sheer incompetence" (185) because "'He might punish you'" (185). Not only is Lieutenant Scheisskopf's wife's fear of divine punishment a marked contradiction to her assessment of God as merciful, her fear of punishment introduces the primary truth of a god-centered cosmos. The *secondary* religious truth is that God-centeredness is inherently repressive in nature, but the text is no longer concerned with that aspect of religion. What is uppermost in the way *Catch-22* dissects religion in the "intellectual conversation" is that it points out that what happens is not determined by laws but is conditional: as Lieutenant Scheisskopf's wife states it "'He *might* punish you'" (emphasis added). As the case of Utnapishtim demonstrates, the gods (or God) also *might* not punish you, the problem being that there is no way of being sure where you stand or what any outcome might be. In the novel the condition of divine indeterminacy is phrased in terms of catch-22: "Catch-22 says they have the right to do anything we can't stop them from doing" (416).

At first sight, *The Gilgamesh Epic* seems a straightforward tale, however, its simplicity is deceptive. The epic is a series of nested narratives, and though Gilgamesh's story is compelling, it is Utnapishtim's memoir that is the core text to which the other texts are subservient. So commanding is what Gilgamesh learns from Utnapishtim that the epic begins with a declaration that the acquisition of this lore is the hero's principal attainment: the opening line of the epic is "He who saw everything [to the ends] of the land," however, the "everything" that Gilgamesh has seen has come to him secondhand, for he has seen it only by virtue of finding Utnapishtim and hearing his narrative. Gilgamesh's triumph is that he has been able to transmit his hard-won knowledge to posterity. The importance of this transmission is emphasized in the following lines: "The [hi]dden he saw, [laid bare] the undisclosed. / He brought report of before the Flood, / Achieved a long journey, weary and [w]orn" (GE 72, lines 5–7). Having learned the secrets that are not the provenance of man, Gilgamesh next finalized his attainment: "All his toil he engraved on a stone stela" (GE 72 ln. 8) Gilgamesh's most important accomplishment was that he learned that the gods attempted to destroy the entire race of man and passed onto men the knowledge of the flood. Utnapishtim's story of the flood overshadows both the great city that he has built and his victorious combat with monsters, for the recovery of Utnapishtim's tale is the appropriation of firsthand evidence of the nature of the world. Utnapishtim was a witness to the wrangling, the pettiness, the ruthlessness, and the arbitrariness that characterizes the gods themselves. In addition, in imitation of Gilgamesh, Yossarian recovers the actual qualities of catch-22 for the people of his time: the agent who delivers this information to him is the old woman, who is substituted for Utnapishtim.

One sign of the subtlety of *The Gilgamesh Epic* is that Gilgamesh does not understand what he is confronted with in the person of Utnapishtim. Gilgamesh is looking for some type of divine warrior, but instead he finds a layabout. Gilgamesh expects that Utnapishtim has been divinized for some individual attainment, but the first revelation that comes to Gilgamesh is that Utnapishtim's elevation is due to something between an accident and a whim: Utnapishtim is privy to a "hidden matter" but it was not by his own doing; he was merely a pawn in the contention between the gods. Kluger states that when we compare Utnapishtim's flood story to the Biblical flood-story

> No human guilt is mentioned here as being the cause of this disaster. On the contrary, Ea afterwards accuses Enlil of destroying mankind *without reflection*, instead of 'putting the sin on the sinner.' So it is divine incalculability and unpredictability which brings about the flood. Ea takes part in the divine plot to destroy mankind, but he at least wants to save one human being. . . . If we compare this with the Old Testament flood story, we see that both these tendencies, the unpredictable decision to bring on the deluge, in which Enlil, the god of the earth, is in the foreground, as well as the other divine decision, personified by Ea, the god of wisdom, namely to save one man, are united in the Bible in the one ambivalent God personality, Yaweh. . . . We can here follow a religious devel-

opment 'in flagrante' so to speak, putting the attributes of two separate gods into the one divine personality. (187–88)

While the characters in *Catch-22* may express disbelief or doubt the existence of God, everyone in Yossarian's culture believes in catch-22. God may seem distant, but catch-22 is immanent. The Assyrian gods are similarly immanent, for they have no regard for belief or disbelief: they exist whether or not they are recognized as deities. Certainly, Yossarian recognizes that the generals and colonels wield godlike powers over life and death, and practically speaking, the arbitrary power that the officers exercise is sufficient to make them gods.

Catch-22 is an imitation of *The Gilgamesh Epic*, a text in which the gods figure greatly, and in imitating that ancient text, Heller has endowed his text with Joycean substitutability, such that without ceasing to be himself, Colonel Cathcart is the god Shamash. It is not until the end of the second chapter that the religious nature of Yossarian's problem begins to enter into the text—though religion is present as the element of unpredictability in the universe. Yossarian experiences unpredictability directly: Yossarian has forty-four missions, "and he sprinted out of the mess hall wildly and ran looking for Doc Daneeka to have himself taken off combat duty and sent home" (22), but, the doctor tells him that "'The colonel wants fifty missions'" (22).

As I have stated previously, we may frame Yossarian's problem as that of not being a god. This is not as absurd as it sounds, for the text supplies specific details that establish that Milo "was the corn god, the rain god and the rice god in backward regions where such crude gods were still worshipped by ignorant and superstitious people. . ." (244). The implication of this passage is that World War Two-era Europe is no more civilized than these remote backwoods, for belief in catch-22 has reduced advanced, modern life to the conditions in a slaughterhouse. Yossarian's desire to be a god are specified in connection with his deflated attempts to control the rain: "If there was no rain at all, there were freakish, inexplicable phenomena like the epidemic of diarrhea or the bomb line that moved" (122). Essentially, Yossarian is no different from the Sumerian gods who generate a flood that destroys all of mankind: his actions are inexplicable. These efforts, though, are little more than comic, and in the end they do not save his friends. Yossarian does become a god, but only when he is transformed inwardly to take responsibility for his actions. In order to do this, he must become a criminal and a madman in the eyes of the authorities. It is only by transcending the outworn morality of the subindividualized "primitives" who control this world that he can jump out of the hopeless and unconscious narrative of the heroic epic and propel himself beyond the "monstrous events" (287) that inform the textual territories inscribed by the modern world.

Yossarian's departure from the script is underlined by the chaplain, who, like Gilgamesh, elects to "stay here and persevere" (463); in doing so he represents a failed attempt to create a divine man. Jeffrey H. Tigay states that "The hymnic description of Uruk looks like a standard temple-city hymn, but placed in the mouth of Gilgamesh, at the end of Tablet XI, it expresses the futility of his quest to overcome death and his reconciliation to immortality-by-reputation-and-achievement only" (249). John Maier seconds this view: "Uruk at the end is seen once again as the house of Ishtar, a final recognition of the feminine. We take the division of the city into one which emphasizes that the uncultivated claypits, source of clay tablets, but also a symbol of the dead, is the fitting comment on life that is, in the words of Martin Heidegger, being-toward-death" (252).

Yossarian chooses to do better than to merely persevere. Significantly, when Major Danby tells Yossarian that he will have to keep on his toes "every minute of every day" (463), Yossarian agrees and promises to keep on his toes every minute. However, in the very act of making his statement, Yossarian falls behind, and Major Danby warns him that he will have to jump: "'I'll jump.' 'Jump!' Major Danby cried. Yossarian jumped. . ." (463).

Chapter 5

Jewish Mysticism in *Catch-22*

Having explored Heller's "Joycean" appropriation of *The Gilgamesh Epic*, it is now feasible to further the discussion of *Catch-22* by showing that although *Ulysses* served as an important intertextual underpinning for Heller's novel, it is to *Finnegans Wake* that we must turn in order to establish what Margot Norris calls the "intellectual orientation" (1) of *Catch-22*. This chapter must first examine Heller's use of Joyce's texts, because the appropriation of Joycean methods did not unqualifiedly determine the teleology of *Catch-22*: Heller was subject to other significant influences—Kafka being one that contributed significantly to the shape of a number of structural components (characterization, tone, symbols, etc.), but Kafka is an even more important influence with respect to the ultimate meaning of the text. Thus, in order to determine the importance of Kafka to *Catch-22*, it is first necessary to examine certain details of Heller's interest in *Finnegans Wake* so that crucial distinctions can be made between Heller's appropriations from Joyce and Kafka.

While it is relatively easy to delineate Joyce's influences on Heller's text once the "Joycean" parallels between *Catch-22* and The *Gilgamesh Epic* have been delineated in detail, Heller's specific appropriations from *Finnegans Wake* are somewhat more elusive. *Finnegans Wake* is such an encyclopedic and innovative text that we must at first balk at the idea that such a comparatively accessible novel as *Catch-22* owes anything substantial to Joyce's challenging work. The curious and paradoxical fact that must be confronted is that although *Catch-22* represents a reduction of the stylistic effect that *Finnegans Wake* produces, without Heller's appropriation of, in a sense, the entirety of *Finnegans Wake*, *Catch-22* would not have become the uniquely popular, highly regarded, and memorable novel that it now is.

It is well known that in writing *Finnegans Wake* Joyce set out to discover a new way to write popular literature, and the result is that Joyce produced a notorious and highly acclaimed failure that has maintained its position as an important work of literature despite a history of remaining largely unread. In writing *Catch-22* as he did, Heller shows every sign of having consciously set out to create the novel that Joyce had intended to write. Not only did Heller succeed in constructing a novel along Joyce's most advanced line of work, but also the novel that resulted was a popular success.

Heller's accomplishment would seem to have been brought about by achieving an astounding balance between content and narrative structure. *Catch-22* possesses a wide-ranging content that, unlike the contents of *Finnegans Wake*, does not intrude upon the surface of the text to the extent that it disturbs the reader. At the same time, the heavily allusive contents of *Catch-22* are paired with a chronologically circulating narrative structure that contributes to the novel's comedic presentation of a fractured reality. In *Finnegans Wake* Joyce's stylistic dependence on various types of "double talk" is so extreme as to render the text virtually unreadable as a novel: Margot Norris states that "Since analysis is impossible within the dream framework of *Finnegans Wake*, Joyce must have decided to make the dream transparent, as it were, by giving the reader access to the repressed material. . . . In *Finnegans Wake* we see the repression and revelation occur simultaneously in the same line of discourse" (103). Speaking of the semiotic freedom that inheres in Joyce's method, Umberto Eco states that "What makes the pun creative is not the series of connections (which precedes it as already codified); it is the decision of the short circuit, the so-called metaphoric one" (quoted in Ulmer 311). For Eco, Joyce's pun, "the principal figure of *Finnegans Wake*" is an "epistemological metaphor" of "unlimited semiosis" (quoted in Ulmer 309). The puns in *Catch-22* are far less visible, and initially the reader is less free: it only requires, however, that the reader penetrate the veil of the surface text to find himself similarly awash in an undecidable text.

An important distinction sets the stage for our discussion of the relationship between *Catch-22* and *Finnegans Wake*, namely that these texts inhabit radically disparate universes. The many studies of *Finnegans Wake* generally agree that the narrative inhabits some form of a collective, sleeping unconscious. Margot Norris states that the *Wake* is a dream about a novelistic story (24), that unilinear time has nearly been abandoned (25), that the repetition of events appears to be compulsive rather than rational (25), that the characters tend to shift and blend interchangeably (30; 74–75), and that the novel's dreamlike humor is unpremeditated and spontaneous (114). Anthony Burgess concludes his detailed discussion of the dream language of the *Wake* by noting that

> We accept the language of dream, then, and the author's laying on of thicker and thicker blankets of dark (with holes in to let in a little light), but now we must ask what the dream is about. Life, yes, but whose life? The answer is: the life of the whole human race—in a word, history. Stephen Daedalus, like Bloom, was oppressed by that nightmare from which he was trying to awake: is he now submitting to the nightmare, settling down to a long sleep the better to be frightened by it? No, because he has rejected Mr. Deasy's vision of history as a long line of events leading to the emergence of God. Time remains the enemy; history must be spatialised. How? By seeing it as a circle, a wheel perpetually turning, the same events recurring again and again. In that 'Nestor' episode of *Ulysses* there is a reference to Vico Road, Dalkey, and it is the Italian historiographer, Giovanni Battista Vico (1668–1744), who shows the way of the wheel. (242–43)

In *Catch-22* Heller demonstrates a disregard for linear time, a blending of characters, and a compulsive repetition that is reminiscent of what is found in *Finnegans Wake*. Yet the action in Heller's novel takes place in the waking world, in history, and is specifically placed in Italy during the Second World War. While sleep is an important motif in Heller's text, the text maintains a consistent distinction between the states of sleep and wakeful consciousness, and characters are often observed as they sleep, either by the narrator or by other characters: thus, we are shown Hungry Joe "screaming in his sleep every night" (26). Significantly, we are also shown the further development of this motif when his nightmares spread to other members of "Major Major's squadron" (where "squadron" may be understood to mean any organized multitude; a legion—in other words—everybody).

Furthermore, we may note that despite the fact that we are made aware of the content of a dream in the case of Hungry Joe's dream of Huple's cat "sleeping on his face, suffocating him" (133), as readers we are denied direct access to the dreams experienced by the characters, in contrast with the reader's immersion in dreams that is sustained throughout *Finnegans Wake*. The implication of dream and nightmare is significantly delimited in the text of *Catch-22* by the fact that Colonel Korn intervenes to "arrest what seemed to him to be the beginning of an unwholesome trend in Major Major's squadron" (55).

Catch-22 contains an entire subtext dealing with literature and "major" authors, and it is through Major Major Major that Heller signals the existence of this fund of allusions and appropriations. This literary subtext is a topic of considerable dimension: at this point, it must suffice to state that by removing Hungry Joe and his dreams from the squadron for four nights a week and putting a halt to the collectivization of the squadron's dreams, Heller indicates that although he has embraced elements of Joyce's (and Lewis Carroll's) methodologies, the perceiving consciousness that orients his text is not located in the dream-world.

Where, then, is the narrative of *Catch-22* located, if not in the world of dreams? The cosmic machinery that determines the events that take place within the narrative of *Catch-22* is the spiritual world of Jewish mystics, the cosmos described in the system of hidden knowledge known as the Kabbalah. The kabbalistic system exists within the text in two independent modes. On one level, the Kabbalah enters the text as allusions to the various components of Jewish mystical practice and as the visions that are the result of kabbalistic mystical practice. On another level the Kabbalah inhabits the text in the form of Franz Kafka's novel, *The Trial*. Kafka's novel constitutes a *further* literary subtext that the novel contains much in the same way that it has been shown to contain Joyce's novels and *The Gilgamesh Epic*. While it is possible to distinguish between these two modes of kabbalistic subtextuality, it is doubtful that doing so will enhance the discussion of this aspect of the novel. It seems likely that the elements of kabbalistic mysticism that are placed in the text independently of what is presented by *The Trial* were done to direct the attention to Kafka's text as a text informed by Kabbalah, an insight which Heller would have had through his background as the son of first-generation Russian Jews, but which was not a part of the critical understanding of the text.

Stephen W. Potts, one of Heller's principal interpreters, notes Heller's statement that it is Kafka in general rather than any one work that influenced him (97). Potts also shows that in the chaplain's letter to his wife he quotes directly from the opening sentence from *The Trial*, (98). Potts reads Kafka as a follower of the proto-existentialism of Soren Kierkegaard and one of the chief originators of "the literary absurd" (61): "If God in Kafka is arbitrary and incomprehensible, an Absolute whose judgments cannot be understood let alone questioned, then human systems attempting to embody divine absolutes are if anything fallible but equally arbitrary gatekeepers standing between the individual and the Absolute" (Potts 61).

Karl Erich Grozinger's *Kafka and Kabbalah* demonstrates that "Jewish elements . . . lie beneath the surface of Kafka's texts" (6) as an "esoterically concealed" (7) content. Grozinger states that

There are many echoes of kabbalistic elements and traditions in Kafka's works. . . . Kafka himself was unable to study the often extremely difficult classical kabbalistic texts in the original Hebrew or Aramaic languages, but he had to have been familiar with certain popularized basic patterns. We know this because they played a role in the daily habits and in the popular teachings of the community. An enormous number of folkloric morality books and collections of homilies popularized the highly mystical theosophical, historiosophical and anthroposophical teachings of the Kabbalah. These works were certainly available to the simple Jew, but primarily the preachers in the synagogues and houses of study (bet midrash) studied them in preparation for their sermons. Such moral writing and folk tales actually defined the general Jewish consciousness in middle and eastern Europe; they were the medium through which each individual living in this milieu received a body of specifically Jewish knowledge, as well as attitudes and world views. That being the case, we should not be surprised to discover parallels between this popular literature and a large number of motifs in Kafka's texts. (7–8)

The discussion of Kafka's relationship to the Kabbalah was commenced in the interest of providing some idea of the nature of the universe depicted in *Catch-22*. Briefly stated, the chief concepts embraced by Kabbalah are: (1) the belief in the unity of all being, but taking the form of ten spiritual forces repeated through four stages of cosmic construction (Grozinger 8)—thus on the spiritual plane, all people are the same (Sheinkin 185); (2) man is in a position to exercise a direct influence on the divine world (Grozinger 10); (3) human life and history are essentially a pendulum swinging between acquittal and judgment (Grozinger 12); (4) the Torah has an infinite number of meanings but each soul has its individual understanding of the text (Grozinger 46-7); (5) the soul ascends to heaven at night where it studies and is judged (Grozinger 49); (6) the soul is reincarnated as many times as it takes until he understands all four levels of the Torah interpretation belonging to the root of his unique soul (Grozinger 49); and (7) creative powers belong to every word composed of Hebrew letters, even to "meaningless" combinations of letters, and to each letter of the Hebrew alphabet (Grozinger 129).

Fundamental to the literary method of Kabbalah is the concept of the hidden *Pardes*, "the garden in which there grows the sacred tree which marks the ascent to God" (Epstein 2). For the Bible is not—as the chaplain says, just a book like *Bleak House* (293). In kabbalistic practice "The letters of the Hebrew word *Pardes* . . . contain the clue to the secret contained [in the Bible]: P represents Peshat, the simple exterior meaning of the Torah; R stands for *Remez*, the homilectical meaning; D is *Drush*, the allegorical meaning; and S is *Sod*, its secret or innermost meaning" (Epstein 3).

Similarly, as indicated by the extended motif of Lieutenant Scheisskopf's parades, we find in *Catch-22* a number of levels—literary, spiritual, mythic, psychological, and historical. Moreover, these parades, described as "the impressive fainting ceremony" (75), appear in the text as a fully developed hermeneutic system with "trained stretcher bearers, . . . spotters with binoculars . . . [and a] tallyclerk" (73). An extended motif in *Catch-22* is concerned with announcing the importance of *Pardes* to interpreting the novel, though Heller's method of revealing the significance of the parade motif is indirect. Heller presents the figure of Scheisskopf and his "monomaniacal obsession with parades" (Potts 44) as a means to work a disguised form of the word *Pardes* into the text. By doing so, he alerts the reader to the multiplicity of meanings that are to be derived from his text. One of the indications that we are to read parades as *Pardes* is that there is little to justify the lengthy treatment of Scheisskopf and his parades in a novel about flying bombing missions in Italy.

The Scheisskopf episode calls attention to itself and brings itself into question, particularly so once we have dispensed with the reading of *Catch-22* as a piece of absurdist literature. The congruence of the parade motif with Clevinger's trial suggests that Heller has constructed a parallel introduction of kabbalistic material: the kabbalistic reading of the word "parades" as *Pardes* doubles the implication of his appropriation of Kafka's "Kabbalist" novel. Moreover, it is Lieutenant Scheisskopf himself who brings Clevinger up on charges before the Action Board (72), thereby generating the parallels between *Catch-22* and *The Trial*.

What is particularly interesting about the way Heller has integrated *The Trial* into *Catch-22* is that his treatment of Kafka's text seems at first to be a parody of *The Trial* and also grounded in an absurdist reading of *The Trial*. Yet once the kabbalistic reading of both *Catch-22* and *The Trial* have been factored into the reading of the surface narrative of *Catch-22*, it is apparent that *Catch-22* treats Kafka's novel quite seriously, and includes it within the text of *Catch-22* as a means of restoring to *The Trial* its kabbalistic semiosis. Considerably more along these lines will be said after the following discussion of Heller's more general incorporation of kabbalistic lore within *Catch-22*.

Kabbalah serves several purposes in *Catch-22*, though perhaps the most crucial is the dismissal of absurdity. This is done through a concealed though nonetheless forceful attack on no less a figure than Soren Kierkegaard—and his attendant proto-existentialism. Kierkegaard is dispatched through Yossarian's dealings with Aarfy. In chapter fifteen Yossarian has been assigned to fly lead bombardier in the first formation;

the enemy's defensive countermeasure is intense, and "Heavy flak was everywhere" (150). Yossarian's response to the barrages of flak is that "He knew at once they were all dead" (151). Kierkegaard's most influential text was *Fear and Trembling*, and this title is conjured up in the text that runs between pages 151and 154; there Yossarian is described as "in aching terror" (151), and "quivering" (153).

However, Kierkegaard is yet more specifically manifested on the linguistic level of the text. Captain Aardvark's name has the distinction of including the same aa dipthong as Kierkegaard. The riddling and linguistic aspect of Aardvark's name is brought to our attention in a series of Joycean puns, in which he is described as "an eerie ogre"(154). Just below this sentence is another in which the "Aard" phoneme is emphasized as Yossarian frantically gives directions to McWatt, the pilot, "I said hard, hard, hard, hard, you bastard, hard!'" (154). Much of the difficulty that surrounds the perception and interpretation of this level of the text is cleared away by Heller in the chapter that follows, when Yossarian encounters Aarfy again in Rome: "Yossarian gaped at him with that same sense of persecuted astonishment he had suffered that same morning over Bologna at his malign and cabalistic and irremovable presence in the nose of the plane" (160). Here "cabalistic" may be interpreted as both an indication that Aardvaark's name is encoded with a hidden or secret meaning and as a homophone of kabbalistic. In any case, the use of the word "cabalistic" in the text, particularly in the episode where it appears, is a further indication of the importance of Kabbalah to the understanding of *Catch-22*.

We are also told that "Yossarian dreaded him for a complex of reasons he was too petrified to untangle" (154)—an approximation of Kierkegaard's proposition that the absolute cannot be apprehended through reason, that a leap of faith is required. Having gotten this far, it is readily apparent that Aarfy's inability to hear Yossarian repeatedly tell him to get back into the body of the airplane is Heller's presentation of Kierkegaard's idea that from the human point of view God is inaccessible: "Punching Aarfy was like sinking his fists into a limp sack of inflated rubber. There was no resistance, no response at all from the soft, insensitive mass, and after a while Yossarian's spirit died and his arms dropped helplessly with exhaustion. He was overcome with a humiliating feeling of impotence and was ready to weep in self-pity" (153). Yet before the episode concludes, a large chunk of flak passes through "Aarfy's colossal jumble of maps" shredding them and filling the cabin with "Thousands of tiny bits of white paper . . . falling like snowflakes inside the plane" (153). By shredding

Aarfy's "maps," Heller dispenses with Kierkegaard's absurd version of an inaccessible God. As a further indication of the significance of the destruction of Aarfy's set of maps, the episode specifically demonstrates the failure of Aarfy-Kierkegaard's epistemology. Aarfy proclaims that Orr's plane has been smashed to bits (155), yet by continuing to search for him Yossarian sees Orr's plane "maintaining altitude and holding a proper course" (156), and in response "Yossarian muttered an unconscious prayer . . ." (156). When Aarfy still persists in attempting to speak to Yossarian despite an intense spate of name calling, "Yossarian put his hand over Aarfy's mouth and pushed him away wearily" (156).

The kabbalistic significance of this series of incidents and puns is that Orr's name is directly attributable to the kabbalistic concept of *Or*, light, (also transliterated as *Aur*), and is related to the initial act of cosmic creation: "Tradition states that God willed to see God and so God's Will, symbolized by light, shone nowhere and everywhere. Thus the EN SOF AUR, the Endless light of Will, was omniscient throughout Absolute All. From God knowing All, God willed the first separation so that, God might behold God. This we are told was accomplished by a contraction in absolute all, so as to make a place wherein the mirror of Existence might manifest" (Halevi *KU* 7–8). On the innermost level of this episode, Heller has presented an ecstatic vision in which the deepest mystery of the universe has been approached. The episode concludes with a coded description of the kabbalistic description of the universe. As we shall see, Heller uses *Catch-22* to present the visionary mysticism of the kabbalistic system, although this can seldom be apprehended from the events that are being narrated in the surface text. Indeed, Heller's method—like Kafka's—is to distract the reader's attention from the subtext by presenting an opposed meaning in the main text: Grozinger states that "Kafka managed to divert his interpreter's attention away from the true background of his thinking and his storytelling by means of transpositions such as [the Altneu Synagogue] into a Christian European setting [a cathedral]" (6–7).

Kabbalistic material appears throughout *Catch-22*. The beginning of the novel implies the creation of the cosmos, a theme that is continued in subsequent chapters. We may understand the entire text as a depiction of the Absolute's plunge into matter and the struggle of the divine element to ascend back to its original level bearing with it the experiences of the lower levels of the cosmos. In the opening chapters of the text Yossarian is depicted giving creative order to the world, yet his creation is disguised as destruction, play, regression, chaos, and death. In specific terms,

Yossarian is in the hospital pretending to be sick so that he will not have to fly any more missions. In kabbalistic terms, Yossarian represents EN SOF AUR, the withdrawal of Absolute All in order to create a place where creation might exist. This topic also emerges in chapter nine, "Major Major Major," where the Major's refusal to see anyone recapitulates the withdrawal of the Absolute. The episode also recapitulates the possibility of the mystic's experience of the divine presence through an inverted parody of Moses's encounter with Yaweh: in *Catch-22* a "madman" (104)—the "prophet" Flume—speaks to Major Major Major from a dewberry bush in reverse of God speaking to Moses from a burning bush.

For the Kabbalists, creation took place through the letters of the Hebrew alphabet: "The first and last Hebrew letters when placed together form a word—*Et*—which is often translated into English as 'the'. . . . Kabbalistically, because the word *et* is comprised of the first and last letters, it has been viewed as a synonym for the Hebrew alphabet itself. Therefore, we can translate this opening sentence as, 'in the beginning, God created the alphabet of the heaven and the alphabet of the earth'" (Sheinkin 57). Yossarian finds that in his withdrawal he must "censor letters" (8), a pun on the kabbalistic understanding of the universe as a descent of the Absolute All into matter (and an additional pun on the creation of the cosmos out of letters), so that the word "censor" can be read as a combination of "sins" and "Or." The passage is a parody of Genesis, as it describes Yossarian on "the first day" (8), though Heller is careful not to count by using numbers, so that his appropriation of the Bible is not readily obvious, and the count continues with "the next day" and the "following day." We do not lose sight of Yossarian's activities as equivalent to cosmic creation, however, because we are told that Yossarian censors the letters "as though he were God" (8). In a culminating gesture towards kabbalistic systematizing, we are told, "Catch-22 required that each censored letter bear the censoring officer's name" (8). Kabbalistically, this revelation is a highly important piece of information in that it introduces the idea of the meditative technique that Abraham Abulafia gave to his students. Abulafia taught them a method in which the seventy-two letters of three special verses of Exodus could be permuted to form the secret Name of God (Epstein 94). Yossarian permutes Washington Irving into Irving Washington (8) in a manner similar to the kabbalist's permutation of Bible verses or the Tetragrammaton (YHVH).

The habit of permutating names that spreads from Yossarian to Chaplain A.T. Tappman and Major Major Major also establishes Heller's allusion to the kabbalistic mystic Abraham Abulafia, who was a master of

letter permutation. Epstein states that "Using a pseudonym corresponding in numerical value to his own name, Abulafia circulated his meditation
manuals under titles like *Splitting of Names*. . . . Influenced by the
intricate kabbalistic style of his mentor, Togarmi, Abulafia freely sprinkled
his texts with codes, acrostics, and number-letter puns to simultaneously
befuddle his persecutors and communicate freely with knowledgeable
Spanish mystics . . ." (*Kabbalah* 81).

Yossarian's game of exploiting "all the possibilities in the letters" (8) is
equivalent to Abulafia's kabbalistic mystical practices: "[He] permuted the
twenty-two Hebrew letters to gain prophetic wisdom" (Epstein 83). The
depiction of Abulafia's career as a mystic and his mystical practice makes
up much of the content of chapter twenty-five, "The Chaplain." One of
the most significant motifs in the chapter is the multiple occurrence of the
word "laugh," introduced by Colonel Cathcart who repeatedly insists that
the chaplain issue a belly laugh. Cathcart says, "'You give me a belly laugh
right now and I'll give you a whole bushel of plum tomatoes'" (289–90).
The phrase "belly laugh" is subsequently repeated. Were "belly laugh"
located among the "earsighted" (FW 143) homophonic puns of *Finnegans
Wake*, where "'we war' unravel[s] to 'hear,' 'he was,' 'Yaweh,' etc." (Attridge
quoted. in Stewart 16), we should have no trouble reading it as [Abraham]
Abulafia's name.

Chapter twenty-five includes several allusions to Abulafia presented as
Corporal Whitcomb's Bible reading and shredding of the chaplain's letters (283). "Mystic phenomena" (94) is the subject of the entire chapter,
as the chaplain attempts to orient himself within a world in which the
"esoteric" (286) and prophetic (294) modes of reality are in conflict with
the skepticism of Corporal Whitcomb and Colonel Cathcart. We can,
however, maintain little doubt that it is the visionary activity of Abulafia
that is privileged in the chapter. The chapter shows the chaplain as a
mystic in pursuit of the highest vision of God by means of Abulafia's
tzeruf, letter contemplation. The chaplain is ascetically isolated from the
world, for he has withdrawn to his tent in the woods in accordance with
standard practice (Epstein 16). Like a traditional kabbalist, the chaplain
meditates on the sexual relationship that he has with his wife ("explicit
acts of lovemaking" [69]) to unify his "male" and "female" selves (Epstein
16).

The chaplain goes back and forth from his tent to Major Major's, but
he cannot attain the vision. The Abulafian Kabbalist always began his
contemplation by starting at the crown or uppermost point of the *sefirot*,
the ten spiritual forces (lights, words) and working his way down; the text

spells out this technique using traditional terminology: the chaplain "plodded along the zigzagging path" (287). The Sefirotic Line of Life is often spoken of as a lightning flash (Halevi *KU* 13), and the path that it takes through the *Sefirah* is a zigzag. Halevi states that "The Sefirot are joined by twenty-two paths. . . . This arrangement is one of the several lesser laws that govern the relative Worlds. Their function is to enable the Line of emanations to circulate generally as against just down the *Lightning Flash*. . . . By this system of *paths*, various minor combinations of flow can occur and so bring about different emphasis in specific parts of the Tree" (Halevi *KU* 16; emphases added). (If we did not have Heller's explanation that *Catch-22* was not the original title of the novel—*Catch-18*—we would implicate the twenty-two paths of the Sefirot as the inspiration for the novel's famous title.)

Thus chapter twenty-five is a detailed exposition of kabbalistic mysticism. Epstein describes the technique of letter contemplation in detail: "the disciple was enjoined to permute the Tetragrammaton according to a formula. . . . If repeated permutation of this kind still didn't bring down the light [AUR], he was told to 'cry and repent,' for it was considered a certain sign of his unworthiness. . . . The final assignment, permutations for the Name inherent in the word *avoa* (I will come) meant that the student had hit rock bottom. 'Be careful not to blame God, the master chided him, 'for the emptiness is in yourself'" (Epstein 97–98). Heller covers this same ground, though concealed under an ironic treatment: "He plodded along the zigzagging path through the forest listlessly, clogged with thirst and feeling almost too exhausted to go on. He was remorseful when he thought of Corporal Whitcomb. He prayed that Corporal Whitcomb when he reached the clearing so that he could undress without embarrassment, wash his arms and chest and shoulders thoroughly, drink water, lie down refreshed and perhaps even sleep for a few minutes" (287). But the chaplain does blame god (293–94) and his thirst persists through his interview with Colonel Cathcart, preventing him from laughing as Cathcart orders (290). The "successive mystical phenomena" (294) with which the chaplain is so concerned throughout the narrative receive a comic treatment, which undermines the validity of spirituality on the surface level of the text. This handling of spiritual material is reversed on the deeper levels, however, and we can see that it receives a treatment that is extensive, detailed, accurate, and specific.

Though the "visions" that the chaplain receives are nothing more than the acting out of a distraught Yossarian and a terrorized Flume, this is not the final word on the subject. Yossarian's playful letter permutation (the sequence of cosmic creation that must be taken seriously on another level of the text) is paralleled by Havermeyer's assassination of field mice. The manic way in which Havermeyer dispatches the mice is yet another imitation of the kabbalistic description of cosmic creation; on yet another level, it is equally the mystical illumination that the chaplain so desperately pursues in chapter twenty-five. The line of string running to the light bulb (31–32) that forms part of the equipment used by Havermeyer in his exaggerated assassination of mice with a forty-five caliber pistol preserves the identical kabbalistic terminology that describes creation. Kabbalists state that manifestation came about when "God willed that the Line of Light should penetrate beyond the First Crown . . . (Halevi *KU* 8). The mystical attainment of "light" is the goal of Kabbalistic study, a condition which is described in terms of Havermeyer's game: "The line was taut as a banjo string, and the merest tug would snap it on and blind the shivering quarry in a blaze of light" (32). As we have seen, this mystical light is named throughout the text, for the Hebrew word for light—*Or* [AUR]—is presented in a slightly permutated form by Orr's name.

The text of *Catch-22* contains many occurrences of abbreviations, such as I.B.M., C.I.D., P.F.C., and R.O.T.C., which may remind of us the centrality of the letters H.C.E. and A.L.P. in *Finnegans Wake*. The name of Joyce's protagonists, Humphrey Chimpden Earwicker and Anna Livia Plurabelle, take many other forms throughout his text, the most often cited being "Here Comes Everybody" for H.C.E. The importance of this linguistic device in the *Wake* alerts us to a similar use of the device in *Catch-22*, and it is apparent that Heller has followed Joyce's lead in constructing a level of the text that depends on attention to the initial letters of words in names, phrases, and abbreviations.

A good example of such a construction is that fairly early in the novel, in chapter four, a piece of comic business involving T.S. Eliot is presented, though no larger purpose for the introduction of Eliot seems to emerge, and, seemingly, the text's concern with Eliot does not long persist. One of the motifs that do figure importantly in the text, however, is Colonel Cathcart's obsession with having his picture appear in *The Saturday Evening Post* (194–201, 288, 290). The equivalence of "T.S. Eliot-poet" and *The Saturday Evening Post* is established by chapter thirty-five, "Milo the Militant," wherein the T.S.E.P. motif reemerges as "Piltdown Man. The Smithsonian Institution" (381). The occurrence of Piltdown Man in *Catch-22* connects Heller's text to *Finnegans Wake*, where the Piltdown Man appears on page 10: "The wagrant wind's awaltz'around the piltdowns and on every blasted knollyrock. . . .") Heller even bridges the disparity between T.S.E.P. and T.S.I.P.M. by presenting the inability of Cathcart and Minderbinder to meaningfully communicate due to the similar pronunciation of "hides" and "hives": the miscommunication motif is not a further indication of absurdity, as it might seem, but instead points toward the unity that lies beneath forms that appear disparate—a concept important in *Finnegans Wake*, Freudian psychology, and Kabbalah.

Chapter thirty-five is also distinguished by the many abbreviations that occur in it. As Milo Minderbinder outlines his activities to Colonel Cathcart he tosses off several: E.O.M., F.O.B., C.O.D., M.I.F., N.M.I.F. The significance of the over-abundance of abbreviations in the text of *Catch-22* may be grasped by noting the relationship between the C.I.D. man and the "ripple of anxiety on some ethereal military echelon" (8) that propels the C.I.D. man into the ward as the direct result of Yossarian's "letter contemplation." Epstein states that "Sometimes the letters sprang to life of their own accord, "speaking" to the mystic for as long and as profoundly as the duration and depth of his trance. To those who permuted them in the form of *Ofanim*, the winged angels, they "flew" forth from the page. . . . Combined names of the powers impelling nature enabled a man to change nature" (98). We must suspect that the proliferation of abbreviations is connected to the practices associated with the permutations of letters. Milo Minderbinder's magical facility with business, then, is the novel's presentation of the kabbalist's mastery over nature through the mysteries of the letters.

Aside from the crucial nature of language and writing in kabbalistic theory, three further kabbalistic doctrines contribute significantly to the structure of *Catch-22*—man's centrality in creation, his freedom, and reincarnation. Man's role in creation is taken up in chapter seventeen, "The Soldier in White." The Soldier in White is attached to two jars containing clear liquid dripped into the soldier and then reversed and fed in the opposite direction. The process is rendered as such a tacitly profitless activity that the artillery captain is motivated to ask, "'Why can't they hook the two jars up to each other and eliminate the middleman? . . . What the hell do they need him for'" (174). It is the assertiveness of the artillery captain's deflation of the soldier in white's maintenance that signals the importance of his question. The comic and somewhat repulsive description of the jars inverts the significance of what this episode is showing, for the episode touches on the great mystery of creation as described by the Kabbalah. In the Kabbalah-Soldier in White intertext, the Soldier in White is cosmic man: as such, he exists because his role is to infuse consciousness throughout the reaches of creation from which God has withdrawn. Thus, Halevi explains that "The reason for the process of human incarnation is that mankind should act as a bridge between the upper and lower worlds. . . . Thus, the planet is gradually lifted in its state of awareness as mankind husbands its surface and resources" (*KU* 195).

In Kabbalah man's freedom is so important that evil is to be understood as originating through Satan—a very loyal servant of God who enables human free will to exist through offering the option of evil. In the universe presented by *Catch-22* man's freedom is communicated through the portrayal of trivial and objectionable activities. General Dreedle is described as a man for whom men were "military quantities" (222). Ironically, it is within the confines of the limited identities that General Dreedle extended to his men that they were invested with whatever freedom they could be said to possess. Thus, the general required that the men serve the "ideals, aspirations, and idiosyncrasies of the old men he took orders from" (222), and "beyond that, they were free to do whatever they pleased. They were free, as Colonel Cathcart was free, to force their men to fly sixty missions if they chose, and they were free, as Yossarian had been free, to stand in formation naked if they wanted to. . . ." (222). Superficially, the presentation of freedom in this episode—and freedom is one of the major themes in the novel—is a mockery of General Dreedle's corrupted conception of freedom. What is striking, however, is that while the passage quoted above takes the approach of black humor to General Dreedle's self-serving, debased, and hypocritical exercise of power, it does so through presenting the general's belief that man is free: Freedom is the subject of the passage.

Thus, Heller's presentation explores the disjunction that exists in the General's understanding of his relationship to his role in the military. We see that, the General does not know what freedom is. However, the General nevertheless voices the question of man's ultimate freedom, even though we suspect that he does not apprehend the meaning of such a proposition. In the existentialism of the Absurd universe that critics see in Heller's novel (Potts 64–66), man is free but his freedom is meaningless outside of himself. The metaphysical freedom vouchsafed by the kabbalistic universe is not privileged by modern thought, which either recognizes man's freedom arising out of the ultimate meaninglessness of the universe or man's lack of freedom arising out of the individual's refusal to recognize that the universe is Absurd in actuality. As we shall see, in line with kabbalistic thought, Heller's view is that man is free and at the same time the universe is meaningful in and of itself. Man's freedom in a meaningful universe is contingent on the individual's discovery of the true conditions of existence. Moreover, man's freedom, rather than reduced by the ultimate preordained structure and meaningfulness of the universe, is miraculous because it does not have to exist, having originated out of God's will to experience infinity—that God should see God (Halevi *KU* 155). In fact, man's freedom is a mystery from which other mysteries issue: man is the only creature empowered "to change levels and accelerate the cosmic processes or even reverse them, should the entity wish to go against God's Will" (Halevi *KU* 156).

Kabbalah embraces the doctrine of reincarnation: correspondingly, the text of *Catch-22* alludes to reincarnation on different levels. In some places reincarnation is approached through experiences of *déjà vu*, such as the chaplain's "weird, occult sensation of having experienced the identical situation before in some prior time of existence" (209). The Soldier in White is described as a mummy, which inescapably touches on the topic of reincarnation. In chapter eighteen, "The Soldier Who Saw Everything Twice," Yossarian substitutes for a soldier who has died, so that whether described or enacted the connection between reincarnation and the motif of "going around twice" is clearly established. The theme of "going around twice," which we are more or less forced to interpret as a pun on reincarnation, is presented in a number of ways. The most literal sense of the action is portrayed by the bombing mission in which Yossarian takes the whole squadron over the target for a second time (described initially on page 141). We also see this motif in Yossarian's repeated sex with the maid in lime-colored panties (169). The motif is reduced to nonsense in the conversation that takes place after Yossarian's bombing mission in which Colonel Korn says "'It seems to me that *we're* going around twice'" (143)—and by now we can recognize in Korn's statement an instance of the device of *inversion* that signals the significance of what is said, not its absurdity. Halevi states that "As a soul becomes incarnated at birth so it becomes discarnated at death" (*KU* 149). The scheme presented by the kabbalistic view of life is of long cycles of lives that ultimately bring the soul to the Kingdom of Heaven, though for some there can be a rapid climb during a few lifetimes or one extraordinary lifetime (Halevi *KU* 151). Between lives the souls either return immediately, though to conditions that reflect their spiritual needs or to one of the Hells of Gehinnom, where the souls are purified. This aspect of the doctrine is particularly important in *Catch-22*. Though there are other appearances of Gehinnom, such as the ditch outside of Major Major's office (104), the most graphic appearance of the Hells of Gehinnom is Yossarian's dream that "he was fleeing almost headlong down an endless wooden staircase, making a loud, staccato clatter with his heels" (369). Yossarian's fall down a staircase depicts a situation that Halevi describes as one in which a soul spends life after life in destructive pursuits "until he suddenly sees that it is only taking him deeper down into Hell and further away perhaps from . . . ordinary humanity" (*KU* 153). As we might expect, subsequent to this dream, Yossarian begins to exert compassion, rebellion, and conscience.

The previous chapters have already said a great deal about the role of allusions to other works of literature in *Catch-22*. The discussion of Kafka's *The Trial* that will occupy the remainder of this chapter argues that *Catch-22* maintains a somewhat different relationship to Kafka's novel than from the other texts that Heller has incorporated in his text. First it must be noted that *Catch-22* may be thought of as a modern analog to Swift's *The Tale of a Tub*, for it engages previous literature with an adversarial intent. We have already seen that Heller has dismissed *Finnegans Wake* and *Fear and Trembling*—banishing the dream world of the *Wake* and reducing *Fear and Trembling* to confetti. On the other hand, there are texts (*The Waste Land*, *Huckleberry Finn*, *Moby-Dick*) that Heller treats more approvingly. *The Trial*, like *The Gilgamesh Epic*, has a particularly privileged place in the scheme of *Catch-22*: *The Trial* occupies nearly as much volume in the narrative as does *The Gilgamesh Epic*, and it interpenetrates the narrative of *Catch-22* from the first to the last chapter.

The Trial enters the discussion of *Catch-22* at precisely this point because, for Heller, Kafka's novel represents a bridge between Kabbalah and postmodern literature—and by implication—postmodern consciousness. It is Clevinger who is put on trial in *Catch-22*, yet his fate is not synonymous with the fate of Joseph K. Instead, he is equated with the prophet Elijah, and he disappeared inside of a cloud (206) in imitation of Elijah's disappearance into the heavens. Thus, Heller seems to underscore the inadequacy of Kafka's ability to depict the kabbalistic universe in *The Trial*. In contrast with Kafka's treatment of similar topics and situations, Heller allows Yossarian to jump out of the way of the knife that strikes at him on the final page, the knife under which Joseph K. dies "'Like a dog!'" (229).

We have already seen that critics recognize that Heller incorporated some aspects of *The Trial* into *Catch-22*. However, the absurdist and black humor readings of *Catch-22* do not allow for an adequate understanding of the intertextual relationship between *Catch-22* and *The Trial*.

The errors inherent in the absurdist reading of *Catch-22* are compounded by the incomplete understanding of *The Trial* that was in effect before the publication of Karl-Erich Grozinger's *Kafka and Kabbalah*: previously, the critical reading of *Catch-22* held that much of the novel consists of nonsense. The view that emerges from the kabbalistic reading of *Catch-22* is that there is nothing in the novel that cannot be interpreted in relationship to some intertext. In the case of *The Trial* intertext in *Catch-22*, much of *Catch-22* that seems to be nonsense may be shown to have been derived from Kafka's novel: the kabbalistic reading of *Catch-22* that is accessed through Grozinger's revised understanding of *The Trial* reveals the spiritual and therapeutic intentions behind Heller's novel.

Grozinger states that

> Kafka . . . is no Kabbalist in the traditional sense of the word. His vision of the radiant transcendental realms of kabbalistic tradition is obscured, and this is why he pulls the whole hierarchical structure lower yet, until it coincides with terrestrial reality. For Kafka, the celestial courts become a second-rate version of the same old petty and dirty story that comprises daily, mundane life. When viewed in the proper perspective, however, this reduction brings him very close to the imagery of the Kabbalists. . . . [T]he courts in Kafka's *Trial* . . . represent a demythologized, at times cynically sarcastic transformation of the ancient celestial hierarchies. Kafka transplanted the lost paradise of the Kabbalists into a European, petite bourgeois milieu. Only once does he dare glance upward. . . . Kafka situates this light in the one place on the European scene that is still capable of evoking a hint of the sacred and the transcendental, namely, in a cathedral. (68)

In order to resolve the question of how the allusions to *The Trial* in *Catch-22* may be understood, it is first useful to notice that in the same way that Joseph K. is arrested without charges in Kafka's novel, "The case against Clevinger was open and shut. The only thing missing was something to charge him with" (73). The ledger in which the examining Magistrate has recorded K.'s deficiencies (*The Trial* 41) appears in *Catch-22* as the pad on which Colonel Cathcart records the "Black Eyes" (217); the "First Interrogation" episode of *The Trial* extends throughout the whole of chapter twenty-one, "General Dreedle" (213–30) of *Catch-22*, if we read the chapter through its relationship to the Kafka subtext. We may also note that just as they go around twice in Yossarian's interrogation into his going around twice, the warder tells K., "So now you're beginning it all over again?" (5). These similarities establish a dispersal of material related to *The Trial* throughout *Catch-22*; we also see that that not only is it true that both Clevinger and Yossarian are Joseph K., but that this is also true for other characters. Additionally, we can see that the discussion of whippings by Lieutenants Engle and Travers (76) alluded to the episode in *The Trial* in which the two warders are whipped in the lumber room.

When Joseph K. visits the court of Inquiry, he faints: in *Catch-22* K.'s fainting spell is expanded and becomes the "fainting ceremony" (75) that provides the system for scoring the parade. Though it is barely recognizable as such without close attention to the trail of associations in *Catch-22*, Scheisskopf's "fainting ceremony" is a parody of the court system described in *The Trial*. The "methodical, practiced, irresistible grip" (Kafka 224) by means of which K. is taken into custody by his executioners appears a number of times in *Catch-22*. In one telling occurrence, when Major Danby is to be summarily executed, two lieutenants seized him under both arms (220); the grip emerges again when Colonel Cathcart is about to faint at the sight of Yossarian naked in the ranks, and Colonel Korn steps behind Cathcart and powerfully grasps his arm (222). Here, in an unusual compression, Heller has combined the fainting motif with the grip motif. The grip motif reappears near the conclusion of *Catch-22*, when Yossarian is arrested for being in Rome without a pass (429).

In contrast with Kafka's treatment of Kabbalah, Heller's novel is suffused with allusions to the ecstatic visions of the Kabbalist mystics: one component of the vocabulary of *Catch-22* makes references to "rapture" (75), "absolute truth" (210), "lightless, unstirring void" (375), "mystic hallways" (250), "mystic phenomenon" (294) "esoteric import" (286), "occult" (209, 275), and "eternal mysteries of existence" (275).

Heller has gone so far as to describe a mystic in the ecstatic state; however, this has been done in such an unexpected context that it is unrecognizable. Nately's whore is described as she waits to have sex with a customer: "Her lax mouth hung open in a perfect 0, and God alone knew at what her glazed and smoky eyes were staring in such brute apathy" (250). Here, the clue to what the passage means is provided by the vocabulary, not the syntax, for it contains the words "God," "knew," It alone," "perfect," and "0." When the words used to describe Nately's whore are removed from their mundane context, they can be seen to refer to the ultimate vision of the Absolute, in which all things are experienced as one.

Heller's treatment of kabbalistic visions also takes the form of the vision of Elijah; Halevi states that "Some great Kabbalists have said that they have been taught by Elijah who is the link between Heaven and Earth" (*Kabbalah* 23). In Kabbalah one for of the highest visions was the direct conversation with Elijah. The mystic Caro stated that "He shall talk to you mouth to mouth and greet you, for he will be your guide and master in order to teach you all the mysteries of the Torah. . . . Elijah clothes himself in a body to be visible to the world" (Epstein 155). Yossarian's description of Clevinger is sarcastic, but "Clevinger knew everything (69). . . . In short, Clevinger was certain to go far in the academic world. In short, Clevinger was one of those people with lots of intelligence and no brains, and everyone knew it except those who soon found it out" (70). This analysis is suspect, however, given the shallowness of Yossarian's understanding of life at the time of Clevinger's trial.

Finally, let us apply to the Kabbalah for some measure of understanding what has been presented in this chapter. The "Lieutenant Scheisskopf" chapter seems to present the disintegration of Clevinger's trial into nonsense of the Lewis Carroll variety as Clevinger declares that he is sure that he cannot be found guilty while the court remains faithful to the cause of justice—and it is at the word justice that the proceedings plunge into a seeming madness. The colonel defines justice as Karl Marx, a knee in the gut, and garroting (82). Read on the surface level, Cadet Clevinger's trial at the hands of the Action Board (77) is not only absurd but it is vicious. However, it is apparent that the literal reading is insufficient, when we realize the significance of the statement that compares Clevinger's recoil from the hatred of his judges (the bloated mustachioed colonel, Major Metcalf, and Lieutenant Scheisskopf) to a blinding light (83). This light is the Ayin Sof Or, the endless light beyond the world, the mystic's vision of the All; beyond the literal and brutal understanding of justice as a form of earthly violence is the celestial scheme where the word "justice" is equivalent to Judgment (Halevi *Kabbalah* 23)—the sixth point on the Sefirot or Tree of Life. Heller's inverted treatment of the Kabbalah through the mundane and celestial modalities of Justice is, perhaps, the novel's most profound evocation of the higher realms of the cosmos.

Reference to the Sefirotic scheme itself demonstrates that at the level of Gevurah or Judgment, the halfway point between the world and the divine has been reached. The celestial courts are not at the highest level of the Tree of Life and do not partake directly of the light of God. The relatively low position of the celestial courts may, then, be understood as a psychological stage in which the initiate develops a conscience—a topic alluded to on the first densely allusive page of the novel, where we are informed that after censoring letters, Yossarian was free to lie around the hospital with a free conscience (7). It follows that Clevinger's trial may be related to stages in both Jung's psychology of individuation and the spiritual psychology of Kabbalah. Since Jung has already been discussed above, we will restrict the comparison to Kabbalah:

> When the student reaches the level of Tiferet [beauty, fifth step] in himself—that is, when he has developed enough will to cross the triad of awakening whenever he wishes—he becomes his own tutor. This is because he comes into contact with the soul triad (Hesed, Gevurah, and Tiferet) that brings the discipline of Justice and the tolerance of Mercy [Hesed] into play. This emotional triad, pivoted upon the self, works at refining a now self conscious soul, sometimes by a touch of Severity [Gevurah, Judgment] from the left and sometimes by a touch of Mercy from the right, which, perceived from the self, brings into balance some discrepancy of emotional expansion or contraction. (Halevi *Kabbalah* 23)

In Halevi's discussion, the setting has been moved inward, into the psyche, as has all of the action circumscribed by *Finnegans Wake*—a text remarkable for its disregard for realism. Because of the sufficiency of realistic elements incorporated into *Catch-22*, we are not prepared to understand that text as having an internalized, psychic reality; however, to some degree the text does make its meaning as an internalized reality. The action that surrounds Cadet Clevinger's trial is a projection of internal processes: the problem of the reality of the trial is further presented when we try to interrogate the relationship between Yossarian and Clevinger. Though Clevinger is on trial, the episode plays out against Clevinger's disappearance into a cloud—the association by which he may be identified as the prophet Elijah. As Elijah, Clevinger is Yossarian's teacher: the trial, then, may be viewed as the means by which Clevinger-Elijah is prepared for his ascendancy into the light. In the novel Clevinger recoils from the light, but as we have seen, Heller habitually reverses the polarity of the events that he narrates, and we, therefore, know that after he has been judged, Clevinger-Elijah goes into the light. Though the teacher has disappeared, he has not gone beyond the fifth level, Tiferet, Beauty—and he is still accessible to any sincere student. From that vantage above the world (but close to the world), the teacher (Elijah) is more efficaciously placed to teach Yossarian-Abulafia how to make his own ascent. In saying this, we must not divorce this mystical scheme from Yossarian's internalization of the whole trial as a psychological process, for the proceedings also describe the formation of Yossarian's conscience.

Conclusion

Earlier in this study I made mention of the contrast between the critical understanding of *Catch-22* as a novel belonging to the Black Humor school and my reading of the novel as a text concerned with the psychic fulfillment advanced by depth psychology and with mysticism. Given my neo-modernist, psychoanalytic, and metaphysical readings of Heller's novel, how are we to account for such disparate elements of its structure as the seeming chaos of its surface text and its unrelenting comedy? How do these and other elements relate to the text's serious purpose and the orderly, progressive, and systematic materials that I have shown to underlie the paradoxical, redundant, and labyrinthine form of the surface text? I believe that the answer is to be found in the "mythical method" from which the text was generated in the first place. Research on the earliest form of the text shows that originally Yossarian was Jewish (Nagel "Two Brief Manuscript Sketches" cited in Nagel JH 10). Moreover, in "The *Catch-22* Note Cards," Nagel's study of an early plan of the novel, Aarfy was originally called Aarky (54) and McWatt was called McAdam [Nagel "Note Cards" 61 n. 10] (57). The suggestion is that the original conception of the novel is that it was to have been a text that made obvious signs of privileging the Bible. Later versions of the novel moved this biblical material out of plain sight.

We also see that since Yossarian will parade unclothed and sit naked in a tree during Snowden's funeral ("Note Cards" 56) that elements of *The Gilgamesh Epic* had been incorporated even at this early stage.

A further indication of the degree to which the earliest conception of the text was invested in the mythical method is the original title of the novel—"Catch-18." The curious story of the original title having been dropped because of its similarity to *Mila-18* and the new title originating from Heller's editor is well known; curiously, the anecdote has seemingly obliterated any interest in why the novel was called "Catch-18" in the first place. Though it is speculative to project an association between "Catch-18" and an origin in *The Golden Bough*, it is interesting that according to Frazer both Set and Osiris were torn to pieces after eighteen days (438). Nagel observes that in the note cards Mc Adam slices Kid Sampson in half and then kills himself and Daneeker [Doc Daneeka] ("Note Cards" 57). The greater prominence of this event in an earlier draft may point toward Heller's prior interest in making it more explicit that his novel was concerned with the motifs of Osiris as a corn-god and as a means to spiritual immortality: corn is certainly a feature included in the final text in that *Catch-22* contains a Colonel Korn, and Milo is a "corn god" (244).

The view of the novel as being predominantly informed by myths is supported by the fact that what Nagel calls the "identity motif'" was prominent in the note cards but was later submerged into the "survival" theme: "In thematic terms, this change is perhaps the most important discovery to emerge from a study of the preliminary note cards" (Nagel "Note Cards" 57–58). What this brief review of Heller's shifts of focus allows us to see is that as the writing of *Catch-22* progressed, Heller worked to make the text increasingly esoteric. Heller's efforts to integrate myths into his text in increasingly inaccessible ways were detected by Nagel. However, Nagel expressed Heller's method in terms of themes that coincided with the absurdist reading of the novel that prevailed at that time.

The structure of *Catch-22* imitates the form of the world, wherein the truth exists on a deeper level of existence than most people are capable of comprehending. In both *The Waste Land* and *Catch-22* we encounter the idea that the world is "unreal" and that its true shape is not available to ordinary men and women. For these people, there is only the law of catch-22 that leads them to destruction, without the hope of renewal. The Tiresias-Madame Sosostris-Old Man axis constructed by the intertextuality of *Catch-22* exists so as to provide a means of salvation for those heroic few who quest for a way beyond the "unreal" level of catch-22. Thus Heller's use of black humor was the medium, the metaphorical dust in which he buried the "bone" of mystical, metaphysical, and transpersonal knowledge.

In essence, *Catch-22* is an application of Eliot's dictum, "We can only say that it appears likely that poets in our civilization, as it exists at present, must be *difficult*" (quoted in Knapp 39). However, *Catch-22* presents specialized and necessary "difficulties" not only the result of numerous allusions but also a discontinuous, fragmented narrative form: the difficulty of *Catch-22* is a formal innovation that accomplishes the transformation of the historical imagination into myth (Knapp 41). James F. Knapp shows how the discontinuous form of modernist literature is related to history by bringing in Joseph Frank's 1945 essay "Spatial Form in Modern Literature":

> Originating in the same perception of the modern world as disordered and chaotic which had so troubled Eliot, Frank's formulation sees the modernists as incorporating that cosmic disorder into their artistic structures. The very act of perceiving patterns of relation among fragments that seem to float in a unified space becomes an escape from time, an artifice of eternity. Discontinuities which in society are frightening become, when reenacted as art, the means to perceive a new order impervious to anything outside itself. (40)

Joseph Frank's description of this method of embodying experience in discontinuous form seems an apt description of Heller's treatment of Yossarian's experience of World War Two in *Catch-22*.

Besides what I am calling Heller's use of Eliot's "mythical method," we may also note that *Catch-22* parallels *The Waste Land* and Joyce's novels in other ways that are useful to assess. While *The Waste Land* is not as famous for its comedy as is *Finnegans Wake*, we have seen that even Eliot's austere and incoherent poem contains burlesques of modern culture and a playful attack upon the reader by means of the recondite and deceptive Notes. In Eliot's poem the fundamental unity that emerges comes about through the poem's complex irony, confusion, and cynicism (Knapp 42)—which are not divorced from the comic-serious treatment of reality that is the net result of the text. *Ulysses* is, without a doubt, an assault upon the reader's sensitiveness, only surpassed by *Finnegans Wake*. In such company, it is hard to see *Catch-22* as anything other than another such assault upon the reader's embrace of comforting illusions and verities. To the extent that this is true, then, *Catch-22* resembles an absurdist text, which is by definition a demonstration that life is formless and without structure beyond what fantasy can lend it. But just as the demonstration has been made, the absurd and the mystical part company, for the vision of the endless light intercedes just at the point of utter darkness, despair, and the abandonment of hope.

The teachings of both depth psychology and mysticism tell us that the world is not as it appears. Very often, in order to bring the subject into the correct view the analyst or the mystic must shatter the subject's habitual world view that has been maintained as a cover for the more profound organization of the cosmos. Thus, in *Catch-22*, Heller shows that the question of the solidity of the war and of the powers of the officers who direct the conduct of the war is based on a dangerous brand of self-aggrandizing nonsense. Indeed, for most readers of the text, this is as far as it goes. Yossarian becomes a "coward" because he has been shocked out of his complacency, and he has grasped something of the sham nature of the vast collective enterprise that has determined the historical shape of his time. However, Yossarian, too, has come to an end: he is still subject to the dictates of the tyrants who control the illusions of the physical world that the men of his time take to be realities.

However, the physical world is subject to the activities of the upper Worlds and what happens on the physical ground of existence results from causes that have come down through all the levels of existence: this means that at various points aspects of the miraculous can break through from the Beyond. One such aspect is the intensely disturbing phenomenon of Orr. Orr is entirely beyond Yossarian's frame of reference. He tinkers with minute components too small to be comprehended. His mind penetrates into the future and plans for the things that he anticipates. Yossarian is afraid of Orr and avoids him, refusing to realize that it is significant that Orr has ditched in the sea several times. Yossarian sees only madness in Orr's behavior in the life raft—making tea, eating, fishing—in short, surviving.

Orr resonates complexly with the subtexts of *The Gilgamesh Epic* and the Kabbalah; his more general significance is brought into focus by Maud Bodkin's association of "the night journey" with rebirth (*Archetypal Patterns* 68). Orr, as the modern cognate of the boatman Urshanabi, knows how to reach the Beyond; Yossarian needs to travel to the Beyond in order that he be reborn. However, he is consciously unaware that the Beyond exists, and he has no means to travel there on his own. Yossarian sees only the meticulously ridiculous, the seemingly purposeless activities that occupy Orr, and because he rejects Orr's foolishness, he will not answer Orr's questions seriously. The repetition of Orr's ditching in the sea conforms to the pattern that critics have noticed in the text: "Not only does the reader learn more as such episodes repeat, but the general tone of each subsequent repetition tends to darken" (Potts 28). Thus the effect of the comedy is generally replaced by the serious purpose beneath the comedy. We laugh because we do not suspect that our laughter is the beginning of our approach to wisdom. Eventually, it becomes obvious that Orr's laughable antics are part of a carefully conceived plan. For the reader, as for Yossarian, when this discovery is made, it is too late to do anything about it. This aspect of the novel is an echo of Eliot's prophetess, Madame Sosostris, who warns the uncomprehending subject. Though it seems that the Tarot card reader's warning should have been more explicit or that Orr's invitation to Yossarian should have been given a reasonable explanation, the fact remains that often one is not able to comprehend words that contain wisdom and salvation until it is too late. The question is not one of the clarity of the warning but of the maturity of the subject's consciousness.

In the course of *Catch-22* Orr is increasingly identified with the use of a life raft. At the conclusion of the novel, we see the "miracle" (459, 458, 461) of Orr rowing to Sweden (an allusion to Emily Dickinson's mystical poem 249, "Wild Nights—Wild Nights!"). Orr's escape is narrated indirectly as Major Danby and Yossarian imagine Orr in a yellow raft paddling out into the Atlantic Ocean, rowing with a tiny blue oar and eating raw codfish as he makes his way to the "sweet" girls and "advanced people" (463) of Sweden. In her discussion of the rebirth archetype, Maud Bodkin points out that a little boat represents something individual and is thereby a symbol of rebirth (*Archetypal Patterns* 59). Bodkin's study was written after years of intensive study of C.G. Jung's work and was published in 1934; while I have no evidence that Heller ever read this work, it is very likely that it played a crucial part in generating elements of *Catch-22*. Walter Sutton states that Bodkin's *Archetypal Patterns in Poetry* was "[a]n important channel for the influence of Jung upon American criticism (176). Bodkin's study contains a chapter on "Rebirth Patterns in *The Waste Land*," so that the work seems to be doubly relevant to *Catch-22*.

Bodkin's assessment of Eliot's poem—a constant presence in Heller's novel, whether as topic, allusion, or cotext—is that *The Waste Land* accomplishes what Jung called "'a translation of the primordial image [of rebirth] into the language of the present'" (APIP 299). This, I believe, is equally true of *Catch-22*, which, in order to reach a contemporary audience, Heller fitted out with a black- comic carapace beneath which may be found what Maud Bodkin calls "the Paradisal love of earth" (APIP 305). Though this inner text is at every point contingent upon the outer text, it is only accessible by means of the resources of the individual consciousness in contact with the text. This, perhaps, accounts for Heller's attitude toward his audience and toward his text. As a worker in the tradition of mythical texts, it would seem that Heller's reticence is a sign that he understands that it does not serve any constructive purpose to intervene in the operation of the text upon the consciousness of the reader, for that is the job of the text, the archetypes, and the imagination brought to life by the language of the text. If the artist has done a good job, we must suppose that there are forces that come into play of their own accord that are more powerful than the author's pontifications and admonitions. Maud Bodkin addresses this nicely in the continuation of the passage quoted above, where she says, "it is for each reader to interpret as he may that indication of a Beyond" (APIP 305).

Bibliography

Adams, Robert Martin. *Afterjoyce: Studies in Fiction After Ulysses*. New York: Oxford University Press, 1977.

Armstrong, Tim. *Modernism, Technology, and the Body*. Cambridge: Cambridge University Press, 1998.

Attridge, Derek and Daniel Ferrer, eds. *Post-Structuralist Joyce: Essays from the French*. London: Cambridge University Press, 1984.

Bal, Mieke. *Narratology*. Toronto: University of Toronto Press, 1985.

Black, Jeremy. *Reading Sumerian Poetry*. Ithaca: Cornell University Press, 1998.

Blair, Walter and Hamlin Hill. *America's Humor*. New York: Oxford University Press, 1978.

Bleys, Rudi. *The Geography of Perversion: Male-to-Male Sexual Behavior Outside the West and the Ethnographic Imagination, 1750–1918*. New York: New York University Press, 1995.

Bodkin, Maud. *Archetypal Patterns in Poetry: Psychological Studies in Imagination*. New York: Vintage, 1961.

Booker, M. Keith. *Joyce, Bakhtin, and the Literary Tradition: Toward a Comparative Cultural Poetics*. Ann Arbor: University of Michigan Press, 1995.

Brooks, Cleanth. "The Beliefs Embodied in the Work." *Storm Over the Waste Land*. Ed. Robert E. Knoll. Chicago: University of Nebraska Press, 1964. 57–87.

———— *The Well Wrought Urn: Studies in the Structure of Poetry*. New York: Reynal & Hithcock, 1947.

Brown, Norman O. *Life Against Death*. New York: Vintage, 1959.

Budge, E.A. Wallis. Ed. *The Book of the Dead*. Seacaucus, N.J.: University Books, 1960.

Burgess, Anthony. *ReJoyce*. New York: Ballentine, 1965.

Burhans, Clinton S., Jr. "Spindrift and Sea: Structural Patterns and Unifying Elements in *Catch-22*." *Twentieth Century Literature*. 19.4 (1973): 239–49. Reprinted in Nagel 1984.

Burnham, Clint. *The Jamesonian Unconscious: The Aesthetics of Marxist Theory*. Durham: Duke University Press, 1995.

Cain, William E. *The Crisis in Criticism: Theory, Literature, and Reform in English Studies*. Baltimore: The Johns Hopkins University Press, 1984.

Craig, David M. *Tilting at Mortality: Narrative Strategies in Joseph Heller's Fiction*. Detroit: Wayne State University Press: 1998.

Deleuze, Gilles and Felix Guattari. *Anti-Oedipus: Capitalism and Schizophrenia*. Minneapolis: University of Minneapolis Press, 1983.

Eliot, T.S. "The Love Song of J. Alfred Prufrock." *The Waste Land and Other Poems*. New York: Harcourt, Brace & World, Inc., 1930, 1962. 1–9.

———— "Philip Massinger." *Selected Essays: 1917–1932*. New York: Harcourt, 1932.

———— Ulysses, Order, and Myth." *Selected Prose of T.S. Eliot*. Ed. Frank Kermode. New York: Harcourt Brace Jovanovich, 1923, 1969. 175–78.

———— *The Waste Land*. *The Waste Land and Other Poems*. New York: Harcourt, Brace & World, Inc., 1930, 1962. 27–54.

Epstein, Perle. *Kabbalah—The Way of the Jewish Mystic*. Boston, Shambhala, 1988.

Fetrow, Fred M. "Joseph Heller's Use of Names in *Catch-22*." *Studies in Contemporary Satire* 1.2 (1975): 28–38.

Fiedler, Leslie. "Come Back to the Raft Ag'in, Huck Honey." *Modern Criticism: Theory and Practice*. Ed. Walter Sutton and Richard Foster. New York: Odyssey Press, 1963. 484–89.

————— *Love and Death in the American Novel*. New York: Delta, 1966.

Fiore, Silvestro. *Voices from the Clay: The Development of Assyro-Babylonian Literature*. Norman: University of Oklahoma Press, 1965.

Forman, Seth. *Blacks in the Jewish Mind: A Crisis of Liberalism*. New York: New York University Press, 1998.

Foster, Paul. *The Golden Lotus: Buddhist Influence in T.S. Eliot's Four Quartets*. Sussex: The Book Guild Ltd., 1998.

Frazer, Sir James George. *The Golden Bough*. New York: The Macmillan Company, 1922, 1972.

Freud, Sigmund. *Civilization and Its Discontents*. New York: Norton, 1961.

————— "The Interpretation of Dreams." *The Basic Writings of Sigmund Freud*. Translated and edited by A.A. Brill. New York: Modern Library, 1938. 181–552.

————— "Infantile Sexuality." *The Basic Writings of Sigmund Freud*. Translated and edited by A.A. Brill. New York: Modern Library, 1938. 580–603.

————— *Standard Edition of the Complete Psychological Works of Sigmund Freud*. *The Basic Writings of Sigmund Freud*. Translated and edited by James Strachey et al. 24 Vols. London: The Hogarth Press, 1953.

————— "Wit and Its Relation to the Unconscious." *The Basic Writings of Sigmund Freud*. Translated and edited by A.A. Brill. New York: Modern Library, 1938. 633–806.

Gibbons, Tom. *Rooms in the Darwin Hotel: Studies in English Literary Criticism and Ideas, 1880–1920*. Nedlands: University of Western Australia Press, 1973.

Graves, Robert. *The Greek Myths*. Baltimore: Penguin Books, 1955.

Grozinger, Karl-Erich. *Kafka and Kabbalah*. New York: Continuum. 1994.

Guillory, John. "The Ideology of Canon-Formation: T.S. Eliot and Cleanth Brooks." *Critical Inquiry*. 10.1 (1983): 173–98.

Halevi, Z'ev ben Shimon. *A Kabbalistic Universe*. York Beach, Maine: Weiser, 1988.

———— *Kabbalah: Tradition of Hidden Knowledge.* New York: Thames and Hudson, 1985.

Hawkes, Jacquetta. *The First Great Civilizations: Life in Mesopotamia, the Indus Valley, and Egypt.* New York: Knopf, 1973.

Heidel, Alexander. *The Gilgamesh Epic and Old Testament Parallels.* Chicago: The University of Chicago Press, 1946, 1949.

Heller, Joseph. *Catch-22.* New York: Dell, 1961.

———— *Now and Then: From Coney Island to Here.* New York: Simon and Schuster, 1998.

———— Letter to Jon Woodson, 27 September 1998.

Hoffman, Frederick. *Freudianism and the Literary Mind.* New York: Grove Press, 1959.

Jackson, Graham. *The Secret Lore of Gardening: Patterns of Male Intimacy.* Toronto: Inner City Books, 1991.

Joyce, James. *Finnegans Wake.* New York: Penguin Books, 1976.

———— *Ulysses.* New York: Random House, 1934.

Kafka, Franz. *The Trial.* New York: Schocken Books, 1968.

Karl, Frederick R. "Joseph Heller's *Catch-22*: Only Fools Walk in Darkness." *Contemporary American Novelists.* Ed. Harry T. Moore. Carbondale: Southern Illinois University Press, 1964. 134–42.

Kluger, Rivkah Scharf. *The Archetypal Significance of Gilgamesh: A Modern Ancient Hero.* Einsiedeln, Switzerland: Daimon Verlag, 1991.

Knapp, James F. *Literary Modernism and the Transformation of Work.* Evanston, Illinois: Northwestern University Press, 1988.

Krafft-Ebing, R. von (Richard). *Psychopathia sexualis: a medico-forensic study.* New York: Pioneer Publications, 1950.

Kramer, Samuel Noah. *History Begins at Sumer.* Garden city, New York: Doubleday, 1959.

Maier, John and John Gardner. *Gilgamesh: Translated from the Sin-Leqi-Unninni Version.* New York: Vintage, 1984.

McHugh, Roland. *Annotations to Finnegans Wake*. Baltimore: The Johns Hopkins University Press, 1991.

Morrison, Martha Oliver-Smith. "The Articulate Monster and His Role in the Public Imagination." unpublished manuscript, 1997.

Mumford, Lewis. *The Pentagon of Power: The Myth of the Machine*. New York: Harcourt Brace Jovanovich, 1970.

Nagel, James. Introduction. *Critical Essays on Joseph Heller*. Ed. James Nagel. Boston: G.K. Hall & Co., 1984. 1–26.

———— "The *Catch-22* Note Cards." *Critical Essays on Joseph Heller*. Ed. James Nagel. Boston: G.K. Hall & Co., 1984. 51–61.

Nelson, Thomas Allen. "Theme and Structure in *Catch-22*." *Renascence* 23.4 (1971): 178–82.

Neumann, Erich. *The Great Mother*. Princeton, New Jersey: Princeton University Press, 1955, 1963.

———— *The Origins and History of Consciousness*. Princeton, New Jersey: Princeton University Press, 1954, 1995.

Norris, Margot. *The Decentered Universe of Finnegans Wake: A Structuralist Approach*. Baltimore: The Johns Hopkins University Press, 1974, 1976.

Olderman, Raymond. M. *Beyond the Waste Land: A Study of the American Novel in the Nineteen-Sixties*. New Haven: Yale University Press, 1972.

Orlando Sentinel. "Joseph Heller Denies Plagiarizing 'Catch-22.' 28 April 1998, A–8.

Pace, Mildred Mastin. *Wrapped for Eternity: The Story of the Egyptian Mummy*. New York: Dell, 1974.

Pinsker, Sanford. "Heller's *Catch-22*: The Protest of a Puer Eternis." *Critique* 7.2 (1965): 150–62.

Potts, Stephen W. *Catch-22: Antiheroic Antinovel*. Boston: Twayne Publishers, 1989.

Pritchard, James B. Ed. *The Epic of Gilgamesh* in *Ancient Near Eastern Texts Relating to the Old Testament*. Princeton, New Jersey: Princeton University Press, 1950. 72(99.

———— Ed. *The Epic of Gilgamesh* in *Ancient Near Eastern Texts Relating to the Old Testament*. Princeton, New Jersey: Princeton University Press, 1955. 72–99.

Raine, Kathleen. *Defending Ancient Springs*. Lindisfarne Press, 1968.

Riffaterre, Michael. *Fictional Truth*. Baltimore: The Johns Hopkins University Press, 1990.

Rosenthal. M.L. and Sally M. Gall. *The Modern Poetic Sequence: The Genius of Modern Poetry*. New York: Oxford University Press, 1983.

Russo, John Paul. *I.A. Richards: His Life and Work*. Baltimore: The Johns Hopkins University Press, 1989.

Segal, Robert A. Foreword. *From Ritual to Romance*. Jesse Weston. Princeton, New Jersey: Princeton University Press, 1993.

Seltzer, Leon F. "Milo's 'Culpable Innocence': Absurdity as Moral Insanity in *Catch-22.*" *Papers on Language and Literature* 15 (1979): 290–310. Reprinted in Nagel 1984.

Sheinkin, David. *Path of the Kabbalah*. New York: Paragon House, 1986.

Smith, Barbara Herrnstein. "Contingencies of Value." *The Critical Tradition*. Ed. David H. Richter. New York: St. Martin's Press, 1989.

Stewart, Garret. "Lit et Rature: 'An Earsighted View.'" *LIT Literature Interpretation Theory*. 1.1–2 (1989): 1–18.

Sultan, Stanley. *Eliot, Joyce, and Company*. New York: Oxford University Press, 1987.

Sutton, Walter. *Modern American Criticism*. Englewood Cliffs, New Jersey: Prentice-Hall, Inc., 1963.

Tigay, Jeffrey H. *The Evolution of the Gilgamesh Epic*. Philadelphia: University of Pennsylvania Press, 1982.

Tindall, William York. *A Reader's Guide to James Joyce*. New York: Noonday Press, 1959.

Trilling, Lionel. *The Liberal Imagination*. New York: Anchor, 1950.

Twain, Mark. *The Adventures of Huckleberry Finn*. New York: Collier, 1962.

———— "Fenimore Cooper's Literary Offenses." *Anthology of American Literature, Vol. II: Realism to the Present.* Ed. George McMichael. New York: McMillan, 1989. 436–42.

Ulmer, Gregory L. *Applied Grammatology: Post(e) Pedagogy from Jacques Derrida to Joseph Beuys.* Baltimore: The Johns Hopkins University Press, 1985.

Walden, Daniel. "Therefore Choose Life: A Jewish Interpretation of Heller's *Catch-22.*" *Critical Essays on Catch-22.* Ed. James Nagel. Encino, California: Dickenson, 1974. 57–63.

Weston, Jesse. *From Ritual to Romance.* Jesse Weston. Princeton, New Jersey: Princeton University Press, 1993.

Whitmont, Edward C. *The Symbolic Quest: Basic Concepts of Analytical Psychology.* Princeton, New Jersey: Princeton University Press, 1969.

Twentieth-Century American Jewish Writers

The **Twentieth-Century American Jewish Writers** series will present the very best, up-to-date, imaginative scholarship. Studies on novelists, writers, poets, essayists, and critics are needed and will be carefully read. New interpretations will be especially welcomed.

All manuscripts should be sent to:

> Dr. Daniel Walden, Editor
> Twentieth-Century American Jewish Writers Series
> English Department
> Penn State University
> University Park, PA 16802

To order other books in this series, please contact our Customer Service Department:

> (800) 770-LANG (within the U.S.)
> (212) 647-7706 (outside the U.S.)
> (212) 647-7707 FAX

Or, browse online by series:

> www.peterlang.com